Navigating the American West

A History

—∞—

Thomas A Permar

Copyright © 2014 Thomas A Permar
All rights reserved.

ISBN: 0990730603
ISBN 13: 9780990730606
Library of Congress Control Number: 2014915060
The Western Sea Press, Morgan, UT

To family: Carol, Jessie, and Matthew

Table of Contents

List of Illustrations vii

Part 1. The Land 1
    Chapter 1. Defining the American West 3

Part 2. Native Americans on Foot 15
    Chapter 2. The First Emigrants 17
    Chapter 3. Equipment, Supplies, and Transport on Foot 34
    Chapter 4. Finding the Way 53
    Chapter 5. Native Trade and Communication 72

Part 3. Mounted Conquistadors 79
    Chapter 6. Supplying an Army in a New World 81
    Chapter 7. Spanish Land Navigation 109

Part 4. French Watermen 141
    Chapter 8. Prelude—Down the Mississippi 143
    Chapter 9. Across the Mississippi and onto the Plains 153
    Chapter 10. Navigating the Rivers and Plains 173

TABLE OF CONTENTS

Part 5. The Americans—Overland by Wagon 183
    Chapter 11. The Way West 185
    Chapter 12. Transport and Supplies 212
    Chapter 13. Jumping Off 227
    Chapter 14. Conclusion 247

Bibliography 257

Index 279

List of Illustrations

Figure 1. Geographical features of the American West. Author's Image. 131

Figure 2. George Catlin, Buffalo hunt on snowshoes." Buffalo Bill Center of the West/The Art Archive at Art Resource, New York. 132

Figure 3. Karl Bodmer, "Mih-Tutta-Hangjusch; A Mandan Village." Bullboats in the foreground. The New York Public Library/Art Resource, New York. 133

Figure 4. "Jackson Staircase," Chaco Canyon, New Mexico. Author's Image. 134

Figure 5. Sighting a Nocturnal. Author's Image. 135

Figure 6. Navigator kneeling with astrolabe, 1635. The Mariner's Museum, Newport News, VA. 136

LIST OF ILLUSTRATIONS

Figure 7. French rivers of commerce, from the Gulf of Mexico to the Great Plains. Fort and post settlement dates in parentheses. Author's Image. 137

Figure 8. Top: Nicolas de Fer, "Les Costes Aux Environs de la Riviere de Misisipi, Decouvertes par Mr. de la Salle en 1683 et reconnues par Mr. Le Chevallier d'Iberville en 1698." Bequest of Richard Koch, Courtesy of the Historical New Orleans Collection. Bottom: Jean-Baptiste Bourguignon d'Anville, "Carte de la Louisiane." Gift of Richard Koch, Courtesy of the Historical New Orleans Collection. 138

Figure 9. Mid nineteenth-century English sextant. The Art Archive at Art Resource, New York. 139

Figure 10. J. Goldsborough Bruff, "Ferriage of the Platte above Deer Creek." This item reproduced by permission of the Huntington Library, San Marino, California. 140

Introduction

By strict interpretation there is no such thing as a "Native American." Go far enough back in history, and we find that the ancestors of every person ever living in the Americas emigrated here from someplace else. In fact, for all but the last twenty thousand or so of the two hundred thousand years of human existence, no one lived in most of the Western Hemisphere. For 90 percent of human history, while people made love and war and traded and traveled across Europe, Africa, and the East, not a single human voice was heard or human foot imprint found within the sixteen million square miles of land now called the Americas. But eventually the first hardy souls headed east from Asia, crossed the Bering Strait, and traveled south along the Pacific coast to populate two continents as far as Tierra del Fuego, the "Land of Fire," at the tip of South America. These were the ancestors of the first people, the first emigrants who traveled to the American West. Many would follow in waves from Asia and, much later, many more from the east.

So the story of the American West is a story of movement. From the first emigrants entering this land tens of thousands of years ago to the not-so-distant past, countless millions traveled the West. They walked the driest, most inhospitable deserts on foot. Some

INTRODUCTION

found their way across plains as flat and featureless as a billiard table without reference or landmark. Others drove heavily loaded wagons over mountain ranges whose peaks topped fourteen thousand feet. Put simply, the story told here is about how they did it—how they were able to find their way and survive on a long journey through the American West.

Navigating means setting a course and guiding oneself or a party—on foot, ship, canoe, horseback, or wagon—from one place to another. To do that a traveler needs an understanding of position—where he is relative to where he wants to go. Navigation requires a means of measuring direction, time, distance, and speed. And assuming the navigator may want to make the same journey again or pass his travel experiences on to others, it requires methods of recording and communicating those experiences.

While the way-finding aspect is important, the process of navigating presented here, in a broader view, includes the means and modes of travel. For an illustration of their significance, we can look back in time to the beginning of westward movement.

Imagine an early morning in the town of San Sebastian, Gomera Island, in the Canaries. It's a fall day near the end of the fifteenth century but still warm in these dots of land off the coast of West Africa, then the edge of the known world. The admiral of a small fleet leaves his lodgings and walks to the harbor, only to find that the ships are gone. He has with him everything necessary to find his way—a compass under his arm, and he knows which direction he wants to travel: west. The admiral steps into the surf and begins to swim south, to open water, and then west, checking his course as necessary. He might make a few miles before he drowns. Suppose, however, that when the admiral reaches the harbor, his ships are there but empty. He could possibly get one underway and sail west for a few days before he died of hunger and thirst. Of course, what really happened on that fateful

INTRODUCTION

September morning was that the admiral went to the harbor and found his ships, his men, and provisions and equipment to last the whole company for a year. With this, his compass, and lots of seagoing experience, the admiral guided his little fleet across thousands of miles of open ocean, discovered a continent, and sailed safely home. Leaving aside the fact that he was sure he had landed on islands off the coast of Japan, or possibly China, it was a remarkable feat. The lesson is the same for any traveler on sea or land. Navigating from one place to another requires much more than the ability to find the way. Without the human necessities of travel—food, water, shelter, and means of transport—the only successful journeys would be very short ones.

Navigating the American West is a story of movement not only through space but also through time, from the mid sixteenth to the mid nineteenth centuries. It shows how four different cultures in four different eras dealt with the ways and means of travel into the land that came to be known as the American West.

Part One of this book addresses the land itself, two million square miles of dirt and rock, the center around which this history revolves and the stage on which all the action takes place. Its geography, to a large extent, determines where and how travelers could travel, and the reader needs at least a glimpse of what the early traveler saw.

The remaining four parts of the book deal with the human element, Part Two with the first emigrants, those here before the arrival of Europeans. These people traveled on a few navigable rivers, but for the most part they walked everywhere they went. They carried what they owned on their backs or packed small burdens on the backs of dogs. They guided themselves over the land in much the same way early European mariners navigated the sea before the compass—by experience and careful observation of natural phenomenon. With the passage of time, the land ceased to be a mystery. Travel for trade and communication carried native

INTRODUCTION

people over innumerable trails, some covering thousands of miles. They migrated or settled primarily near geographical margins—along the boundary between mountains and plains, where rivers cut the open prairie, or where the land met the sea, and understood their importance for survival.

Part Three looks at the mid sixteenth century, when the Spanish entered the American West: Francisco Vasquez de Coronado traveled from Mexico to present-day Kansas with his force of three hundred soldiers and one thousand Aztec warriors, and Hernando de Soto led his expedition from Florida into Texas. They found their way using native guides and rudimentary navigational instruments—the astrolabe to calculate latitude and the compass for direction. From thriving Spanish ranches and livestock farms in the Caribbean and Mexico, they shipped horses and mules to ride and to use as pack animals. Behind mounted conquistadors came cattle, sheep, and pigs—portable rations on the hoof. They moved across the land primarily in search of gold. Their reputations proceeded them, and one native chief, at their first meeting, told Hernando de Soto, "I have long since learned who you Castilians are...To me you are professional vagabonds who wander from place to place, gaining your livelihood by robbing, sacking, and murdering people who have given you no offence" (Garcilasco de la Vega, *Florida of the Inca*, 1605).

Part Four opens in the eighteenth century, with French claiming 1.2 million square miles, all the land drained by the Mississippi River and its tributaries—over one third of the land mass of the current continental United States. Moving south from the Canadian High Country, they established new settlements along the Gulf of Mexico. From there, French explorers paddled west along the Gulf Coast in their bark canoes loaded with trade goods, entered Lake Pontchartrain, crossed the waterways of present-day Louisiana,

INTRODUCTION

and emerged from tiny Bayou Manchac into the Mississippi River, just south of where Baton Rouge now stands.

Going upriver on this great water highway, they reached the Red, the Arkansas, and Missouri Rivers and found their way out onto the Tallgrass Prairie. But western waterways were different than the land of lakes and rivers known to the French voyageur and the Coureur de Bois of the far north. There were fewer of them, they were filled with water hazards, and most were only seasonally navigable. And where the rivers ended, French watermen had to learn the skills of the plainsmen.

Better educated than adventurers of the past, usually in Jesuit schools, French navigators and surveyors made careful notes of their travels to send back to cartographers in Paris. A major improvement in map making came during this period with recently published logarithm tables and the surveyor's technique of triangulation. This new procedure made it possible to stand in one spot and calculate distances to and between any object that could be seen, no matter how far away. Officially, the French presence in the American West ended in 1762, in the later years of the French and Indian War, when the Louisiana Country was secretly ceded to Spain. Unofficially, individual French, French-Canadians, and their descendants continued to play major roles in the exploration of the Great Plains and the Rocky Mountains for many generations.

Part Five covers the greatest mass migration in American history, as western emigrants gathered at frontier towns along the Missouri River in the mid nineteenth century. From jumping-off points like Independence, Saint Joseph, and Council Bluffs, travelers left the United States and crossed into land held by native tribes, heading for the valley of the Great Salt Lake, California, or the Oregon Territory. For most this was a family affair—including men, women, and children—so the logical choice of transport

INTRODUCTION

was by wagon. Wagons were the most efficient means of overland travel of the era; a draft animal could pull twice the weight in a wagon as what could be packed on its back. Wagons provided shelter from the storm, defense against attacks, and transport for children, pregnant women, the elderly, the wounded, and the infirm. Wagon companies headed west to the Promised Land guided by unemployed mountain men, published guidebooks, letters from relatives who had gone before, celestial navigation, gossip, and blissful ignorance and faith.

The mid nineteenth century was an era of unprecedented advances in western travel and communications. Toll bridges, river ferries, and trading posts sprang up along the trails, making travel easier and more predictable. In 1857 the federal government finally stepped up to the plate, allocating a whopping $300,000 for improvements on the Pacific Wagon Road, a route between central Nebraska and California. By the following year a paying passenger could take John Butterfield's Overland Mail Company stages from Saint Louis via the Southern Route, traveling day and night, never stopping longer than ten minutes except for meals, to arrive in San Francisco in twenty-five days. In '61, a telegraph line strung from coast to coast provided instant communication between easterners and the Pacific Coast. And before the end of that decade, workmen graded a wide, nearly level road from Omaha, Nebraska, to Sacramento, California, crossing the Great Plains, two mountain ranges, and the deserts between. It was billed, in the parlance of the day, as a "rail road." On it, for the first time by mechanical means, travelers crossed the American West. With the spiking of the last steel rail, passengers could move from East to West and back in a matter of days, on an unalterable course, without guidance from compass or star. And there is where this story ends.

It may be necessary to add that this work was not intended as a textbook, academic reference, scholarly exposition, or analysis of the American West. It was not intended as a general history of the

West. Its goal is to provide just enough background to give a sense of historical position to the four eras covered. What this work was intended to do was simply tell the story of what it took for travelers to find their way and survive a long journey across the West, hopefully in a manner interesting to the informed reader.

Part 1

The Land

Chapter 1

Defining the American West

Most boundaries of the American West are relatively easy to define. The Pacific Ocean obviously establishes a western limit, and to the north and south it wouldn't be hard to accept the borders of Canada and Mexico respectively; these can be arbitrary because the lands on each side of these borders are the same. To the north the Great Plains, Rocky Mountains, and the Cascades run well into Canada. To the south the Chihuahuan and Sonoran Deserts of the American Southwest are mirrored below the Mexican border. But where the eastern boundary lay is an open question. The obvious choice might seem to be the Mississippi River. East of the river is the East, and west of the river is the West. But geographical features cloud the issue. Prairies would certainly be considered a typical western landscape and dense hardwood forests typical of the East.

In sixteenth-century America, however, prairies and eastern hardwood forests existed on both sides of the Mississippi. Grasslands blanketed most of what is now Illinois, as well as parts of northern Indiana; forests of eastern hardwoods covered the southern half of Missouri, eastern Oklahoma and Texas, and all of Arkansas and Louisiana in a wide westward arc from where the City of Saint Louis now stands in the north through Tulsa, Dallas, and Houston. Leaving behind these two anomalous inconveniences and crossing the Mississippi River, our West begins where the traveler breaks free of woodland entanglements for the open, uncovered grasslands of the Great Plains. From that point to the Pacific Ocean, the land area of the American West spreads across two million square miles, four times as much territory as the combined countries of Spain, England, and France—the homeland of the majority of early European immigrants and settlers. Within the boundaries of the American West, two great mountain chains separate the land into three distinct regions. Moving from east to west, the Rocky Mountains separate the grasslands region of the plains from the Intermountain Region of deserts and highland plateaus. The combined Sierra Nevada/Cascade Mountains define the border between the Intermountain Region and the narrow strip of the Pacific West Region.

The Great Plains alone made up half of the American West, about a million square miles of grasslands. But long before the grass, a vast inland sea covered what is now Middle America. When the waters receded, this great central lowland, remnants of the ancient seabed, became fertile land. Along what would one day be the western boundary of the Great Plains, geological forces squeezed the earth's crust until the Rocky Mountains rose up out of flatland like toothpaste from a tube. Even as the land rose, wind, water, and ice tore at the young mountains. Eons of erosion followed, bringing sand and gravel washing down from the mountains into eastward-flowing rivers. Along the flanks of the Rockies, sediment from individual rivers formed huge plumes—alluvial fans—that spread out over the land until they converged into one continuous high plain across the entire western part of the old seabed. These vast, coalescing plumes of sediment sloped gently eastward from the foothills of the Rocky Mountains at six thousand feet to an elevation of fifteen hundred feet, intersecting what remained of the eastern lowlands, roughly along the one-hundredth meridian—or a north-south line between Bismarck, North Dakota, and Abilene, Texas.

The further west across the grasslands a traveler went, the drier the land got. Clouds moving in from the Pacific Ocean dropped their rain before crossing the Rockies, creating a "rain shadow" across the high plains where little moisture fell. With little rain and only seasonal snowmelt for river flow, western plains were flatter, less rolling, than the eastern plains and were only occasionally cut by rivers. On this semiarid land, short, shallow-rooted bunch grasses—buffalo grass and blue grama—grew in clumps, leaving exposed, barren ground between. Only a few taller plants stood out to break the monotony of the landscape—yucca, cholla, prickly pear cactus, saltbush, and (in the southern plains) scattered mesquite. Between bunch grass—in uncovered, sandy soil—high winds carved out thousands of shallow basins. Early European explorers believed buffalo formed these land features they called "buffalo wallows." But as natural moisture collectors, these shallow depressions formed intermittent ponds, in and around which more prolific vegetation grew, and so were obvious gathering places for herds of grazing animals (Bloom 1978, 331).

In the eastern plains, beyond the mountains' influence, rainfall was more plentiful. There, fertile soils supported lush grasslands (bluestem, Indian, and switch grass) and wildflowers (yellow goldenrod, black-eyed Susan, purple prairie clover, and coneflowers). Tall grass grew as high as a man's head and so thick that the movement of the wind could be followed through the undulating grass, flowing like waves across the sea that once covered this land. Below ground, dense root masses held dark soil in a solid mat of sod. With greater rainfall to the east, rivers, gullies, creeks, and streams cut the landscape like branches of a tree, forming the vast drainage systems of the Missouri, Platte, Kansas, Arkansas, Canadian, and Red Rivers, giving the eastern prairie its distinctive rolling feature. Few trees survived on the Great Plains. Those that did grew along moister, protected river bottoms with cottonwood trees most prominent. Scarce and unpredictable rainfall, grazing animals, and incessant fires kept grasslands from supporting larger vegetation. Lightning strikes caused some fires; native people deliberately set others. Fire cleared away old growth, and ashes provided nutrients for young succulent grass to grow. Strategically set fires, and the resulting new grass, lured buffalo and other grazing animals to waiting hunters.

Buffalo were the defining resource of the Great Plains, providing meat for food; hides for shelters, sleeping robes, packs, bags, clothes, and boat coverings; sinew for binding and thread; dried dung to use as fuel for cooking and heat; and horn and bone for utensils and tools. Migrating herds on the grasslands were enormous, with estimates ranging between twenty to sixty million buffalo alone. Add herds of deer, pronghorn antelope, elk, and the predatory wolf packs that shadowed them all; spread these over a million square miles of grass and sky, and it would have been a grand panorama of nature that will never be seen on this planet again.

Moving west of the plains, across the mountain barrier of the Rockies, and into the Intermountain West, the land could be characterized by one controlling feature: water. There was little of it. The air was dry, and the land was dry. There were few rivers. Vegetation was sparse except along rivers and at higher elevations of the plateaus and mountains. The climate ranged from semiarid to desert. Two major watercourses cut the intermountain region, defining two widely separated highlands, one to the north, near the present-day US-Canadian border, the other far to the south, centered roughly around the four corners area, where the borders of Utah, Colorado, Arizona, and New Mexico now meet. And between the two plateaus, a huge basin striated with low mountains and wide, sagebrush-covered valleys.

In the northern Intermountain Region, and far back in time, ancient volcanic activity spewed molten rock from cracks and crevasses across eastern Washington and Oregon to form one massive basaltic highland, the Columbia Plateau. Later, during the ice ages, glacial lobes crept slowly south, cutting off Columbia River flow, impounding enough water behind dams of ice to fill Lakes Erie and Ontario. Periodically the ice dams gave way, and the ensuing floods gouged out massive amounts of rock and soil along the course of what is now the Columbia River (Bloom 1978, 245). These catastrophic natural disasters began the metamorphosis of the plateau into a gigantic bowl, with the river at its center. With the end of the Ice Age, the central plateau remained as flat grasslands, rimmed along the higher elevations of its outer edges with western pine forests. Blue-flowered camas and other plants with edible roots flourished in the open mountain meadows called flats. Where the Columbia River entered the eastern flank of the Cascades on its path to the Pacific Ocean, a narrow gorge created a series of rapids and waterfalls later named "the Dalles." In addition to being a natural gateway to the Pacific, the Dalles were the most prolific salmon-fishing grounds along the Columbia River. What the buffalo were to the plains, salmon were to the Columbia River and its tributaries—from the Pacific Northwest eastward through the Columbia Plateau—and a particularly important resource through the dry sagebrush and bunchgrass of the plateau's central lowlands, where few other food resources were available.

Below the Columbia Plateau were some of the driest and most desolate lands of the American West—the Great Basin, Mohave, and Sonoran Deserts. Like the dry western Great Plains in the rain shadow of the Rocky Mountains, east-flowing clouds crossing the Sierra Nevada dumped most of their rain long before they reached the lands between the two great mountain chains. Add clear air and plenty of sunshine, and what little moisture did fall was quickly lost through evaporation. Geologically, these deserts were basin and range landforms, remnants of rugged fault-block mountains separated by narrow V-shaped valleys formed during an earlier period from pressures along the margins of two great plates of the earth's crust. Over time, and in a wetter climate, erosion carried sand and gravel from the mountains to the valley floors below, simultaneously lowering the mountains and raising the valleys until only scattered remnants of low, north-south trending ranges remained, separated by wide, gently sloping valley basins. The Great Basin desert covered southeastern Oregon, southwestern Idaho, Nevada, and western Utah. Most northerly of the three intermountain deserts, and the highest in elevation, the Great Basin was a cool desert with little summer rain. What little water was available came from winter snowmelt. In these dry basins, scattered, shrubby plants like sagebrush and shadscale formed a low, even vegetative layer without cover or shelter and having little food value for grazing animals. Squat piñon pine and juniper grew along the upper, moister elevations of the scattered mountain ranges. On the higher slopes, piñon pine nuts provided a food source for man and beast, and game was more abundant there than in the basins below.

Moving south into the Mohave Desert of southeastern California and the northern tip of the Sonora Desert of southern Arizona, the scattered ranges are lower in elevation, and the basins between the ranges widen, making up more of the total land area, while the ranges take up less (Krober 1963, 190). Temperatures rise in the creosote bush desert of the Mohave, being the hottest and driest area of the Intermountain West. And yet the Mohave gives the appearance of supporting scattered forests, though populated with a giant yucca, the Joshua tree, an almost inconceivable plant in such an inhospitable environment. Joshua trees reached heights of forty-five feet and could live for hundreds of years, some over a thousand. And like the trees of a proper forest, the Joshua Tree provided cover and habitat for desert wildlife.

Of all the American deserts, the Sonora Desert of southern Arizona was blessed with the greatest diversity of plant life. While the Great Basin and Mohave Deserts had cooler climates and precipitation, as rain and snowfall primarily in the winter months, the Sonora had both summer and winter rains and a milder winter. Varieties of cacti covering the Sonora ranged from the tiny, six-inch fishhook cactus to the giant saguaro, which could top out at fifty feet. Dry-land trees, like desert ironwood and the green-barked palo verde, along with tall yucca and agaves, provided food and cover for wildlife. Mesquite grew across all the dry lands of the Southwest from the southern plains of Texas to the Mohave of California, diminishing in size across its range from a fair-sized tree on the plains to a shrub in the Mohave. Ripe by late summer or early fall, its six- to eight-inch pods, filled with large, protein-rich beans, were a favorite browse for grazing animals and were ground into a nutritious flour by native people. The large, dense-fibered taproot of mesquite, dug up and dried, was one of the few good sources of firewood available across deserts of the Southwest.

To the east, sandwiched between the Great Basin and Mohave Deserts on one side and the Rocky Mountains on the other, lay the geologically uplifted highlands of the Colorado Plateau. Larger in land area than the Columbia Plateau to the north, it covered eastern Utah, southwestern Colorado, western New Mexico, and northern Arizona—roughly centered where the four borders of those states met. These mesas, buttes, and canyon lands of the Colorado Plateau, with their brightly colored sandstone bands layered in shades of red, yellow, white, pink, and tan—what native people called land of the sleeping rainbows—have come to typify what most consider to be the American Southwest. From this region the Colorado River and its tributaries—the Green, San Juan, and Little Colorado Rivers—cut and drained the highlands westward through the rim of the plateau at the Grand Canyon, emerging into the arid lands of the Mohave Desert then flowing south across the Sonora Desert to empty into the Gulf of California. Where the Colorado dissected the high plains of the plateau, the river's course created shear-walled canyons and thundering rapids. River canyons, in places a mile deep, forced land travelers in some areas to travel hundreds of miles to find accessible river fords. High above the rivers course, the dry, flat plains of the Colorado Plateau, at an elevation of around five thousand feet, supported little vegetation other than desert grasses and low shrubs. But climbing to the higher elevations around the rim of the plateau, major changes in vegetation and habitat occurred over relatively short distances. Temperatures dropped and rainfall increased at higher elevations. A short distance horizontally, at an elevation of six to seven thousand feet, the land was covered with low piñon pine and juniper trees. Another short trip upward to around nine to ten thousand feet, vegetation changed to 150-foot-tall stands of ponderosa pine interspersed with flowered mountain meadows. By moving upward in elevation over relatively short distances, a traveler would encounter the resources of a wide variety of habitats that would take hundreds of miles of overland travel to find. This was a fact of nature all native peoples living in transitional areas between lower and higher elevation understood and exploited.

West of the intermountain deserts, across a formidable wall of granite, in places topping fourteen thousand feet, was a geographically isolated land. Access to the Pacific West from any point would not have been easy. To the west was the planet's largest ocean. To the north the rugged, heavily wooded Pacific Northwest and to the south the Mohave Desert, a most inhospitable landscape. The Sierra Nevada and Cascade Mountains on the east ran from the Mohave well into Canada. Climbing high mountain passes or crossing an arid desert would have been the only options for those on foot. Once within these boundaries, the traveler found a narrow sliver of land, about twelve hundred miles long and not more than 125 miles wide. Compared in land area with the Great Plains and the Intermountain West, which made up well over 90 percent of the American West, this strip of Pacific coast would have been unimpressive. But its importance to human populations was grand. Long before dust-bowl Okies headed west in their broken-down jalopies or ragged pioneers in their wagons, even before Spanish soldiers and priests traveled on foot and horseback, back into the ice ages, for tens of thousands of years people had been migrating to the Pacific West because of its geography and resources.

The Pacific West was a case study in geographical transitions. A condensing of many different geographical features and ecosystems along a narrow strip of land between the Pacific Ocean and the mountains made it as close to a land of plenty as could be found in North America. In what is now California, north of Los Angeles, native people had at their disposal all the resources of an ocean, its shoreline, the varied habitats that come with changes in elevation of both the low coastal ranges and the high Sierra Nevada, and a large central grassland with rivers and marshes—all within a relatively short east-west distance. Summers were dry in California; there was not enough rain to support domesticated crops. But with such a diversity and abundance of resources, the intense labor required for growing domesticated crops would have been an unnecessary burden. Along the Pacific coast was all the bounty the ocean provided: fish, shellfish, and sea mammals. And nearby forests of redwood, cedar, and hemlock furnished the wood for large sea-going dugouts and plank boats with which to harvest the resources of the ocean. The coastline provided shellfish and seaweed for food. And seaweed could be boiled down as a source of salt.

PART 1 — THE LAND

On land, by far the greatest resource was oak trees. They grew everywhere, forming park-like groves along the flanks of the coastal ranges and the Sierras, in the chaparral that bordered the central valleys, in large stands along rivers and streams, and up into the redwood forests of the north. Oak trees produced millions of acorns, the most important land-based food source.

Along California's Central Valley, marshes of the San Joaquin and Sacramento River valleys filled with migrating waterfowl, while herds of deer grazed the grasslands that surrounded them. The foothills of the Coastal and Sierra Nevada Mountains surrounding the valley yielded a rich harvest of pine nuts from digger pines and, higher in elevation, cones of the coulter pine weighing four to five pounds.

The bounty of the Pacific West continued north into western Oregon and Washington, but the geography changed. With the exception of the Willamette Valley in northeastern Oregon, a continuous sea of mountains flowed west from the Cascade Range to the Pacific Ocean. Towering headlands jutted out into the ocean itself, making overland travel along the isolated beaches impossible. Inland, the rugged terrain and dense northern rain forests of the Pacific Northwest limited overland travel to a few narrow woodland trails. Winds flowing inland off the ocean kept the climate relatively mild for these northerly latitudes. Plentiful rainfall, overcast skies, and high humidity provided enough moisture to cover the land with thick stands of red cedar, hemlock, fir, and spruce trees. Cedar, like the redwood farther south, was a soft wood and easy to work, with natural oils that made it resistant to rot and, thus, prime timber for boat building. Huge seagoing dugouts riding Pacific swells and smaller vessels plying the straights and sounds of the inland seas of Northern Washington had access to the prolific marine life—otters, seals, halibut, sturgeon, salmon, and whales, and, along the ocean shore, oysters, abalone, and mussels (Kopper 1986, 201). The broad Columbia, the only major east-west-flowing river of the Pacific West, provided a water route inland, a passage through the Cascade Mountains, and a gateway east to the Columbia Plateau of the Intermountain region.

The Rocky Mountains, dividing the Great Plains from the Intermountain West, and the Sierra/Cascades, separating the Intermountain West from the Pacific West, are the only western land features left to describe.

Western ranges with jagged peaks topping fourteen thousand feet were younger, less worn by time than North America's eastern mountains. High mountain passes, often blocked by heavy snows, made mountain ranges barriers to east-west travel for a good part of the year. That meant long trips around the mountains or waiting until spring or (in some cases) summer thaws to move from one region to another.

The easternmost of the dividing mountain systems, the Rockies, ran for thousands of miles, from northern New Mexico far into Canada. Over a hundred individual mountain ranges—sandwiched between the Front Ranges facing the plains and mountains facing the Great Basin and deserts of the Intermountain West—made up the Rocky Mountain system. But the Rockies, unlike the Sierras, had a relatively easy passageway between its many ranges. Travelers on foot followed the trail across the Wyoming Basin, in what is now central Wyoming, for thousands of years. The same trail, in time, would be rutted by the wagons of hundreds of thousands of settlers moving west to reach what would become California and Oregon.

To the west, the Sierra Nevada/Cascade Mountains separated the Intermountain and Pacific West regions. On a map these two distinct mountain systems appear to form one continuous line from Southern California north into Canada. But to any land-bound traveler, their differences are obvious. Running roughly four hundred miles along the eastern edge of what is now California, the Sierra Nevada had a steep, formidable wall of rock on its eastern

PART 1 — THE LAND

flank. Catching first sight of such a fortress of granite must have been a heart-stopping experience for travelers moving across the low sagebrush-covered valleys to the east. Native people believed that this area was once covered with water and that the Spirits created the Sierras to hold back the ocean. Unlike the Rockies, there were no easy passages through the Sierras, but for those who made it to the crest, the mountain had a gentler, though canyon-gouged, westward slope down into California's Central Valley grasslands.

The uplifted, wedge-shaped Sierras ended in northern California and gave way to the Cascade's conical volcanic peaks along seven hundred miles of eastern Washington and Oregon.

The towering Cascades cut off massive storms moving ashore along the coast of the Pacific Northwest. Up to twelve feet of rainfall per year deluged the mountain's western flank, while empty clouds whirling over the peaks on the dry eastern side yielded less than eight inches annually. Like the Rockies, the Cascades had one relatively easy passageway, the Columbia River, a water trail for travelers moving east-west.

With the exception of large mountain valleys, the harshness of winter climates eliminated mountains as places to live. But in the spring and summer, native populations along the lower margins migrated up into the heights to dig edible roots, pick ripening berries, hunt, and fish. Mountains were also storehouses of materials, like wood for building and stone for tools and weapons.

All of the land features of the American West combined—mountains, deserts, and grasslands—provide the foundation on which the chapters that follow have been overlaid. These physical regions—their features, resources, and climates—shaped and directed human action from the moment the first emigrant entered this land many thousands of years ago.

—∞—

Part 2

Native Americans on Foot

Chapter 2

The First Emigrants

Possibly as far back in time as twenty to thirty thousand years ago, and in successive waves thereafter, the ancestors of the American Indian began migrating east across a temporary land bridge connecting Asia and North America. Slowly, generation after generation, they made their way south, following big-game herds—mammoths, mastodons, musk ox, and the long-horned ancestor of the bison—along the edge of retreating glacial ice sheets (Jennings 1983, 45). Small groups of family and friends eventually populated the habitable parts of the Americas. The first people established cycles of annual migration. There was a season to follow game herds and hunt, one to travel to where ripe berries and edible roots could be gathered, another to be on the river to take the fish that swam upstream to spawn, a season to have nets ready to trap migrating geese and ducks, and another to find shelter from the coming winter in some protected canyon or river bottom. Small groups coalesced into tribes large enough and strong enough to claim and defend hunting grounds and berrying spots

PART 2 — NATIVE AMERICANS ON FOOT

for their own exclusive use. New immigrants, making their way east and south from the Old World, clashed with established peoples of the New World. The strongest tribes took up the best lands until reduced by disease or starvation or overpowered by others more technologically advanced. Century after century passed as waves of migrating bands took over new lands or were displaced by others, until the native population of the North American continent was a multicultural swirl of peoples with several hundred different languages. Wild plants were domesticated, and small groups began to settle fertile, well-watered lands along river valleys. Advanced civilizations developed, thrived, and collapsed. The survivors moved on, and the earth kept to its annual passage around the sun: spring, summer, fall, and winter.

Where and how a particular native tribe lived was an ever-changing phenomenon, and no one knows for sure how many native peoples actually lived in the American West before the entry of Europeans. The unknown variable in that equation was the spread of European diseases into the Americas. The premise that European diseases entered native life before European people seems highly possible. What effect this may have had is speculative. Trade networks and communications among native peoples were extensive, and trading canoes made regular runs between the Caribbean and Florida. It is possible that smallpox and other European diseases were introduced through native trade networks from almost the moment Columbus first stepped ashore. Although these numbers are not known, it has been estimated that within the thirty years following Hernando Cortez's defeat of the Aztec Empire, recorded epidemics spreading through Mexico reduced the native population from twenty-five million to three million. The spread of new diseases through an even more extensive network of trade trails linking Mexico with what is now the American Southwest would seem likely. What first contact Europeans saw in terms of native populations might have been significantly different than what would have been the norm.

While population numbers are not known with any certainty, relative population numbers, or the question of where most native peoples lived and why, can be addressed. Native populations might be broadly characterized by two lifestyles: those that were migratory and those that settled in a fixed location. And it needs to be quickly added that defining the lifestyles of native peoples as settled or migrating is more for the sake of simplicity than accuracy. Even cultures that relied primarily on domesticated crops traveled for annual hunts, from summer quarters to more protected winter quarters, or to gather wild plant foods.

Populations were most condensed where farming people lived. The ability of these settled peoples to produce excess quantities of domesticated crops, and their relatively fixed location, made their towns natural centers for trade, attracting surrounding migratory tribes. When game was scarce and there was nothing to trade, or when the lure of abundance called, raiding migratory bands took what they wanted by force. And certainly this was a strategy not lost on the Spanish invaders who followed, their large mobile armies moving from one native agricultural center to another to use as sources of food, supplies, and shelter.

In some areas settled peoples relied on growing domesticated crops, and in others they kept the hunter-gatherer lifestyle. The quantity, variety, and accessibility of natural food resources determined whether a hunter-gatherer culture could settle in a relatively fixed area or led a migratory lifestyle. Support of large populations in an area meant it had to have a plentiful supply of food, and it had to accessible. Buffalo herds on the Great Plains were about as plentiful as game could get, but for hunters on foot, buffalo were difficult to kill, and that limited population on the plains until the introduction of the horse. After the horse entered the scene, accessibility to the great migrating herds of the Great Plains increased dramatically, along with native population on that land. The less abundant food sources were, the more likely the inhabitants would have to move from place to place to find enough to survive and the wider that potential area of travel would have to have been. But as long as the native traveler remained on foot, that range of territory was limited. To cope with these mutually incompatible circumstances, successful native peoples tended to live or migrate close to geographical margins or boundaries. Variety of resources in different geographical or ecological areas meant to native people then what the principle of diversity means to a sound investor today. Each habitat—river, river valley, lake, grassland, mountain, marshland, seacoast, and ocean—had a unique value as a potential food resource. Relying on multiple resources was a plan more likely to ensure survival and success for a native population than banking on any single food resource. A native clan living far out in the plains and relying on a good buffalo hunt alone was more vulnerable if the hunt was unsuccessful than a clan that lived along the margin of the plains and the Rocky Mountains, where they could move on to the plains to hunt buffalo and also up into mountains to gather berries and dig roots. If one food source failed, there would still be another to fall back on.

But any effort to describe a particular native culture, where they lived, or how they lived would be like cutting a single frame from a reel of film and presenting it as the whole movie. Each frame presents a different part of the story, and what that story was depends on where along the reel it was cut. What is presented here is the picture of a single frame in the history of the American Indian, the one just before the first European entered the western scene.

The list of tribes that were not present on the Great Plains at the opening of the seventeenth century might be surprising to aficionados of the Hollywood Western. Most on the list farmed and hunted the eastern woodlands between the Great Lakes and the Ohio River valley, and most were driven west by pressure from more powerful native adversaries or expanding white settlement. In the early seventeenth century the Osage left their eastern homeland to settle along the Little Osage River near the current Arkansas/Nebraska border. About that same time a band that would become the Crow split off from the Hidatsa, traveling as far west as Montana. The Cheyenne and Arapaho followed in the middle of the same century. The Sioux didn't arrive on the grasslands west of the Mississippi for another hundred years. Moving east from the Rocky Mountains, a band split from Wyoming's Shoshoni in the late seventeenth century and migrated to the southern plains. Acquiring horses along the way, they became the Comanche. And it was likely that the movement of so many eastern tribes west, along with their many spoken dialects, spawned a new common language, a sign language, making it possible for new and old plains dwellers to communicate (Malinowski et al. 1999, 826).

Before these new arrivals the central grasslands were a lot less crowded. Plains Apache hunted buffalo across the southern grasslands on foot before the arrival of mounted Comanche. The Wichita farmed and hunted in what is now Oklahoma for thousands of years. The Pawnee, a branch of the Wichita, raised corn, squash, and beans along the Platte River valley. The plains' most prolific agriculturalists, the Mandan and Arikara, raised corn, beans, squash, sunflower, and amaranth along the Middle Missouri River, roughly between present-day Pierre, South Dakota, and Bismarck, North Dakota. These river villages of the Middle Missouri were major trade centers. The inhabitants not only sold their own goods but acted as middlemen in trade between the woodland dwellers of the east and buffalo hunters to the west. On the Upper High Plains, Kiowa hunters followed buffalo from the Black Hills into Montana, while the migratory

PART 2 — NATIVE AMERICANS ON FOOT

Blackfeet ranged from the headwaters of the Missouri north into today's Canadian provinces.

To supplement a steady diet of meat, migrating bands of the western grasslands moved into the mountains to gather ripening berries and dig plant roots. Along the more numerous river bottoms of the eastern grasslands, hunter-gatherers found wild plums, grapes, chokecherries, rosehips, and a variety of berries and nuts. But one resource all these plains dwellers had in common was the buffalo. Even those who settled and farmed along river valleys traveled the plains for an annual hunt. Buffalo alone could provide everything needed for survival—food, clothing, footwear, shelter, and tools. But buffalo hunting on foot was a tricky business. With skill, luck, and the wind in his face, a skillful hunter crawling under cover of a buffalo hide might get close enough to take one of these animals with a bow and arrow. Taking enough buffalo to support a group of any size needed a different technique—the use of "jumps" and "pounds."

A buffalo jump was a cliff, most often a bluff along a river, over which native men drove buffalo. Pounds were natural enclosures among rocks, a dry wash or coulee, where herds could be confined and individuals picked off, one by one, with arrows and spears. But first hunters had to get buffalo close to the area of the kill. Deliberately setting fire to grasslands near the jumps and pounds lured buffalo into the traps. Ashes from old grass fertilized new succulent grass toward which buffalo naturally migrated. In the area leading in to a pound or jump, hunters built rock walls and blinds as diversions. When the time was right, a group of men behind the herd began a stampede toward the killing grounds. Along the rock walls and behind blinds others waited, listening for the distant drumming of hooves moving toward their positions. Sounds of the herd, snorting and bellowing, and clouds of dust intensified as the herd grew nearer, until even the ground itself seemed to move. Funneled toward the slaughter by manmade diversions, the buffalo would be driven faster and faster. Men jumping from behind blinds shouting and waving animal hides whipped the herd into a frenzy until, even as the lead buffalo saw the trap, they were pushed forward by the panicked animals behind. At the bottom of a jump, those animals not killed outright by the fall were quickly finished off. It was a risky business and one that had to be well organized.

However, according to one legend passed on from generation to generation across the plains, there was another, much easier and safer way of taking buffalo. The ancient story was told of a mythic figure called Old Man, who lived long ago when animals could still talk. Old Man and didn't like to work or hunt. One day Old Man saw Fox walking by. Old Man was lazy, but he was also clever. He had a plan. Old Man asked Fox if he could pull all the hair off Fox's body except for one tuft on his tail. After much persuasion, Fox finally agreed. Old Man pulled all the hair off Fox except one tuft on his tail, and Fox continued on his way. After some time Fox came to where Buffalo was grazing. When Buffalo saw Fox, he dropped dead from laughter (Gill and Sullivan 1992, 223).

Regardless of the technique, if everything went right, a good hunt meant fresh meat now and dried meat for winter, clothes and shelter from the hides, bone tools and utensils. And after a flurry of skinning, feasting, drying meat, and pulling sinew for sewing and bindings, the people moved away, leaving what remained and the scent to scavenging bears, wolves, coyotes, vultures, flies, and ants. And with them they carried what was the premier trade item of the plains: the buffalo hide. Cured with the thick hair still on, these warm—and surprisingly heavy—robes provided protection from the coldest weather or comfort as a mattress or sleeping robe. A good buffalo hide could buy a lot of trade goods. Since incessant warfare along the Mississippi River valley had dampened trade between that region and the plains (Vehik and Baugh 1994, 266),

PART 2 ~ NATIVE AMERICANS ON FOOT

buffalo hunters of the south and central plains would most likely trade with the Pueblos of the America Southwest.

This was the region—today's Arizona, New Mexico, West Texas, and Northern Mexico—that the Aztecs called Azatlan, the land of their revered ancestors. It was hot and dry, the Sonoran Desert to the west and the Chihuahua in the east, interspersed with a few fertile river valleys. In this land advanced cultures—Mogollon, Hohokam, and Anasazi—formed, spread over large areas of the Southwest, then collapsed, most likely from overpopulation and changes in weather patterns (Lipe 1983, 473). Their descendants consolidated along more reliable water sources of the Rio Grande, the lower Colorado, and their tributaries in what first-contact Spaniards called pueblos and rancherias.

Traveling west from the plains, migratory traders might first encounter the Pecos Pueblo, situated in a pass along the southern tip of the Sangre de Cristo Mountains, halfway between the grasslands and the Rio Grande Pueblos to the west. It would have been an impressive sight for plains dwellers traveling along the stream valley approach—suddenly looming ahead, stone and adobe covered buildings spread over a low ridge, four and five stories high, with hundreds of rooms.

Or further south, at about the center of present-day New Mexico, plains traders would find the Salinas Pueblos—Quarai, Abo, and Gran Quivira—bordered on the west by the Manzano Mountains and to the east, glimpsed through a few outlying foothills, the unbroken grasslands of the high plains stretching hundreds of miles beyond the horizon. Las Salinas, the name the Spanish gave these pueblos, came from the nearby Estancia Basin, a group of intermittent lakes, usually dry, where these pueblos gathered their most important trade item, salt. Pueblo farmers also raised the traditional "three sisters"—corn, beans, and squash—for trade, along with cotton for clothes and blankets. According to early Spanish sources, linens from the pueblos of the Southwest were as fine as anything made in Spain. In exchange for their goods, the pueblo traders received slaves, flints, dried buffalo meat, and the highly prized buffalo hide. And what these easternmost pueblos didn't keep for their own use made its way west as trade goods to the pueblos lining the northern half of New Mexico's Rio Grande valley. Native towns along that river were the most densely populated in the American West, most likely due to the fact that they also had some of the most productive farmers. Spanish explorers reported one pueblo of that region having stored enough corn to supply the town for three years. Pueblos of Upper Rio Grande valley were also adept at producing cotton well north of its normal growing range. Here all that was needed to overcome the limitations of nature were an abundant supply of rocks and lots of sunshine. Native farmers cleared potential cotton fields of trees and brush and then covered the field with large flat rocks placed close together. In the cracks between the rocks, they planted cottonseed. The rocks acted as mulch, retarding weed growth and soil moisture loss. More importantly, during the day, the rocks absorbed heat from the sun. At night, when temperatures dropped to levels that would normally kill the plant, the rocks gave off stored heat, creating a warmer microclimate in which cotton could survive (Ford 2000, 217).

In addition to the other trade goods mentioned, native miners dug valuable turquoise from the low hills of the Cerillos, south of what is now the City of Santa Fe. From the Rio Grande Pueblos, turquoise and other trade items moved as far south as the Aztec capital in Mexico or west to the Pueblos of Acoma and Zuni in New Mexico and the Hopi of Northeastern Arizona.

Other settled native peoples of the Southwest grew domesticated crops in small, scattered farm communities along the rivers of western Arizona that early Spaniards labeled "rancherias." In the Sonoran Desert of southwestern Arizona, the Pima and Papago cultures farmed the Salt and Gila River valleys using flood plain irrigation. Though often dry, these rivers were subject to sporadic flash floods, great waves of water that surged down river valleys then quickly disappeared. To provide a more reliable source of water, native farmers dug canals to funnel off floodwaters into manmade catchment basins—holding ponds to store water until needed. Radiating out from the basins, irrigation ditches supplied water to surrounding fields. Yumanspeaking natives who settled along both sides of the southern Colorado River practiced a similar style of irrigation. The Mohaves, part of this group, were said to have traveled widely, establishing a trade trail all the way to the Pacific (Malinowski et al. 1999, 473).

In the vast, unoccupied territory outside the settled pueblos and rancherias of the Southwest roamed small migratory bands of Athabascan-speaking hunter-gatherers. These tribes slowly filtered south from Canada beginning in the fourteenth century, some reaching the Southwest barely ahead of the first Spanish entrada moving up from the conquered Aztec Empire. On their long journey south, part of that Athabascan group, what would become the Navajo, broke off and headed west to settle in northern New Mexico and Arizona by the early sixteenth century. The rest, the Apache, ranged from the southwestern plains of Colorado through parts of west Texas, all of New Mexico except the northwestern quadrant, and into central Arizona. They survived the arid deserts of the Southwest hunting deer, rabbits, and other small game. Wild plant foods added to their diet—mesquite seeds, cacti, yucca, and agave. The last two were particularly useful plants. Dried leaves of yucca and agave were food sources that could be stored for long periods and often used as travel food. Pulverized yucca root made soap for washing and as a shampoo. Soaking and pounding the leaves separated stringy leaf material from the soft tissue, and, when dried, native people wove the tough fibers into string, rope, nets, mats, and sandals.

To the north, the cold desert lands of the Great Basin of Nevada, Utah, southern Oregon, and Idaho had once supported a settled agricultural lifestyle similar to the early pueblos of the Southwest. Natives of the Fremont Culture lived in pit house settlements, grew corn, hunted game, and gathered wild plant foods for hundreds of years then disappeared around the thirteenth century. At the opening of the sixteenth century, the Great Basin, for humans, was the most demanding environment in the West. Those who survived in this harsh climate followed the hunter-gatherer lifestyle. The Shoshoni, thought to have migrated from the Southwest between one and two thousand years ago, roamed through Idaho's Snake River, Central and Northeastern Nevada, and Northwestern Utah (Malinowski et al. 1999, 353). Around the time of the collapse of the Fremont Culture, Utes moved south from Canada to settle parts of the eastern Great Basin and the Colorado Plateau. Bands of Paiute occupied the western Great Basin from Eastern Oregon south through Nevada and into the eastern tip of California.

In these dry basin and range lands between the Rocky and Sierra Nevada Mountains, game was scarce, and migrating hunter-gatherers had to cover long distances on foot to find enough resources to survive. Relying most heavily on plant foods, women harvested tiny seeds of sagebrush and lamb's quarters growing along basin floors using special conical seed baskets and gathering fans that looked something like wicker paddles. With the mouth of the basket against one side of sagebrush, a woman would beat the other side with her gathering fan, separating the seeds from the plant. Tossing these tiny seeds in the air from a shallow winnowing basket carried away the lighter husks and chaff in a light breeze, while the heavier seeds fell back to the basket. Gathered seeds were eaten fresh or made into cakes (Mason 1894, 459).

PART 2 — NATIVE AMERICANS ON FOOT

The Great Basin had another plant resource that, in all around utility, rivaled the buffalo of the Great Plains. This humble plant grew along the marshlands that surrounded the rivers and lakes of the region. Tule was a type of bulrush that grew up to twelve feet tall and provided everything a human needed to survive. Its seeds and roots could be eaten. The stems, tied together, made mats for resting on and as shelter covers. Tule was woven to make clothing, sandals, cord, baskets, packs, cradle boards, and duck decoys (Kopper 1986, 191). Tule even made serviceable watercraft; bundles of its buoyant, hollow stems lashed together made rafts or reed canoes. Although not waterproof, these craft could float a fair-sized load.

Along the north-south trending ranges of the Great Basin, vegetation increased with elevation, and in late summer hunter-gathers moved out of the basins and up into the scattered mountains. Pine-juniper forests covering the upper levels of the ranges were a place to harvest seeds of the piñon pine, a major food source for the area. Individual hunters in the region took what limited game they could find, but once a year small bands, each with a section of net made from plant fibers, came together for an annual rabbit hunt. Individual nets tied together formed one long barrier strung out across a sagebrush-covered basin floor. People moved over the ground in long lines, driving rabbits in front of them into the net trap. The catch was shared among the bands, and then each went its own way (Kopper 1986, 191). Such a harsh environment couldn't support the needs of a large group for long.

But along the northern fringes of the Great Basin there was one abundant and highly valued resource—obsidian. This dark-colored, glass-like byproduct of volcanism could be chipped to an edge sharper than modern surgical steel. Shaped as tools for hunting, war, or household chores, they were packed in bundles by traders who started down the long trail, skirting the western flank of the Wasatch Mountains, over the southernmost tip of Nevada, and across the Mojave Desert to trade for shells on the Pacific coast of present-day California.

For the traveler from the Great Basin, the Pacific coast would have been an example of ecological diversity in the extreme, its bountiful resources easily accessible and concentrated in a narrow strip of land little more than 125 miles wide, from California into the Pacific Northwest. The Pacific West was the most densely settled region of the West, supporting approximately one quarter of the total native population of what is now the continental United States (Krober 1963, 136). Culturally and geographically, the Pacific coast could be subdivided roughly along the latitude passing through Cape Mendocino, California, where the Sierra Nevada curve westward to merge with the Cascade and Coastal Mountain Ranges. South of this line, including most California to the thirty-fifth parallel just below Bakersfield, lay the resources of the Pacific Ocean and two mountain ranges separated by the broad plain of the Central Valley.

In California's Upper Central Valley, the Sacramento River flows south to meet the lower valley's north-flowing San Joaquin in a broad marshy delta that emptied into San Francisco Bay. The Yahi and Yana tribes in the Sacramento River valley and the Yokuts of the San Joaquin Valley followed migrating game herds across broad grasslands and snared waterfowl in the marshlands using nets made from hemp. They harvested the rivers using extracts from California buckeye, a type of neurotoxin that, when spread over the water, stupefied the fish and caused them to float to the surface. In the foothills of the Sierra Nevada to the east and the Coastal Range to the west, native gatherers collected the California staple, acorns, in huge quantities from park-like groves of oak. And climbing upward from the foothills of either range, they followed the seasonal progression of food sources changing with elevation: serviceberries, huckleberries, and pine nuts. Central Valley dwellers could also travel through the low passes of the Coastal Mountains westward to harvest or trade for resources of the Pacific coast.

Tribes along the California coast also followed the hunter-gatherer lifestyle but had the added resource of an ocean to fish and from which to take sea mammals, along with all the food sources of the tidal margins—clams, scallops, mussels, and oysters. Costanoans who settled between today's Monterrey Bay and San Francisco had all this, and they could move inland to gather plant foods along the western slopes of the Coastal Mountain Range—acorns, fruit, berries, and nuts. Near today's New Almaden, California, Costanoan natives mined cinnabar, from which they prepared the red pigment vermillion, a valued resource that drew traders from as far away as the Columbia River.

South of Costanoan territory, along a two-hundred-mile stretch of coast, roughly centered on current-day Santa Barbara, Chumash people navigated the Pacific coast in brightly colored cedar-plank boats (Malinowski et al. 1999, 997–998). In Chumash society, boat builders were placed in the uppermost class. And they were the only native people who constructed plank-built boats. Local cedar was a soft wood, easy to split, with natural oils that inhibited rot. Split planks, tied together with sinew and caulked with naturally occurring asphaltum, made a seaworthy craft that gave the Chumash control of most of the Southern California coast.

North of San Francisco Bay, from the coast east to Clear Lake and the Russian River, was Pomo territory. Like most coastal societies, they harvested the bounty of the ocean, but they also moved inland to fish the rivers using the same technique as the Yokut of the Central Valley, stunning fish with extracts of California buckeye. But what made Pomo people unique was their ability as traders who manufactured their own money in the form of circular seashell disks and colorful beads from the mineral magnesite. Keeping track of money forced Pomos to develop a system of counting far beyond other native people (Malinowski et al. 1999, 1114).

Transitional tribes, sharing cultural characteristics of Upper California and the Pacific northwest, settled Southern Oregon and Northern California. Among these were the Hupa and Chilua of Northwestern California, who moved into that region from the north some thirteen hundred years ago. Pacific coast Athabascans, related to the Apache and Navajo of the Southwest, migrated south from Canada to the Rouge and Umpagua River region of Southwest Oregon.

Above the Cape Mendocino parallel, geography changed dramatically; the uplifted Sierra Nevada gave way to volcanic peaks of the Cascades crowding in on the Coast Ranges to form a densely wooded, rugged, and mountainous terrain that made overland travel difficult. Even along the coastline massive forested headlands broke out into the sea, blocking north-south travel along the beaches. Native populations in the Northwest tended to congregate along the Pacific coast on flat deltas, where the mouth of a river emptied into the ocean, or inland along major rivers, particularly the Columbia (Kopper 1986, 203).

Dozens of tribes of Coastal Salish settled from lower British Columbia to Northwest Oregon, moving along the coast in canoes of every size, hunting marine mammals, fishing, and collecting shellfish from the shore. The Tillamook, once the most powerful tribe along the Oregon Coast, formed the southernmost colony of Coastal Salish (Santoro 2009, 380).

Chinook people lived along both banks of the greatest of these inland waterways, the Columbia River, now the boundary between the states of Washington and Oregon. Chinook economy relied heavily on their control of commerce and trade that moved along that river highway from the Pacific, through the Cascades, to the interior Columbia River Plateau of the Intermountain Region, and the Great Plains beyond. As on the Great Plains, interaction of such a wide variety of cultures over such a long range necessitated the development of a common trade language, and that was Chinook jargon, a combination of Chinook and other native languages.

Travel by water was a distinguishing feature of the people of the Northwest coast, among whom boat building reached its highest level. From huge oceangoing boats with high sides and tall bows to slender, low-riding canoes used for river travel, native craftsmen designed and built a wide variety watercraft for trade and transportation. During the winter most coast dwellers of the Pacific Northwest lived in longhouses made from split cedar planks. When warm weather arrived, native travelers prepared for the annual trip inland to hunt, fish, and gather wild plant food. Planks taken from winter longhouse shelters and fastened across pairs of canoes made catamaran-like vessels for the journey up navigable rivers loaded with men, women, children, and equipment. When they arrived at their inland destinations, cedar planks from their vessels were recycled to build shelters for temporary summer camps.

Native populations from California to the Pacific Northwest were a bit of an anomaly: hunter-gathers who lived in relatively fixed villages. Why then, in this densely populated and limited land area, weren't domesticated crops grown to support the people? In short, it was because natives of the Pacific West probably couldn't and wouldn't but most definitely didn't have to. They couldn't because of environmental factors. During the summer growing season, California is too dry to support domestic crops even in the fertile central valleys. Further north, along the western coasts of Oregon and Washington, rain is plentiful. But there, with the exception of Oregon's Willamette Valley, the Cascade and Coastal mountain ranges coalesce into one rugged, densely forested land scarcely penetrable by man and therefore unsuited for agriculture. Native cultures of the Pacific West probably wouldn't have turned to growing domestic crops even if the environment had been favorable because of intensive amounts of labor involved in agriculture compared to hunting and gathering. Traditionally it was held that hunter-gatherer cultures would naturally evolve into agricultural cultures if the proper resources were available. But considering that those who grow domesticated crops spend twice as much time in acquiring their food as hunter-gatherers do, it may be that an agricultural way of life was something adopted out of environmental necessity (Kopper 1986, 50). There certainly was little environmental necessity for using domesticated crops as a food source in the Pacific West. Easily accessible and abundant natural food sources from a diversity of environmental zones were enough to support a large and stable population.

No matter what region the first emigrants roamed, the land they crossed had a profound effect on where, how, and why they traveled or settled. Its features could invite or exclude—and sometimes both. For those on foot, a river was an obstacle to cross. In a dugout, a traveler saw the same river as a water highway. In the summer mountains were places to travel to for a wide variety of resources; in the winter, covered with snow, they were barriers not to be crossed. Mineral, water, plant, and animal resources—or lack thereof—across the grasslands, mountains, and deserts of the American West determined where people lived and the lifestyles they had to adopt to survive. And, in time, the lifestyles and cultures of the first people had a profound effect on the travels of the European emigrants who followed.

Chapter 3

Equipment, Supplies, and Transport on Foot

Native people had been traveling the American West for many thousands of years before the first Europeans entered the scene. The land was not the trackless waste portrayed in the journals of early European explorers. Travel trails covered the West. Using ancient memory aids, native people moved over trails, crossing vast expanses of territory without printed maps, guided only by information imprinted in their minds—where water could be found, where game was scarce or plentiful, where friends and enemies lived, the various land features that had to be crossed, and which landmarks to use as guides. And when necessary they could make long overland journeys on foot with everything needed to survive carried on their backs.

If land travel prior to the European introduction of the horse meant walking then it would follow that one of the most important pieces of travel equipment was foot cover. In many cases native

EQUIPMENT, SUPPLIES, AND TRANSPORT ON FOOT

peoples went barefoot locally, but long-distance travel required some type of protective footwear—a pair of moccasins or sandals.

Moccasins made from animal hides had stiff rawhide for soles and buckskin or some other tanned and pliable hide for the upper parts. Summer moccasins had the animal hair removed; winter moccasins came from hides with the hair on and turned in for warmth. Sandals woven from plant material didn't provide cold protection and so were most common in the warmer climates or during warmer weather. Yucca was a widely available plant that grew in the Southwest and the Great Plains as far north as the Dakotas. The long fibers of its pulverized and shredded leaves, woven into cordage and rope, also made sandals. Agave leaves and Indian hemp, among other plants, served the same purpose. Marsh reeds, like tule, provided a ready material for sandal making. Unlike the small fibers of the agave and yucca that had to be first made into cordage then woven into sandals, the larger-diameter marsh grass could be woven directly into footwear.

When snow fell, travel required specialized footwear. With well-made snowshoes, an experienced winter traveler could cover up to fifty miles a day skimming over the snow (Mason 1894, 381). Without them, winter journeys would be short and exhausting, if not impossible. Basic snowshoes were a wooden frame covered by a netting of animal sinew or rawhide or cordage of woven plant material. They ranged in size from small and rounded to teardrop-shaped shoes as tall as a man. The purpose of the trip, and the type of snow the traveler crossed, determined snowshoe design. Snowshoes used for travel were smaller than those used for hunting. Those for dry, powder snow had close web netting. Wet, soft snow needed wider netting.

For hunters the first snow of the year was a reason to celebrate with religious ceremonies and dancing. Game was much easier to track through snow, and a snowshoe-clad hunter, moving quickly over drifts, had a definite advantage over large, heavy prey like buffalo that had to founder through them (figure 2).

Long-distance travel for native people meant providing some means of carrying all the paraphernalia of life: food, water, cooking utensils, tools, weapons, shelter, clothes, babies, children too young to walk, and even puppies. Devices for burden bearing had to be light and rugged. Heavy wooden storage boxes and chests carried in native canoes of the Pacific Northwest would have been impossible for overland foot travel. Nor would the breakable pottery containers used by settled tribes of the Southwest and other regions have been practical. Packs and containers made from animal hides or plant materials carried the necessities of life in overland travel. Most common were woven burden baskets made from an endless variety of plant materials and in a variety of designs. Every region had some indigenous material adaptable to this purpose. Where wood was available, baskets were woven from spruce roots, cedar bark, thin strips split from tough, straight-grained hickory, or supple willow branches. Where wood was not available, cordage and ropes made from fibrous grasses like native hemp, fibers processed from desert leaves of yucca or agave, or rushes and reeds harvested from marshlands made serviceable burden baskets.

Early French explorers gave the name *par fleche* to another type of native carrying case, common where animal hides were abundant. Par fleche was rawhide, usually buffalo. The process of turning an animal skin into rawhide started by staking it out flat, scraping off the fat, then soaking it in an alkaline solution made of wood ashes or crushed lime rock. The alkaline solution helped loosen hair so it could be scraped away. The result was rawhide, which when dried was very stiff, not supple like tanned hides. When wet, though, soggy rawhide could be shaped into par fleche cases of whatever size and shape needed. Dried rawhide became stiff once more, holding the desired shape. A common style of native par fleche case looked something like a large folded wallet tied together with thongs. In camp, par fleche cases were used for storage, and for traveling they could be made as backpacks for humans or packs for dogs, if dogs were available.

Mothers carried babies, up to about one year of age, on their backs in specialized burden baskets. Like all other burden baskets, these carrying cradles were made from whatever native materials were abundant in a particular region—wood, hides, reeds, plant fibers, or any combination of these. Carrying cradle design might include a hood as protection for the baby from sun, snow, and rain or a wooden hoop that functioned like a roll bar to protect the baby's head in case the cradle was dropped or tipped over. In place of diapers, native mothers used strategically positioned absorbent plant materials—dried moss, shredded bark, or fluffy "wool" from seedpods—inside the carrying cradle. Children over one year but still too young to walk, or walk very far, were carried on the backs of mothers in shawl-like slings or, on the open plains, hauled on dog travois (Mason 1894, 537).

Packs and burden baskets of all types had to be supported for carrying, and usually this was done with a trump line of leather straps or cordage that passed under the bottom of the load, up the back, and around the forehead of the carrier like a sling. This arrangement transferred some of the weight of the load from the back to the head. Where the trump line passed over the head, padding or netting was added for comfort. Sometimes chest or shoulder straps gave additional support. Raising and lowering a heavy pack was tiring, and experienced carriers looked for a tree or rock to lean the weight of a burden against and remain standing during rest breaks. Another strategy was to carry a forked walking stick that could be wedged up under the pack when resting. Sticks gave the heavy burden bearer something to lean on when walking or climbing and doubled as a weapon when necessary. Sometimes burdens were carried balanced on top of the head. A head carry, most often a method used by women, had the advantage of bringing the center of gravity of a given load in line with the vertical axis of the body, which made it easier to carry. Head pads or doughnut-shaped head rings made of plaited animal fur or plant fibers helped cushion the load.

Of all the supplies that had to be carried, water was the most important. Without it no human, or any other animal, could go far. But the weight of water, over eight pounds per gallon, made carrying it long distances something to be avoided whenever possible. For that reason most trails followed rivers and streams or went from one waterhole or spring to another. But sometimes the need to extend the range of native travel beyond known water supplies made carrying water a necessity. Fragile pottery water containers or pottery canteens used by settled people were not a good option for long-distance travelers. Closely woven baskets made water tight with pitch were stronger, less breakable water containers. In some areas of the West, waterproofing material came from naturally occurring surface deposits of tar-like asphaltum. The gum of pine or fir trees served the same purpose. A dried gourd with a hole drilled in one end and stoppered with a corncob made a handy canteen. Some gourds, specially grown as canteens, had constricted middles so that carrying straps could be easily attached. Bladders and intestines of animals, made pliable by tanning, could also be used to transport water. One sixteenth-century Spanish journalist recorded a more creative means of thirst quenching where water was scarce.

> *When these Indians kill a cow [buffalo] they clean a large intestine and fill it with blood and put it around their necks to drink when they are thirsty. After they cut open the belly of the cow they squeeze out the chewed grass and drink the juice, which remains on top, saying that it contains the substance of the stomach (Hammond 1940, 262).*

Finding water was a problem in strange territory or in overland travel that strayed from established routes. When no water was available, native travelers chewed on cattail roots or mesquite beans as a temporary means of allaying thirst. But sooner or later some water source had to be found. One possibility was to follow game trails that might eventually lead to water. And plants reflect the environment they live in and so can tell a story if a traveler knows how to read them. Shrubby willows and mesquite only grew where groundwater was relatively close to the surface. The presence of these indicator plants meant the possibility of water, which could be found with a little digging. Another indicator was the flight of pigeons and doves heading toward water for an evening drink. Being aware of this, and following their course, the traveler could find water too.

The dove in the story of Noah and the Ark, from the Christian Bible, was an ancient parallel for the use of birds as navigational devices. Before the invention of the compass, it was in fact a common practice for sailors to carry caged birds to sea. If seamen wanted to find land again once it dropped below the horizon, a bird was set loose. The bird, from its vantage point circling high above the ship, searched the horizon. If no land was visible, the bird landed on the ship. But if the bird spotted land, it flew off in that direction with the seaman following behind on the same course. In that case seaman used birds to find land, while in the former example landsmen used birds to find water.

In the hierarchy of important travel supplies food follows closely behind water. To supply this need the native traveler had three choices: carrying food, foraging for food, or relying on the kindness of strangers. On regularly traveled trails, food from a friendly village might be relied on either through hospitality or trade. In many cases, though, food had to be carried, hunted, or gathered along the way, and often it had to be a combination of all these. Hunted and gathered food would be whatever might occur

PART 2 — NATIVE AMERICANS ON FOOT

naturally in the land traveled. The most likely food sources were near water. Not only man but also all kinds of migrating game concentrated near water. Around water a hungry traveler might find waterfowl, birds, turtles, eggs, fish, roots, tubers, eatable plant leaves, berries, fruit, nuts, seeds, insects, and grubs.

Even in what would seem the most inhospitable desert lands, food was available—for those who knew where to look. One plant, notable because it was both a benefit and a nuisance, was the prickly pear cactus. This hardy cactus grew over America's dry, grassy midlands from Texas as far north as Canada. It had edible flowers and fruit when ripened and in bloom, and its flat segments, or paddles, were a food source any time. Prickly pear also had a rather unique quality: it could be used to purify water. Individual cactus paddles were easy to break loose with a stick, knock to the ground, and roll in the dirt until enough of the spines were broken off to make them safe to handle. A small cactus paddle split open and dropped into a container of muddy river water could, with a little stirring, turn river water silty enough to plow, clear as a mountain stream. On the other hand, as a nuisance, sharp spines of the prickly pear pierced the moccasins of many an unwary traveler.

In the desert Southwest, a hungry traveler happening on a stubby barrel cactus cut off its top and scooped out the insides to make a hollow container. Into this natural cooking pot he'd add water and any plant or animal food found, including edible parts of the cactus itself. Dropping fire heated rocks into the mixture made a hot stew without the necessity of dragging along a lot of heavy kitchenware. As an added bonus, one species of barrel cactus was a natural compass, its tip always growing with a definitive lean to the south. And in an emergency a very hungry traveler might even resort to stripping bark from a tree and eating the mucilaginous layer next to the wood. A very, very hungry traveler could scrap lichen off a rock. Boiled lichen made a foul-tasting, malodorous slime, and on the scale of human food sources it might possibly be considered a small step above cannibalism. Beyond that, crossing uninhabited lands where foraged food was scarce, or under travel conditions where speed was a priority, food had to be packed along the trail.

The types of foods carried by native travelers for thousands of years would look familiar to modern hikers and campers. Packed foods were almost always dried. Foods with the water removed were lighter, took up less space, and drying was a method of preserving foods for long periods. This was true for meat, fish, and plant foods. Fresh meat with the fat removed, cut into thin strips, and dried under the sun or over a fire became jerked meat. It lasted for years, making it an important staple for travelers. Dried meat was also ground into a meal or flour-like consistency. Grinding made it possible to utilize poorer quality, tougher meats generally considered uneatable. Water added to the powdered meat made it swell and, cooked with anything else edible found along the trail, provided a variety of diet. Pemmican was a popular and widely used type of travel food, also made with dried, ground meat. A single pound of pemmican had the food value of ten pounds of fresh meat. Most common native recipes called for grease or fat and dried berries, or ground roots or herbs, mixed with the meat meal. Pemmican could be stored for long periods, made a nutritious meal, and was eaten as is. It didn't require the time or fuel to build a fire. In the Pacific Northwest, where fish, particularly salmon, were common, a variation of pemmican substituted dried fishmeal for meat.

The list of plants, wild and domesticated, that were processed as travel food was substantial. One of the most widely used was parched corn. Dropping corn with the hulls removed into a flat, woven basket with heated stones or coals, and just the right amount of agitation, parched the kernels without burning the basket. Winnowing removed any wood ashes that got into the mix. Parched corn was eaten as is or ground into a fine meal. Adding other ingredients like dried fruit or berries to the grinding mix provided a varied diet. The same process was performed on any number of plant roots, leaves, fruit, and seeds. The ubiquitous sunflower grew everywhere and under the worst possible conditions. Its seeds—parched, ground, mixed with grease, and made into cakes—were a nutritious, portable, and long-lasting food source. As travel food in the American Southwest, native travelers carried roasted agave leaves pressed flat, dried, and tied into bundles. In mountain valleys, dried and ground meal of bitterroot, camas, or arrowhead roots were a favored travel food. Two or three ounces of dried plant meals mixed with a cup of water were considered a meal. While travel food added to the burden, it was also an insurance against unexpected hunger and a means of extending how far and how long a traveler could journey and the types of terrain over which he could move.

In harsher climates not only food and water but shelter was a necessity. Native travelers sought protection from the elements by carrying along portable shelters or by taking advantage of whatever resources were found at the end of a day's travel. Hides or rolled-up mats carried from one camp to another formed the usual portable shelter. On the plains portable animal hide shelters were common. Buffalo hides thrown over poles made the familiar tepee. Native women made these shelter covers during the summer because hides taken from buffalo during warm weather were thinner and lighter. Tanning made the hides soft and pliable, and a smoky fire burning inside a new tepee cover set up on poles helped preserve the leather and make it waterproof. On the plains, where wood was scarce, rocks gathered from the surrounding area anchored the bottom of the tepee cover. Thousands of these tepee rings are still visible throughout the West as partially covered rock circles.

But even the lightest buffalo hides were heavy, and before the introduction of the horse, weight limited what migrating hunter-gatherers could carry on their backs. Besides the weight of the hides, tent poles had to be carried, too, not to mention all the other necessities of life. Hollywood representations to the contrary, weight limitations meant animal hide tepees had to be small, light, and therefore cramped throughout all but a final and brief period of migrating native history.

Native travelers throughout the West carried mats made from plant materials more often than animal hides to make their shelters. Cut to size and sewn together side by side, mats made of stems of reeds and rushes gathered from river bottoms, marshes, and lakes could be rolled up when traveling and then thrown across poles or piles of brush to provide shade or shelter from wind and rain. The same type of mat doubled as a seat or something to sleep on.

When portable temporary shelters weren't available or necessary, native travelers relied on whatever natural resources they could find. In mountainous regions of the rugged Intermountain West, undercut rock faces along old riverbeds, caves, and rock outcroppings afforded a night's shelter from the elements. Since the migratory patterns of people inhabiting a given region remained the same, as long as resources were available, these rock shelters could be used year after year. Further south in warmer climates, temporary shelters didn't have to be elaborate. A night might be spent in a hollowed space in the sand with rocks or brush piled to one side as a windbreak.

There were two possible means of transport that could help lighten the load for burden-bearing native peoples traveling on foot. The most significant and widely used was the domesticated dog.

Native dogs were large, bred that way to carry heavy burdens. The load a dog could carry varied substantially depending on the size of the dog and whether the load was packed directly on the dog or pulled behind on a travois. Pack dogs carried loads directly on their backs in leather saddlebags or cases lashed to padded packsaddles. A cinch passing underneath the dog along with a chest strap stabilized the load in the same manner as on European pack animals. Large pack dogs carried thirty-five to fifty pounds, but a dog pulling a travois could carry twice that weight. A dog outfitted with a travois could carry more weight because part of the burden was transferred from the dog's back to poles resting on the ground. A travois consisted of two poles or two sets of multiple poles fastened together—one set suspended on each side of the dog and fastened to a pad cinched behind the dog's forelegs, along with a chest strap. Poles of a dog travois were about eight feet long and made from aspen or other springy wood to help absorb the shock of a bouncing load. Several feet of the poles extended forward of the cinch pad crossing out over the dog's head. The rear section of the poles spread out behind to a width of three or four feet. Four or five parallel sticks fastened to the poles with rawhide, or a large wooden hoop interwoven with sticks and rawhide resembling the oversized head of a tennis racquet, provided the load platform on a travois. Either load platform was fastened to the travois poles about half way between the back of the dog and the back end of the poles. Adding willow-framed domes covered with animal skins protected the load from rain and sun. At the end of the day, travois poles turned into tepee poles with a hide or woven mats thrown over them for shelter. The poles of the travois made it possible to carry a much heavier load but were also its greatest disadvantage. Spreading out behind the dog, travois poles were easily hung up in vegetation or rocks. To be passable by travois, trails had to be wide, clear, and relatively flat—areas like the open grasslands of the Great Plains or the flat bowl of sagebrush-dotted land of the Great Basin. Across rocky mountain passes, rough and broken ground, brushy land, or narrow forest trails of the Pacific Northwest, only the narrow profile of pack dogs traveled.

A man hunting might take a single dog to carry provisions or return to camp with meat from a kill. At the other extreme a migrating tribe formed long trains of dogs, packing or pulling travois, when a village moved. The earliest Spanish explorers, crossing the high plains of eastern New Mexico, recorded a meeting with native tribes on the move.

> *These people [Plains Indians] have dogs similar to those of this land [Mexico], except that they are somewhat larger. They load these dogs like beasts of burden and make light packsaddles for them like our [Spanish] packsaddles, cinching them with leather straps. The dogs go about with sores on their backs like pack animals... When these Indians move—for they have no permanent residence anywhere, since they follow the cattle [buffalo] to find food—these dogs carry their homes for them. In addition to what they carry on their backs, they carry the poles for the tents, dragging them fastened to their saddles (Hammond 1940, 311).*

Moving an entire village was a complicated affair, beginning with a council meeting to work out details. If the purpose of the move was to be closer to a food source like buffalo, scouts were sent out to find a herd. Men from police or soldier societies organized people and maintained order during a move and picked a campsite at the end of the day. On the day of the move, rawhide cases had to be loaded with food, clothes, household gear, and other supplies. Tents were struck, babies secured in carrying cradles, and excited children rounded up. When a pack dog was unwilling, a woman straddled it backward, clamping the animal's head tight with her knees to keep it still while the heavy burden was loaded. If the job wasn't done right, if the load slipped once on the trail and the dog let out a howl, the whole village would know until it was put right. Moving a village was like a military maneuver, with two outer columns separated by a protected inner column. Single file, women, children, and dogs made up the inner column. One woman started off with the lead dog. Other women followed, leading dogs and children. Armed for defense against enemies or for hunting game, men traveled in columns on each side of the center at a distance from but always within eyesight of the women and children in the middle. On foot, with the elderly, infirm, small children, and heavily loaded dogs, a day's march couldn't be long, about five or six miles.

In winter with snow on the ground, overland transport was often by sled. Sleds made of wood or bone had a mixture of water and blood—blood made the mixture stick better—applied to their runners, which, when frozen, created a very slick surface. The great advantage of the sled was its load capacity. It was easier for a man to haul a 150-pound load on a sled than to carry one-third that weight in a backpack (Mason 1894, 546). In addition to their use in hauling equipment and supplies, sleds were one of the few viable ways of moving people. Loaded with the sick, wounded, elderly, or children, sleds carried human cargo over considerable distances in winter. Covering such distances was a feat next to impossible at other seasons of the year. Surprisingly, in most of the American West, one purpose dogs were not used for was hauling sleds in winter. Humans hauled sleds by lines attached to a chest strap or padded collar across the forehead or both.

There was a third option for dealing with heavy objects or excess burdens—not to transport them at all. Migrating people (and other native travelers) who followed a regular pattern of movement, returning to the same places year after year, solved the problem of limited transport by using the cache. A cache was a place to store or hide food or supplies for later use. It could be as simple as a rock crevice or a hole under a boulder or as complicated as a large underground storage pit. Any cache that was to be left unattended for long periods had to be well hidden. Returning to a raided food cache could be catastrophic for a people low on food. Camouflaging small caches in or under rocks was simple enough but hiding large underground storage pits required a little more effort. A well-designed cache pit kept the amount of visibly disturbed soil to a minimum. So underground pits were bell shaped, with a narrow opening at the surface and a space below that widened toward the bottom. Branches and brush lined the inside walls. Once filled and covered, the disturbed ground over the site had to be hidden. On grassy ground, sod could be carefully removed and laid aside before digging then replaced after the pit was completed. Water poured over sandy soil disguised disturbed ground. And if all else failed, the ashes of a campfire built over the storage pit kept the location secret (Hodge 1907, 643).

Anything could be cached—food, water, supplies, or equipment. In the pine-juniper forests of the Great Basin highlands, rather than carrying surplus piñon pine nuts along when they moved, natives stored them in caches for later consumption. A heavy object like a stone pestle, used by California natives to grind acorns, was much easier to cache than carry back and forth to the same oak groves each season. Native hunters cached excess equipment like spear points, arrowheads, and knife blades to be picked up later for use. Water was a particularly heavy burden at over eight pounds per gallon, and it could also be cached to make travel possible over lands that would be impossible to cross otherwise. Sixteenth-century Spanish explorers, the first Europeans to view the Grand Canyon, recorded this native practice. Moving along the dry south rim of the canyon with native guides and unable to reach the waters of the Colorado River a mile below, they wrote,

> *The party did not continue farther up the canyon of the river [Colorado] because of lack of water. Up to that time they had gone one or two leagues inland in search of water every afternoon. When they had traveled four additional days the guides said that it was impossible to go on because no water would be found for three or four days, that when they themselves traveled through that land they*

PART 2 — NATIVE AMERICANS ON FOOT

> took along women who brought water in gourds, that in those trips they buried the gourds of water for the return trip, and that they traveled in one day a distance that took us two days (Hammond 1940, 216).

Considering that the Spanish soldiers may have traveled fifteen to twenty miles a day total, daily side trips of roughly three to six miles in search of water would have slowed them down considerably. And considering the last line of the quote above, this lack of progress seems to have been a source of impatience for their native guides.

Native people weren't limited strictly to land travel. There were waterways, but they were relegated, with a few exceptions to the fringes of the West. Moving people and supplies by water was a much more important mode of transport along eastern rivers than rivers between the Plains and the Pacific. The difference came from the source of the water that flowed through them. In the East, rivers were fed by accumulated snowmelt of winter as well as summer rains. For many eastern rivers, together they maintained runoff at flow levels that were navigable by canoes for most of the year—except when blocked by ice. The West was dry; what little rain fell came in the winter, not the summer. Western rivers relied primarily on snowmelt for their water supply, and once snow packs in the high mountains melted completely, many rivers and streams went dry or had flow levels too shallow to navigate. There were, however, two notable exceptions: the Missouri River of the Great Plains and the Columbia River in the Pacific Northwest.

The Missouri was the most navigable river of the plains and the water gateway to the Northwest. A huge river, the Missouri had a muddy flow that changed the clear waters of the Upper Mississippi, from their confluence near Saint Louis all the way to the Gulf of Mexico. Missouri River flows supported canoe travel in all but the ice-covered winter months. From the Missouri's confluence with the Mississippi River, a river traveler could move west across the present State of Missouri, northward along the Kansas-Nebraska border, through the Dakotas, and west again, crossing Montana—and a distance of over twenty-four hundred miles—before coming to a major obstacle, the Great Falls of western Montana.

The other great western river of transport was the Columbia. It, too, was a water gateway for commerce between the Pacific West and the Intermountain Region. From its headwaters high in the Canadian Rockies, the river flowed south into the Columbia Plateau of eastern Washington and Oregon then west to the Cascade Mountains, where falls and rapids of the Dalles blocked river traffic. Portaging around this obstacle, river travel continued westward through the Cascades until the water of the Columbia crossed the bar at present-day Astoria and flowed into the Pacific Ocean. The Columbia was the only major east-west river artery between the Pacific coast and the Rocky Mountains.

Few other western rivers were navigable for any great distance. In some cases rivers were entrenched and inaccessible, like the section of the Colorado River running through southern Utah and northern Arizona. There the river flowed through a series of canyons—Cataract, Glen, Marble, and Grand—in places over a mile deep. Travelers in that part of the country had to detour hundreds of miles to find a place to cross the Colorado. Numerous rapids and falls made this river, and others, impassable for river traffic but most simply lacked enough summer water flow for river transport.

Where water travel was possible, the watercraft of choice was the dugout. Carved from a single tree, native dugout canoes ranged in sophistication from a stubby log with a hollowed center used for river travel on the plains, to the sleek and finely built, seventy-foot oceangoing vessels of the Pacific coast. The simplest dugouts came from cottonwood trees common to river bottoms of the plains. This tree had soft wood that was easy to work.

Cottonwood dugouts were also heavy and unwieldy, but they were rugged, and they needed to be to take the rocks and snags in the rivers that flowed east across the Great Plains.

The Pacific coast was the busiest region for boat building, and there native craftsmen produced the most advanced forms of dugout canoes. The coast had all the natural resources for building very large dugouts, plus an ocean to float them in and the well-watered Columbia River for moving trade goods inland to the east. Giant trees—spruce, fir, redwood, and cedar—grew in forests from the northern half of California far up into the Pacific Northwest. All four species were soft and easy to work, but cedar and redwood had the advantage of containing natural resins that made them resistant to rot. And considering the tremendous amount of time and labor involved in producing a large oceangoing canoe, boat builders wanted them to last.

Huge redwoods grew in the narrow fog belt that inundates the northern half of the Pacific coastline from the central California north to southwestern Oregon. Coast redwoods were not only the right wood for boat building, but they grew in the right place. Building a large boat was one thing; moving it to water was another. A solid log, massive enough to hew an oceangoing dugout seventy feet long and eight feet wide, wasn't going anywhere easily. Where the tree grew was the building site, and that site had to be close enough to water that the heavy vessel could be moved to it. Fortunately for native boat builders, coast redwoods, the world's tallest trees, grew near water and, in some places, in pure stands.

There, wandering through the misty gloom of cathedral-like coast redwood forests, crews of native boat builders searched for a tree of the right size and in a position to be moved to water. Staring upward into the crown of a tree as tall as a twenty-five-story building, even a heart tempered by experience must have skipped a beat at the thought of bringing one of those monsters to the ground. Amazingly, this was accomplished with small fires and pieces of bone or stone tied to sticks. Giant redwoods were literally scraped to the ground. The effort began with small fires built around the base of the tree. When the fires were extinguished, the remaining soft, charred wood was scraped away with stone tools. Workers moved through the massive tree inch by inch, scraping and burning, over and over, until that process finally brought a coastal redwood crashing to the ground. After felling, more fires and scraping at each end of the tree produced a log the proper length. Then the hull began to take shape as stone wedges and wooden mauls split sections of wood off the outside of the log. More fires and scraping smoothed the hull into its final shape. The thickness of the hull, from outside in, was gauged by drilling small holes of a prescribed depth along the sides and bottom. Then from the top of the log, small fires controlled by dams of wet mud began the process of hollowing out the inside of the hull with burning, scraping, and chopping until each of the predrilled gauge holes in the hull were reached. When the hull was finished, wooden plugs, driven from the outside in, permanently closed the gauge holes. The final step in boat building widened the beam for greater cargo capacity and stability at sea. By filling the inside of the hull with water and dropping in fire-heated stones, the upper hull became pliant enough to force apart with wooden crosspieces to the desired width. The crosspieces stayed in the dugout to serve as seats (Kopper 1986, 210). Boat building completed, native men dragged the finished craft over peeled log rollers to the nearest water at high tide. Once in the water, large vessels like this could coast the Pacific shore carrying cargo from Canada to Mexico and far up the broad Columbia River into the Cascade Mountains.

Native people along the major rivers of the eastern plains employed a far different type of watercraft, primarily for ferrying across rivers and short distance travel. Around river settlements, where crossings were made on a near daily basis, people used bullboats. These odd-shaped watercraft resembled large, round-bottomed washtubs, similar in construction to the coracle built by ancient Britons. Bullboats—large enough to carry three men and baggage and light enough to be carried by a single woman—were simple and fast to build. A buffalo hide, rawhide for lashings, and poles or saplings of a subtle wood like willow were all that was needed. It was built upside down, and construction began by burying pole ends in the ground in a circle the desired size of the finished boat. The tops of two poles from opposite sides of the circle were bent and lashed together. This process continued until each opposing set of poles was tied together and a dome-shaped top formed. At the bottom of the poles, close to the ground, a horizontal pole circling the frame and lashed to it formed be the upper rim of the boat. With the finished frame covered in a water soaked hide and the pole ends dug out of the ground, the craft was ready for river travel (figure 3).

When not on the river, bullboats made handy coverings for smoke holes of the timber-and-sod lodges along the riverbanks of the eastern plains, keeping them dry during downpours.

A thousand miles to the south and west, natives along the lower Colorado River used similarly shaped craft as river ferries, but instead of animal hides and poles, their river craft were made of woven saplings and branches. The finished products looked like giant baskets with coatings of tar-like asphaltum to makethem waterproof.

—⁂—

Chapter 4

Finding the Way

With the exception of water travel along the Pacific coast and a few inland rivers, western travel was on foot and usually on an established trail. Native people had been crossing the deserts, climbing the mountains, and traveling the forests and plains of the American West for thousands, in some cases tens of thousands, of years. North America was crisscrossed with trails from coast to coast, from Canada in the north to Mexico in the south. In heavily populated areas like California, finding a trail wasn't as great a problem as knowing which one to use among the confusing array of trails that led to a desired destination. Local trails were everywhere—trails connecting villages; trails leading to water holes, creeks, or rivers; and trails to resources like stone quarries, salt sources, or berry patches. Long-distance trails of commerce connected major population centers. In the Pacific West the oldest native trail ran from Canada, along the Pacific coasts of Washington, and into Oregon, where it split, one trail continuing along

PART 2 — NATIVE AMERICANS ON FOOT

the coast, bowing eastward around San Francisco Bay, and continuing south to Mexico. The inland leg of the trail followed the Willamette Valley of Oregon south along the rivers of California's Central Valley, joining the main trail once again along southern California's coast. A native trader of the Pacific Northwest who wanted to reach the Intermountain Region followed the Columbia River through the Cascade Mountains into the Columbia Plateau and eastward along the Snake River valley of southern Idaho. Heading eastward toward the Great Plains, the trail crossed the Wasatch Range of the Rocky Mountains north of the Great Salt Lake and entered the relatively level Great Divide Basin of Wyoming. Rounding Wyoming's Wind River Range at its southern tip, it followed the gradual rise of South Pass over the Continental Divide of the Rocky Mountains. Crossing Wyoming along the Sweetwater and North Platte Rivers and moving into Nebraska, the trail passed along both sides of the Platte to its confluence with the Missouri then continued down that river to the Mississippi River near present-day Saint Louis.

About midway along the Pacific coast, another east-west trail from the Sacramento area crossed the Sierra Nevada and ran down into and across the Great Basin, following Nevada's Humboldt River toward the Great Salt Lake of Utah. North of the Salt Lake, this trail met the trail from the Pacific Northwest and continued eastward to the plains.

On a third east-west route, shell traders from the southern California coast headed east across the Mohave Desert to the Colorado River near present-day Needles on the Nevada-California border. From there the trail split, a northern eastern leg following the transition between the Great Basin and the Colorado Plateau diagonally across Utah to the Great Salt Lake. From Needles an eastern leg ascended the Colorado River to the Little Colorado and on to the settlements of the Hopi and Zuni below the Southern Rockies then east again to the Rio Grande Pueblos of Northern New Mexico. Needles was also the junction of a trail following the Colorado River south, one of three major trade trails up from Mexico. Along this trail, through Colorado River rancheria settlements, passed shells from the Gulf of California for trade, along with many other items. A middle trail from Mexico ran west of current-day Bisbee, Arizona, following the eastern border of Arizona to another major trail junction near the Zuni Pueblos. Trade among the Aztec Empire of Mexico, the Rio Grande Pueblos, and points east followed a third route up the Rio Grande River, through El Paso, into Northern New Mexico.

Native travelers moved from the Southwest to the Great Plains along a continuation of the trail from the Rio Grande Pueblos that ran around the southern tip of the Rocky Mountains and on to the plains then followed eastward flowing rivers—the Arkansas, Canadian, or the Red to the Mississippi. Along the margin between the eastern flank of the Rockies and the Great Plains, a series of north-south trails connected the lands between Canada and Mexico. Further east, footpaths followed two great rivers, the Mississippi north from the Gulf of Mexico to the mouth of the Missouri near present-day Saint Louis, up the Missouri within fifty miles of the Canadian Border then westward, crossing the Bitterroot Range of the Rocky Mountains of eastern Idaho to connect with Columbia River trails to the Pacific Ocean. These were only a few of the major native trails, not to mention the lesser trails connecting them, travelers followed through America's "trackless" western lands.

The route that a particular trail followed from one point to another was generally along the easiest line of travel, avoiding as many obstacles as possible. The easiest line of travel rarely meant the most direct line of travel, and the course of a trail was influenced by many factors. Water was by far the most important factor determining trail position. Where there was no water, there were no trails. Water was heavy and hard to carry for a people traveling on foot. Native trails followed streams and rivers whenever possible, and those that didn't ran from one spring to another, even if this meant adding many miles to a journey. The Shell Trade Trail through the Mohave Desert of southeastern California was one of the most desolate landscapes in the West, but even there the traveler was never more than a day's walk from water. Where there was water, there was food. Water sources attracted game—deer, buffalo, antelope, smaller mammals, and birds. And around water, wild plant foods—berries, nuts, roots, and seeds—grew. Wooded fringes along rivers, lakes, and springs provided fuel for cooking and heat as well as materials for shelter. Besides providing basic human needs, rivers and streams were aids to travel. As a way-finding device, the course of a river didn't vary—at least in the timescale of man—and always lead to the same points. The chances of getting lost following a river were slim compared to traveling over unfamiliar, open, or heavily wooded ground. Where rivers cut canyons through mountain ranges, travel was usually easier than climbing the slopes to a mountain pass.

But many areas of the Rocky and Sierra/Cascade Mountains had no river canyons to follow. Then the only choice was to climb up and over. Trails that crossed mountain ranges did so at the lowest possible point. Even so, heavy snows closed many mountain trails for the majority of the year, sometimes up to eight months. These two great mountain systems created an effective seasonal barrier to travel between western regions. Snow-packed mountain passes limited travel to a north-south direction. Mountain slopes had another feature that affected the placement of trails. Slopes were usually covered with deep ravines cut by runoff from snowmelt in the spring and summer. Treelike drainage systems formed along mountain slopes with multiple ravines at the top converging into a common trunk at the bottom. Straight-line travel up or down slope meant a tortuous path constantly climbing into and out of many deep ravines. But different drainage systems never crossed, so there was always a continuous dividing ridge separating each drainage system that ran from the peak of a mountain to the foothills below. Finding this dividing ridge going down slope was close to impossible. From the top of a mountain, a traveler would be faced with a myriad of ravines branching downward. Ridges separated each branching ravine, any one of which could be the dividing ridge between two drainage systems. On the other hand, finding the dividing ridge was easy when starting at the bottom of the slope, where the drainage branches converged into a single trunk. The ridge between each trunk was the beginning of the dividing ridge. A knowledgeable traveler would start his climb on that ridge and stay on it to the top, without having to spend the extra energy of climbing into and out of numerous ravines. Naturally, mountain trails followed these dividing ridges as much as possible.

Trail placement followed the same pattern across a large segment of the Great Plains and for the same reason. Picture the plains as a low mountain with its peak at the foothills of Rockies and descending very gently eastward. The streams and rivers that cut the seemingly flat plains actually flow downhill eastward from about six thousand feet at the foothills of the Rocky Mountains to approximately fifteen hundred feet at the hundredth meridian and beyond, creating a washboard landscape of ridges and valleys. As on mountain slopes, treelike branches of river systems drained eastward (downslope) from the High Plains toward a common trunk in the Central Lowlands of the Mississippi River valley. Rather than follow the more strenuous straight-line path climbing into and out of endless gullies, coulees, and ravines, prairie trails also followed the more level but longer route of the single unbroken dividing ridge that snaked its way between drainage systems (Blakeslee and Blasing 1988, 18).

PART 2 — NATIVE AMERICANS ON FOOT

While moving up and down the rivers and streams might be a reasonable means of travel and transport, moving across rivers was a burden for the traveler on foot. A traveler by land would view a river crossing as a delay at best and a danger at worst. Trails avoided areas were many river crossings were necessary, but when crossing was necessary the traveler searched for a ford, or shallow place, to cross. In well-traveled crossings, rocks taken from the river bottom and piled across the stream made wading easier and marked the edge of the ford. Near settlements where rivers were too deep or the current too swift to ford, a native traveler might find a bridge. Although native bridges haven't left much of an archaeological record, they did exist and are mentioned in the journals of mid sixteenth-century European explorers. At Taos Pueblo in northern New Mexico, the Rio Grande River ran through the center of town and was "spanned by wooden bridges built with very large and heavy square timbers...The river was deep and had a swift current, without any ford" (Hammond 1940, 244). Traveling through what is now Arkansas during the same period, another source wrote, "After passing several [Indian] villages, they [Spanish] spent the night in one. And the following day they crossed a swamp over which the Indians had thrown a well-constructed bridge, broad and very cleverly built" (Bourne 1973, 139).

Too deep to ford and without a bridge, river crossings could be treacherous. Babies and children too young to swim might be put in waterproof baskets and towed across a river by a swimmer. Rafts were simple and quick to build out of almost anything that would float: animal hides from tepee covers, logs lashed together with brush or mat decking, cane, or bundles of reeds and bulrushes like tule. Add a sapling or two for poling, and people and baggage could pass relatively dry to the opposite bank. Sometimes in more populated or heavily used river crossings, rafts were kept permanently for ferrying travelers.

Trail travel meant overcoming obstacles besides river crossings. In the American Southwest, trails added a curious feature, one that would seem completely out of place to a modern traveler. But before beasts of burden and wagons entered the West, a native traveler crossing the high desert could follow a trail cutting through sagebrush and rock until it appeared to dead-end at the base of a towering mesa front—an obstacle stretching across the horizon as far as the eye could see. As the traveler moved closer, a fissure in the rock face eventually came into view. Finally, on reaching the very base of the mesa, he could just make out, in the dark shadows of the fissure, handholds or steps cut into rock leading to the top. Stairways as part of a road system might seem odd, but with no pack animals or carts, it would have been much easier for a native traveler to go up and over these obstacles rather than a long distance around them. Jackson Staircase in Chaco Canyon, New Mexico, is a notable example of stairways incorporated into road systems. Named after the man who first photographed it, Jackson Staircase probably dates back to somewhere between 900 and 1100 AD. The dark spots beside each of the steps are handholds—holes chiseled into the rock with a lip on the lower side providing a good grip for climbers. The lower parts of the steps have eroded away over time. The beginnings of a second set of stairs are visible in the upper right corner of the mesa front (figure 4).

Physical structure of trails depended on the region through which they passed. Trails through the heavily forested Pacific Northwest were narrow, just wide enough for a human to pass through. Trails across the western Great Plains were wide, where even groups of travelers with dog travois could spread out across the open land.

When traveling overland away from established trails became necessary, the distance covered in a day would be cut significantly, by as much as one half. And if the purpose of travel was to make war, travelers avoided established trails, along with unplanned

PART 2 — NATIVE AMERICANS ON FOOT

contacts with the enemy. But off the trail or on, when moving long distances across unfamiliar terrain, native travelers had the means of finding the way.

Early European explorers marveled at the Native American's ability to navigate their own land. Native navigational skills, particularly over long distances and through unknown territory, were often subscribed to some inherited instinct or unconscious skill mysteriously passed from one generation to the next. But the ability to travel across the land from one place to the next without getting lost was very much a learned skill. It was taught by elders to the young, recorded by memory, and honed by experience and careful observation. In many ways the land navigation of the Native American was analogous to earlier European navigation of the sea before the invention of the compass. A land traveler at sea, standing on the deck of an early sailing ship, would be just as lost as the seamen suddenly set down in the waving tallgrass of a western prairie. Yet each in his own element could find his way using a similar process. Before navigational instruments, the key to way-finding, on land or sea, was by careful observation of the natural surroundings and the cycles and patterns of nature. To a landsman who sees nothing but endless ocean and sky, the early seaman's ability to navigate would seem nothing less than magic. But for the observant and experienced mariner's eye, signposts were everywhere: in the sky, cloud patterns, flights of birds, wind direction, the sun, the moon, and the stars. On the water and below, the color of the sea, shape and duration of waves, depth of the sea, and type of sea bottom—sand, gravel, or mud—showed the way. The leadline sailors used to measure the depth of water and pick up small samples of the bottom allowed them to "see" the physical geography of the ocean bottom, the shallows and troughs, and guide on these familiar features.

On his home ground, the native land traveler, too, oriented on known and conspicuous features of the land, mountains, valleys, and rivers. In unknown territory, though, native land travelers, like the early mariner, used natural signposts, the wind, clouds, plants, animals, insects, birds, the sun, moon, and stars to help guide their way. From the North Star to the orientation of an ant mound, the signs were there for anyone who knew how to read them. The native western traveler did have a distinct advantage over his seagoing counterpart in that on land he could supplement natural landmarks with manmade ones when it was necessary. The simplest and most widely used manmade navigational aids were piles of rocks called cairns. Cairns could range from a few rocks to substantial mounds, the size and height depending on what was needed to make them visible to the traveler. While rocks made the most permanent trail markers, travelers might guide on piles of buffalo bones, sod, or even buffalo chips. Cairns marked trails across the featureless plains, where no natural landmarks were visible, or across hard ground or rock of the Southwest, where unmarked trails were nearly invisible. At the top of a mesa, a rock pile could mark the place were a carved stair step trail descended to the valley floor below. Rock cairn markers were used in rough landscapes, where a limited line of site made trails hard to follow. Cairns marked trail junctions, paths to water holes, and trails to mountain passes. In canyons they marked access points between ridge and valley trails. Some rock cairn markers served double duty as religious sites, where small offerings were made by native travelers to ensure a safe trip.

Trees were as scarce as water in most of the West, but travelers into the higher mountain elevations or the heavily timbered Pacific Northwest might find "blazed" trees, trees with patches of bark chopped away, to mark a trail. In winter a rock placed in the low crotch of a tree served the same purpose and was visible even during heavy snows.

Another possible form of navigational aid may have been the mysterious figures recorded as petroglyphs and pictographs.

PART 2 — NATIVE AMERICANS ON FOOT

Petroglyph figures were those chiseled on rock surfaces, while pictographs were painted figures on any material: rock, trees, or even hides. These figures were quite common on rock faces on or near major trails, and it is possible that some of them were used to guide the way to water or mountain passes or as trail marks. Or they may have had religious meaning. Or they might also have been symbols used to mark a tribe's territory. And some could just as likely have been native graffiti, something done in an idle hour to pass the time or for amusement. Their true meaning remains a mystery.

In some areas of the American West, there were no prominent natural landmarks, no mountains or hills, no trees, not even a manmade pile of rocks to guide on when traveling. Without a compass or any visible feature, setting a direction of travel and sticking to it would have been next to impossible. Like the invisible ocean current that pushes a ship off course, unseen forces push the land traveler veering to one side or another. If the forces are strong enough or the journey long enough, the traveler might find himself right back where he started, simply walking in circles. One cause is the physical makeup of the travelers themselves. A walking human usually favors one side of the body over the other. One arm might be more developed, or a leg might cause a slight inclination in one direction. An unbalanced load or heavy object carried on one side can cause the same inclination. Outside forces such as driving rain, snow, wind, or sandstorms will also push a traveler off course (Gatty 1958, 61–62).

There was no better example of lands without landmarks than the Llano Estacado of West Texas and eastern New Mexico. There, on the southern High Plains, nothing breaks the flat, monotonous, and bunchgrass-covered horizon, with the exception of an occasional bristling cholla. In the mid sixteenth century, when the first Spanish explorers crossed the Llano Estacado, migratory Teyas Indians inhabited the land. Their unique method of navigating these featureless plains was recorded in the journal of Pedro de Castenada in 1541.

> *Being people who travel continuously in that land, following the cattle [buffalo], they are familiar with it. Their method of guiding was as follows: early in the morning they watched where the sun rose, then, going in the direction they wanted to take they shot an arrow, and before coming to it they shot another over it, and in this manner they traveled the whole day until they reached some water where they were to stop for the night (Hammond 1940, 242).*

The Teyas method of maintaining a straight line of travel was the same as sighting on natural landmarks. But their manmade landmarks were portable. They began by orienting their line of travel relative to the easterly rising of the sun. Shooting an arrow in the desired line of travel acted as a temporary guide. Keeping themselves in a direct line with the arrow, they walked toward it, but before they reached it they shot another arrow in the same direction. Repeated over and over in this flat, featureless land, the arrows acted as artificial landmarks guiding them along a straight line for each leg of their journey until they reached their final destination.

The aspect of native travel that probably added the most mystery to native navigational skills, at least in the eyes of Europeans, was the lack of maps to help find the way. Yet they could make complex journeys over seldom-traveled or even unknown country. All cultures consider travel experiences as useful information worth preserving, and Native Americans were no different. Maps are distillations of travel experiences, recording the most important points to help guide the way. Physical maps, drawn and labeled, were the usual way this information was passed on by European explorers who entered the West. But prior to the arrival of Europeans, the idea of a physical map as a travel guide would have seemed an unnecessary burden to native people traveling on foot. It would have been just one more thing to carry for a people who had to travel light. Native people could produce a usable map and often did at the request of Europeans. They traced them in the dirt or painted them on a hide. For themselves, they considered a physical map a temporary device, useful only to make a point or for instruction. All the important detailed travel information was stored in the mind, a memory map. The scope of Native American memory maps was often noted in journals of early European explorers. Map information memorized by native peoples sometimes covered thousands of square miles, describing types of terrain (deserts, mountains, plains, grasslands, or forests), location of water (rivers and their fording places, major rapids, lakes, and waterholes), location and type of game available, locations of other tribes and their villages, and whether they were friends or enemies (Warhus 1997, 2). All of this information was passed on through songs or stories or as direct instruction from someone who had traveled the territory. In the nineteenth century, a US Calvary officer recorded how map information was passed on by direct instruction from an old Comanche scout. Although a relatively recent source, it is a likely representation of one technique for developing memory maps. The scout described how a group of young men prepared to travel into country they had never visited before. They began by consulting older men who knew the territory and who could instruct them in the necessary landmarks to be found on the way to their destination.

> *All being seated in a circle, a bundle of sticks was produced, marked with notches to represent the days. Commencing with the stick with one notch, an old man drew on the ground with his finger, a rude map illustrating the journey of the first day. The rivers, streams, hills, valleys, ravines, hidden water holes, were all indicated with*

reference to prominent and carefully described landmarks. When this was thoroughly understood, the stick representing the next day's march was illustrated in the same way, and so to the end. He further stated that he had known one party of young men and boys, the eldest not over nineteen, none of whom had ever been in Mexico, to start from the main camp on Brady's Creek in Texas, and make a raid into Mexico as far as the city of Monterey, solely by memory of information represented and fixed in their minds by these sticks (Dodge 1959, 551–552).

Like all skills, the mysterious way-finding ability of native travelers was a combination of training, experience, and careful observation.

It is important to note that the old Comanche scout did not explain the length of the journey as a defined interval of space, like the European league or mile, but in intervals of time—days of travel. The duration of the trip would be more influenced by the conditions of the territory over which a journey was made than a defined distance. A village fifty leagues across a flat plain would be much closer—in time—than one at the same distance but with a mountain range in between. So travel time, as affected by travel conditions, was a more useful measure of how far away a destination was than some unit of spatial distance, like a league or mile, which did not take into consideration travel conditions.

And timekeeping wasn't only a means of measuring the length of a journey but a necessity for determining when to travel, the conditions of travel, and, once on the trail, the traveler's position relative to a starting point or final destination. Knowing when to travel was something that required timekeeping on a long-term basis. Time had to be tracked to understand when berries in the mountains and cactus fruit in the desert would be ripe, when to begin the long climb to a mountain pass without finding it still clogged with snow, or the time of the salmon run, the buffalo migration, or the communal hunts by clans. And a trader loaded with goods needed to arrive at a trade fair on time to sell his goods.

The most ancient methods of timekeeping followed the natural cycles or seasons of the year. Native Americans recognized many more seasons than the four we have today. There were seasons for the migration of birds and animals, for the appearance of insects, and for the blossoming time of different fruits and berries. There were the seasons animals mated and gave birth, the seasons of the different winds that blew, as well as the seasons of weather (Nilsson 1920, 46). But timekeeping by seasons was inaccurate; the length and occurrence of a season fluctuated with changes in weather. Rain or the lack of it, prolonged summer heat, or the severity of a winter and other factors could cause unusual gaps or overlapping of seasons. Keeping time by the varying duration of natural phenomena often lead to misinterpretations of time of year and when certain seasons began or ended.

A more accurate method of timekeeping was available and used to varying degrees by native populations of the West. Overhead, the changing patterns of the sun, moon, and stars acted like a giant clockwork and calendar in the sky. The overhead world moved with certainty and precision. There, time moved in a continuum, without gap or overlap from fluctuating conditions or human error. How native observers used this celestial timepiece depended a great deal on whether they were settled or migratory.

Native people who could make daily observations from a fixed position tracked the annual passage of time by following the shifting positions of sunrise or sunset. In the pueblos of the Southwest, anyone rising before dawn and watching the sunrise would see a backlit horizon marked with mountain peaks, valleys, undulating mesa fronts, buttes, and spires. Standing on the same spot day after day, and using landmarks along the horizon as markers, it would soon become apparent that the daily position of the sunrise was changing. The sunrise would be moving either to the right (south) as winter approached or to the left (north) going into summer. Its shifting position, relative to known landmarks on the horizon, read like the pages of a calendar. Careful observers who followed the sun's movement through a complete annual cycle noted the two points along the horizon where the sun stopped shifting to the right or left and reversed its direction. The northernmost limit of the sun's travel, to the left when facing the sunrise, came at the end of the third week in June. This limit marked the summer solstice and the time when the shifting position of the daily sunrise would reverse its direction and begin moving south. In six months' travel, the sun would reach its southern limit of travel at the end of the third week in December. Here, at the winter solstice, the sun was in its "winter home," and a time of concern for native observers. As the sun reached either of its limits, the summer or winter solstices, the movement of the sun seemed to slow, its shift in the position becoming smaller day by day until it appeared to stall at the solstices. Worshipers used ceremonies and prayers to coax the lingering sun out of its winter home. If they were successful, the sun began its slow move north once again, and the annual cycle once again brought warmth and life back to the land. The same horizon calendar could just as easily be based on sunsets—the setting positions along the horizon marking various seasons of the year. Settled agricultural people used sun positions at certain horizon landmarks to begin tilling land and planting seeds as well as to determine the time to leave their villages to forage and hunt.

Other timekeeping variations also followed the annual pattern of the shifting sun's position. In Northern California the sunset behind an extinct volcano cast a shadow that marked positions on an easterly mountain range. The shadow moved north as the sun set farther south and south as the sun set farther north, marking the time of year on its distant mountain landmarks. It was, in fact, a giant sundial, with the volcano peak acting as the sundial gnomon

PART 2 — NATIVE AMERICANS ON FOOT

(the part that casts the shadow). In New Mexico the famous sun daggers of Chaco Canyon came from the orientation of large rock slabs positioned so that between their shadows a narrow shaft of light was visible, moving with the sun across rock-etched patterns marking the changing seasons. In other areas, native timekeepers followed the changing shadows cast by stone monoliths or circles of wooden poles set in the ground.

Migratory people, and other travelers who couldn't make celestial observations from a fixed position, looked to the stars for long-term timekeeping. There are hundreds of recognizable stars and star patterns visible throughout the year, but only half are visible on any given night. The other half are blotted out by the brilliant glare of the sun as an earthbound observer rotates from night to day. At the same time the earth is rotating around its axis, it moves through space in an orbit around the sun, so each night the earth is moving toward some stars and away from others. Each of the visible stars and star patterns surrounding the earth will appear and disappear—as observed from earth—sometime during the earth's annual trip around the sun (with the exception of the pole stars directly overhead). The time of year that a star is visible depends on its position relative to the earth and the sun.

The sixteenth-century native timekeepers would not have been aware of that grand scale of celestial motion. What they were aware of, standing on the bank of the Platte or among the sagebrush of the Great Basin, was that by carefully watching the eastern sky in the dark hours just before dawn, they might be able to get a glimpse of that most delicate of observable celestial effects, the first faint twinkling of a familiar star, lost for half a year. On its first rising the star would shine for a minute or two before being blotted out by the light of the dawning sun. The following morning the star would appear a little higher in the sky and be visible a little longer before sunrise. Gradually, the star would make its arc across the sky, appearing a little higher each night, until it eventually disappeared over the western horizon. One first rising of a star to the next first rising marked one year. Since there were many recognizable stars and star patterns flowing across the night sky, the exact time of their first rising, along with their last sighting before they disappeared, marked the different periods of the year. Together, many stars made a star calendar. One of the most universally followed star patterns throughout the northern hemisphere was that of the seven closely positioned stars the Greeks called the Pleiades. Some Native American cultures considered these stars to be lost children. They first appeared in October, marking the beginning of fall; their disappearance in March marked the beginning of spring. The nightly wandering of the lost children, slowly shifting from east to west across the sky, kept track of the progress of seasons from fall, through winter, to spring. Other native cultures believed prominent stars were ancient chiefs of the first people who had long ago crossed the Milky Way, the trail to the sky world. And in the darkness of night, their benevolent spirits guided their earthbound descendants below.

Like the sighting of stars, following the phases of the moon was a practical means of timekeeping on a smaller scale for anyone, settled or on the move. A complete cycle of the moon involved four distinct phases—the invisible new moon, followed by the right half lit first-quarter moon, then the completely lit full moon, and finally the left half lit last-quarter moon. Each moon phase had a time interval of between seven and eight days. A full cycle of moon phases marked slightly less than thirty days.

Understanding the phases of the moon had obvious, and practical, applications for travelers besides timekeeping. Phases of the moon might well determine when travel should be done. If the purpose of a journey were a peaceful night crossing of a desert, avoiding the heat of the day, traveling by the light of a full moon would make sense. If the purpose was war, a night raid during the darkness of a new moon would make the trip safer (for the warriors). Combining two or more astronomical observations, like a moon phase and the position of the rising sun, gave a fairly accurate time of the year. As an example, "the first moon after the sun rose due east on its journey to its summer home" established a fairly narrow and specific timeframe within the year. The sunrise is due east only during the spring or fall equinox. The sun being on "its journey to its summer home" meant the season was moving from winter to summer, and so the time of year was the first full moon after the spring equinox, or the end of the third week in March, plus the time to the next full moon.

Although marking the passage of twenty-four-hour days, or "sleeps," was easy enough, there was no universal method of measuring time for less than one day. Even without a standard, however, there were ways to dissect time, both day and night. When a party of Spanish and native allies was attacked in the early sixteenth century, one native survivor later reported the battle beginning "when the sun was lance high" (Baldwin 1992, 59). Everyone knew the length of a lance and so understood the relative time of the attack in the morning. Someone pointing from one position along the sun's path to another would be understood as defining the specific amount of time it would take for the sun to move from one position to the other.

When the sky turned dark, there was a more accurate way of tracking time. Looking skyward, an observer would find the dimly glowing North Star and the Big Dipper, called "The Star That Does Not Move" and the "The Seven Stars," respectively, by some native cultures. High enough in the sky to be visible throughout the darkness of night, stars of the Big Dipper pivot around the North Star like the hour hand of a giant clock, a quarter of a rotation marking six hours of time, a half rotation twelve hours, and one complete revolution taking place every twenty-four hours. It was a handy way to mark the passage of time in the dark—if the night sky was clear. Particularly observant, and patient, native night-sky watchers also realized that the position of the Big Dipper, relative to a given time, shifted counterclockwise slightly each night. They saw that it took an entire year for the Big Dipper to rotate back into the same position relative to that given time. With the knowledge handed down through the generations, and some careful observation, a native traveler had, in the night sky, a calendar, a clock, and a compass.

Chapter 5

Native Trade and Communication

Among native societies, the two occupations that required the most sustained travel were those dealing in trade goods and information. Extensive trade networks and a system of runners or couriers provided a means of interaction between different regions and cultures of the American West.

In the early sixteenth century, a visitor to the Taos Pueblo of Northern New Mexico might find a man wearing decorations crafted from abalone shells that had traveled a thousand miles from where they had been harvested along the Pacific coast of Southern California. Inside his dwelling, it wouldn't be surprising to see the family pet, a brightly feathered macaw, from the tropical jungles of Mexico. Far across the plains, along the banks of the Mississippi River, a woman might be shaking the dust from a cotton blanket woven by the man from Taos. Along the Missouri River valley of the Dakotas, a native farmer might be handing over a string of Dentalia shells from the Pacific Northwest in payment for hides taken from a buffalo killed on the Great Plains by an obsidian arrow point that came from the Yellowstone Park area of Wyoming.

Commerce moved over well-established trails throughout the West, and the variety of trade items stretches the imagination: obsidian and Knife River flints for arrow points, spear points, knives, scrapers, and drills; turquoise from the Cerrillos Mountains of New Mexico; shells from the Pacific and Gulf of California; animal pelts from Canada; copper from the Great Lakes, Canada, and Mexico; parrot and macaw feathers from Mexico; salt gathered from the dried lake beds of the Southwest. There were pottery, baskets, cotton cloth, buffalo hides, corn, cornmeal, beans, squash, gourds, pumpkins, piñon nuts, walnuts, hickory nuts, acorns, syrup from maple and box elder trees, tobacco, slaves, pipestones, dogs, turkeys, grizzly bear teeth and claws for decoration, iron crystals, pigments for decoration, cedar wood, canoes, fish oil, dried fish, dried meat, dried fruit, berries, and roots, to make an incomplete list. Depending on the tribal politics of a region, trade goods might be carried over long distances by a single trader or from one tribe to another traveling long distances by a series of short hops. Commerce and traders were usually protected to a certain degree by intertribal laws (Hodge 1907, 332) or a periodically declared trade truce so people could come together to exchange goods. Traders, in general, usually relied on a certain amount of protection not given to other travelers. But like most cultures, there were those who didn't follow the rules. Alone or in small groups, traders engaged in a risky business. Patterns of trade, like the populations themselves, were constantly shifting. As illustration, by the early sixteenth century, just before the arrival of Europeans, trade from the plains to the Mississippi River valley had all but collapsed. Along the Mississippi River Valley and further east, the use of agriculture had been intensifying for many years. Greater reliance on crop production led to increases in populations and eventually the most fertile lands were taken.

PART 2 ~ NATIVE AMERICANS ON FOOT

Powerful eastern chiefdoms fought incessant wars over limited land resources. To avoid hostilities in the East, plains trade shifted west to the benefit of the pueblos of New Mexico.

Exchange of trade goods occurred in a variety of ways—by itinerant tradesmen, one tribe visiting another, or on the grandest scale, a regional trade fair. For the lone trader the most profitable trade items were lightweight, high value, and exotic, like paint pigments for personal decoration or blanks cut from the flat part of an abalone shell. Only the most valuable parts of the shell were kept to save weight on the trail. Craftsmen traded for the blanks and turned them into exquisite pendants of fanciful bird and animal forms, greatly adding to the value as each item continued along the trade network. The load that a single trader was able to bear was remarkable. One late-nineteenth-century naturalist, who actually weighed an itinerant native trader, reported him carrying nearly his body weight in trade goods and still able to cover thirty to forty miles a day on foot (Kelly 2000, 137–38).

Intertribal trade was common between migratory and settled tribes. Upon arrival in a settled village, the visiting tribe of hunter-gatherers set up camp in a designated space safely outside the host tribe area. Ceremonies, speeches, and gift giving came next. Then various chiefs and their councils met to discuss the value of each trade item. Only after prices had been agreed on did trading begin, with hopeful vendors' wares spread out on the ground for inspection by potential buyers, strolling "window shoppers," excited children, and stray dogs. Social as well as economic needs were a part of these gatherings. With the conclusion of business, and official ceremonies out of the way, people had time to relax and enjoy the festivities: sports, games, and dances (Mason 1894, 587).

The format of the regional trade fair was similar to trade between tribes but on a much grander scale. Some of the larger trade fairs could count on attendance in the thousands. Regional trade fairs were usually in fixed locations determined by a variety of factors. Food was an important requirement; there had to be enough available to support the temporary influx of large numbers of people. Most trade fairs occurred in or near large, fixed population centers; along the margins of geographical or ecological transitions, where a variety of resources were available; or at major trail junctions, where goods were redistributed. The Dalles, on the Columbia River where it begins to cut its way through the eastern flank of the Cascade Mountains, was one example that met all of these requirements. One of the most prolific salmon-fishing spots along the river, it provided an ample food supply. The falls and rapids at the Dalles were impassible to canoe traffic, so goods traveling east or west along the river had to be unloaded, moved around the falls, and reloaded to continue the journey upstream or down. The Dalles was also a population center, and traders from the Pacific coast, Great Basin, and as far away as the Great Plains met there to carry on trade. Other important fixed regional trade fairs occurred at the settled villages along the middle Missouri River in the Dakotas and at the pueblos of the Southwest. Both were agricultural areas with enough surplus domestic crops to support large gatherings. Both were situated along major trade trails. The Missouri River location was the hub of commerce from the eastern woodlands, from Canada to the north, and the Great Plains to the west. Pueblo trade fairs of the Southwest were actually a series of trade centers along a network connecting the Great Plains with the Colorado Plateau, the Great Basin, the Pacific coast, and south into Mexico. Wedged between the Sangre de Cristo Range of the Rocky Mountains and the Colorado Plateau, Taos Pueblo on the northern Rio Grande River hosted one of the largest trade fairs in this region.

 An important exception to the fixed trade fair scenario was the large regional trade fair held each year somewhere within the general area bounded by the Great Salt Lake on the west, Wyoming's Great Divide Basin on the east, and south of Idaho's Snake River.

It was a movable feast; one year it was near Green River, Wyoming, another in Cache Valley, Utah, and another at Pierre's Hole, Idaho (Pritzker 2000, 238). It was an annual event that promoted commerce between the Great Basin, Rocky Mountains, and the plains.

Native trade was not only an exchange of goods and resources but also a conduit for ideas and information. Along with buffalo hides, dried salmon, and spear points came new beliefs, innovation, and idle gossip. But, when needed, there were even faster means of moving information over long distances.

Systems of native runners or couriers were common throughout the Americas, and they carried messages with surprising speed and range. Complexity of these courier systems varied depending on the culture. The most advanced were to the south, in the empires of the Aztec of Mexico and Inca of Peru, but native couriers of all cultures shared common characteristics. Couriers enjoyed high status and were supported by the communities they served. Training usually began in childhood and required almost religious devotion. It was the life of a trained athlete: careful diet, regular exercise, and, often, celibacy. Reliability, honesty, and accuracy were qualities as valued in a courier as endurance and stamina. It would have been an appealing profession for any adventurous young man with a desire to move fast and see the world. Depending on the trail and terrain, a runner might cover between six and eight miles in an hour; experienced runners traveled a hundred miles or more in a single day.

For a native courier, like the Pony Express rider of the future, weight was everything. He carried only what was absolutely necessary to complete his mission. He wore moccasins with double rawhide soles to take the heavy wear of a long-distance run. He carried a leather belt around his waist covered with pictograph messages, a small leather pouch with cornmeal or high-nutrition seeds as food rations, and, when necessary, a knotted cord or bundle of sticks to mark time. He ran alone and unarmed. Across the open, short-grass-covered plains or as a tiny speck among the towering mesas of the Southwest, a runner moved forward mile after mile and hour after hour, without stopping, even for the occasional pinch of cornmeal or seeds to restore his energy. The measured breathing he practiced so often at home carried him on into the night, and in darkness, a familiar star or constellation guided his way.

At the end of the journey, an eager audience waited. On the runner's belt, each symbol represented part of a message carefully rehearsed and memorized before he left his village. If part of the message was some future action, the knotted cord or bundle of sticks he carried acted as a timepiece, a knot untied or a stick discarded represented the passing of a single day. If, for example, the message was that two tribes should meet in ten days, the courier carried a bundle of ten sticks or a cord with ten knots so that the receiver of the message knew that when all the knots were untied, or sticks discarded, the meeting would take place.

Relays of runners covered even longer distances and at greater speeds than a single runner. Each relay runner made shorter, but faster, runs before passing messages on to the next relay. Maintaining a system of relay couriers required considerable social organization like that of the Aztec Empire in Mexico. Early-sixteenth-century Aztec leaders kept contact with all their lands through a system of roads with post houses built every five to six miles. Relay couriers passed messages from post house to post house with remarkable speed (Prescott 1998, 39). And so on a spring day in 1519, a runner with a startling message left the lowland jungles along the gulf coast of eastern Mexico. Relay after relay carried the message up and over the Sierra Madre and down into the mountain rimmed bowl that held the Aztec capital city of Tenochtitlan. There, Emperor Montezuma heard the news of a landing on his shores of bearded, white-skinned foreigners. The messenger would have been trying to describe the indescribable, things their language had no words for: horses, guns, and sailing ships. The distance from where the foreigners first landed (near present-day Vera Cruz) to the throne at the Aztec capital where Montezuma sat was 260 miles. Less than twenty-four hours after Hernan Cortez first stepped on Mexican soil, Montezuma, in his capital, knew it.

In a few short years the Aztec Empire would be gone, and, not long after, native runners would carry similar messages into the pueblos of the American Southwest.

Part 3

Mounted Conquistadors

Chapter 6

Supplying an Army in a New World

The first Spanish journey into the American West began, by accident, in what is now Tampa Bay, Florida. From those shores, in 1528, a force of three hundred soldiers, under the command of Pánfilo de Narváez, launched an attempt to explore the ill-defined lands of La Florida. Traveling overland as far as the Gulf Coast just south of present-day Tallahassee, Narváez's force encountered fierce opposition from the native inhabitants. Having lost contact with their supply ships, and therefore their passage out of that hostile land, the embattled and starving Spaniards attempted an escape in crudely built open boats, sailing westward across the Gulf of Mexico toward what they hoped would be the safety of New Spain. A storm scattered the little flotilla. One boat made it as far as Galveston Island in Texas before breaking up in the surf. The sole survivor of that boat, Alvar Núnez Cabeza de Vaca, crawled ashore, only to be captured and enslaved by natives. As time passed he heard reports of three other survivors held captive by neighboring tribes. It took several years, but Cabeza de

PART 3 — MOUNTED CONQUISTADORS

Vaca eventually united with the Spanish prisoners, and on foot they made their escape, heading westward in an epoch journey. Eight years after landing in Florida, the four, traveling overland, arrived safely at a Spanish outpost along Mexico's western coast.

While traveling across the American Southwest, Cabeza de Vaca's party had heard from native sources of large cities of many-storied stone buildings and great wealth to the north. It wasn't long after the survivors reached New Spain that the stories they told bred what appear today as outlandish tales. Where facts were missing, Spanish imagination filled the void. They had become what Bandelier called "a kernel of fact enveloped by a shell of exaggerated fancies" (Bandelier 1893, 112). The kernels of fact were the pueblo trade centers along the northern Rio Grande River and west to the Hopi settlements in northeastern Arizona. The shell of exaggerated fancy was born from an ancient Spanish legend conceived during the Moorish invasion of Spain. As the legend goes, during that period seven Christian priests escaped the Moorish invaders by ship, sailing westward to mysterious islands far across the Atlantic. Each of the seven priests founded a city in the new lands, and all prospered. Their wealth became so great, it was said, that even common people ate their meals from golden plates. These were the lost Seven Cities of Gold.

Every sixteenth-century Spanish adventurer knew the fortunes of Cortez sailing westward from the Caribbean to conquer the land of the Aztecs in the 1520s. How, deep in the interior of Mexico, he'd discovered in a great bowl of a valley, Tenochtitlan, a city his soldiers described as the most beautiful in the world. Everyone knew of the wealth of gold and precious jewels taken there. And a decade later, how the Pizzaros moved south to Peru to discover and conquer the Incan Empire, and how the captive Inca Emperor, Atahuallpa, filled a large room with gold in a fruitless attempt to gain his freedom. So why not now, in the 1540s, go north to unexplored lands and new cities of gold? These were the kind of fantasies that lured two large, well-organized Spanish armies of discovery and conquest into the sixteenth-century American West, one by circumstance and one by design.

First to depart was the army of Hernando de Soto in the late spring of 1539. What followed their landing on Florida's Gulf Coast was a four-and-a-half-year journey, wandering north through Georgia and the Carolinas, west into Tennessee, southward to Georgia, into Alabama and Mississippi, and across the greatest river highway of North America. They marched and fought their way west through Arkansas, Louisiana, and Texas as far as the Great Plains before starvation and lack of supplies forced them back to the big river. In homemade boats, the survivors, half the original army, rowed and sailed down the Mississippi into the Gulf of Mexico then west again toward the settlements of New Spain.

Less than a year after de Soto's men splashed ashore on the beaches of Florida, a second Spanish force, commanded by Francisco Vasquez de Coronado, left New Spain's outpost at Culiacán on the west coast of modern Mexico. Coronado's army headed north along the native trade trail, "a wide and well-traveled road" (Baldwin 1992, 56). They went north to present-day Guaymas, Mexico, then inland along the eastern edge of Arizona to Cibola, just south of present-day Zuni, New Mexico, which was reputed to be the first of many elusive Seven Cities of Gold. At that dusty pueblo the only thing of value for the starving Spanish army was food. From there Coronado's force moved east, toward the Rio Grande Pueblos of Northern New Mexico. On the Rio Grande, Spanish soldiers heard stories of another city of gold, Quivira, even farther to the east. On the move again, Coronado's army traveled across the featureless flat lands of the Llano Estacado of New Mexico and West Texas, north across the panhandle of Oklahoma, and into Kansas, crossing the Arkansas River east of what is now Dodge City. Closing in on what they believed to be the fabulous wealth of Quivira, the Spanish made

PART 3 — MOUNTED CONQUISTADORS

a forced march into central Kansas, there to discover nothing more than a collection of grass huts, a temporary camp of wandering hunter-gatherers. For Coronado this was the final disappointment, and the army returned to winter at the pueblos of the Rio Grande. The following spring, after two years on the trail, Coronado's once-formidable army retraced its steps back to Mexico with empty pockets.

The story of how these Spanish soldiers made their way into the West begins with a completely new means of transport introduced to the Americas: the sailing ship.

By the opening of the sixteenth century, Spanish sailing ships made regular voyages to the Americas. Early European arrivals believed these western continents—made up of an unbroken land mass running north and south some nine thousand miles—to be scattered islands off the coast of Asia. It was a notion that began with Columbus and lasted for many years. As Spanish adventurers island hopped through the Caribbean and touched along the coastlines of the Gulf of Mexico and Central and South America, the greatest accomplishment of any explorer—not counting the discovery of gold, silver, or some other source of immediate wealth—would have been to locate a strait, or channel, or inland sea that could carry their ships through to the rich trade of the Indies. What the Spanish conquistadors didn't know then, and what those who followed wouldn't realize for centuries after, was that the only sea passage to the Pacific lay far to the south in the treacherous waters between the tip of South America and Antarctica. No matter how far and in which direction Spanish ships sailed, when they turned west that first image of land—a dark, broken thread, shimmering mirage-like along the horizon—eventually appeared to block the way.

Since they couldn't sail around or through the Americas, exploration had to continue overland, and in the Spanish experience that meant traveling with large armies. And large armies required large amounts of equipment and supplies. Across the Atlantic, in the Old World, moving large quantities of equipment and provisions by sea had been the most effective means of supplying land-bound forces for thousands of years. Even a little Spanish caravel—small, maneuverable, and shallow drafted enough to anchor close in to shore—could disgorge enough cargo to pack a thousand mules.

In the Old World mariners sailed to established ports, carried reasonably accurate maps or sailing directions, and had some idea of the bounds of land and seas that surrounded them. In the great question mark of the Spanish sixteenth-century New World, none of these conditions existed. There were no established ports or manmade landmarks to guide on. Maps were few, and those that were available were as likely drawn from myth and wishful thinking as fact. As long as a land force traveled close to the sea and made a successful rendezvous with their supply ships, they were reasonably assured of provisions and, if necessary, a way back home. But having an army and its supply ships rendezvous at the same time and same place, in a new world, was not an easy task.

Even maintaining contact with a mobile land force was a tenuous proposition in the vastness of the sixteenth-century Americas. Spanish soldiers had no idea of the size of the North American continent or even its relative position on the earth. According to one Spanish chronicler traveling with Coronado from Mexico to the native province of Tiguex in northern New Mexico, "If one wishes to go to Tiguex in order to turn west from there in search of India, one should follow the route taken by the army, because, even though one might wish to take a different route, there is none" (Hammond 1940, 281–282). Although technically true, the Indies were west of New Mexico; what that writer and other explorers of the day didn't realize was that seven or eight hundred miles of land and the widest ocean on the planet separated the Indies from the native province of Tiguex. And at the time of Coronado's

PART 3 — MOUNTED CONQUISTADORS

entrada into the American Southwest, it was believed his supply ships could sail up the coast of Mexico to the army's destination of Cibola, along what is now the border of Arizona and New Mexico.

Complicating matters even further in the early years of Spanish exploration was that there were usually no set plans for travel. Since the main objective was the search for gold, silver, or anything else of value, an expedition might start in one direction based on rumors of great wealth in some native province. Arriving at that destination, conquistadors might find nothing but more rumors—stories from native sources of even greater riches over the next mountain range or across a jungle or desert. The purpose of these rumors was to move these interlopers on to some other province as quickly as possible, and preferably into the province of some hated enemy. Since movement was haphazard, Spanish armies could end up many hundreds of miles inland with little clue of where they were relative to the outside world. Even so, attempts had to be made by land forces to maintain communications with supply ships, send reports to superiors, and pass information between separated detachments and the main army, even while all were on the move.

The most obvious method of communicating was by message carrier. This the Spanish did themselves, but they also quickly learned to made use of the established system of native runners. The viceroy of New Spain instructed one expedition leader to "try always to send reports through Indians, telling how you are faring, how you are received, and particularly what you find" (Mendoza 1940, 60). Native runners were given messages that they might carry hundreds of miles on foot before they could be delivered. The other common means of communication was by posting, defined in the archaic sense as leaving a letter or message in a prominent place for others to find. How this was accomplished is best described in sixteenth-century words.

> *Captain Juan de Añasco and his soldiers searched in the hollows and under bark of trees in an earnest attempt to ascertain if letters had been left which would disclose what their predecessors had seen and noted, it being a very usual custom for the discoverers of new lands to leave such announcements for those to come, and many times these announcements had been of major importance (Varner 1951, 192).*

Spanish explorers left messages for those who followed them or those who might be searching for them, using the commonly accepted methods of the day. Trees were the most likely places for posting messages. Such a tree had to be in a prominent location and noteworthy in itself either because of its height relative to other trees near it or because it stood alone. Between two or more land parties, messages buried at the foot of trees at trail junctures, along trails a second party would be known to follow, or some prearranged meeting place was one way of maintaining contact. If messages were to be relayed between land parties and ships, they would be left at a prominent tree at the mouth of a river, a suitable harbor, or at headlands (Mendoza 1940, 60). To mark a post tree, the bark would be chopped away, and the sign of the cross or a short message cut into the blaze. It was understood, or written above, that the full message was buried at the foot of the tree. Anything that could be made watertight could hold the message—a sealed jar or even a hollowed-out pumpkin or gourd.

Trees, unfortunately, had the habit of only growing where it suited them, and in some areas they simply refused to grow at all. If no convenient tree could be found, another method of posting messages was to bury them at the foot of a cross. A cross could be erected anywhere it was needed. In addition to message posts, crosses served the purpose of trail markers where landmarks were scarce.

The captain of Coronado's supply ships was instructed to leave messages in this manner along the western coast of Mexico, and

> *If you should fail to hear from him [Coronado] there, you should send some one to examine the landmarks you have left to learn whether they have been found. If so, the general will know where you are, and if he should be unable to reach you, he can leave information in writing at posts, which will be found by your men, and thus a means of establishing communication from the sea and with you might be established (Hammond 1940, 119).*

Once a ship or land party posted a message, it was necessary to return to the place of posting to check for a reply. A typical message, if it could be found, might include what the sender had done, what they planned to do, and where and when they planned to be in the future. But with limited knowledge of the country and ineffective communication, once the land and sea forces separated, there was a fair chance they would not meet again.

That was the fate of Coronado's army after it left the Spanish outpost of Culiacán on the west coast of Mexico and headed north in the spring of 1540. Earlier expeditions into this country had spread the rumor that in the lands to the north they would find the fabled Seven Cities of Gold. Arriving for a rendezvous at the port of Culiacán in May, supply ships under the command of Hernando de Alarcón found that Coronado's army had left a month earlier. As instructed, Alarcón continued up the coast, leaving landmarks and messages at all the harbors, along his route in an effort to communicate with the land expedition. By August the ships found themselves land locked at the head of a gulf. Into the gulf from the north, a formidable river (the Colorado) flowed, and beyond that was unknown territory. Leaving his ships, Alarcón started upriver in small open boats in the hope that this river would lead them to Cibola and Coronado's army. They traveled northward for fifteen days along shores well populated with native villages. From villagers Alarcón learned that strangers like themselves had been sighted ten-day's journey to the east. Cibola, in fact, lay over three hundred miles to the east as the crow flies and even farther as the trail unwinds. Alarcón called for volunteers to attempt to carry a message to Coronado, but no one came forward for such a dangerous trip. Receiving word from the gulf that the wooden hulls of his ships were being eaten up by shipworms, Alarcón had no choice but to abandon the search. Faced with the loss of his ships, Alarcón headed south. Along the coast he revisited the places he had left messages and landmarks for signs that the army had discovered them. He found them untouched. About the time Alarcón's ships were heading south, an overland scouting party, under orders from Coronado himself, was heading north along the same coast in search of the ships and their much-needed supplies. That party, under command of Captain Melchior Diaz, traveled up the west coast of Mexico and above the mouth of the Colorado River before he found one of Alarcon's messages. According to a chronicler with the Coronado expedition,

> When Diaz's party reached the place where the boats had come, which was more than fifteen leagues up the river from the mouth of the bay, they found written on a tree: "Alarcón came this far; there are letters at the foot of the tree." They dug up the letters and from them they learned how long the ships waited for news from the army and that Alarcón had returned to New Spain from there with the boats because he could not proceed any further, for that sea [Gulf of California] was a gulf which extends toward the Island of Marquis, which is called California. They reported that California [Baja California] was not an island, but a point of the mainland on the other side of that gulf (Hammond 1940, 211).

PART 3 — MOUNTED CONQUISTADORS

By then, of course, it was too late. Alarcón had come and gone; the land and sea parties never met.

Remarkably, during that same period supply ships of Hernando de Soto were scouring the eastern Gulf Coast in search of his army. A year and half had elapsed since that Spanish force had gone ashore in the shallow waters off west central Florida. Since the day the empty transport ships headed south, returning to Cuba, there had been no further contact. What followed for de Soto's army, as in the case of Coronado, was aimless wandering in search of elusive wealth. The army had moved inland, cut off from the outside world, traveled north through the Florida peninsula, wintered near present-day Tallahassee and in the spring headed north again through what are now the states of Georgia, South Carolina, and North Carolina. Then they headed west into Tennessee and finally south to central Alabama by the fall of 1540. There, at the fortified native town of Mauvilla, well past the time set for the first rendezvous with supply ships along the coast, the army found itself engaged in one of the most desperate battles they would face in their four and half years of hardship and suffering across the continent.

Although the Spanish eventually routed native forces—with heavy losses—in the ashes of the town were most of the army's extra weapons, clothes, and equipment. Outside the smoldering town wounded and dying Spanish soldiers lay in open fields without medicine or shelter. During the month the army spent recuperating, a native runner arrived with confirmation that ships were still waiting on the coast—just six days march to the south. De Soto took the message in private, swearing the messenger to secrecy on pain of death. The message informed him that Captains Diego Maldonado and Gomez Arias were indeed waiting with men, provisions, weapons, ammunition, horses, livestock, and even seed and farming equipment. But the loyal captains would search the coast for de Soto and his army the rest of that year until the threat of winter storms drove them back to Cuba. Returning again, for the next three years they sailed west along the Gulf as far as Mexico and as far north along the Atlantic Coast as what they called "the land of the codfish" in an attempt to locate the missing army. Like Coronado, de Soto's land and sea contingents never met.

Unlike Coronado, what kept Hernando de Soto from his supply ships wasn't geography. He, in all likelihood, deliberately avoided them. After the battle at Mauvilla, when the wounded were sufficiently recovered to travel, de Soto informed his men that since it was now mid-November, they needed to find winter quarters where there were enough provisions to carry them through to spring. He then turned what was left of his army and marched north for a month, away from the coast and away from his supply ships.

A hint of why de Soto made what appeared to be such an illogical move came later when the army had taken up winter quarters. Early one morning, native forces attacked the Spanish position, beating drums and firing burning arrows. A cold north wind fanned the flames in the grass huts the army had built for shelter. Confused men stumbled from their sleep half dressed. Smoke and fire blinded them, while riderless horses ran panicked through the camp. On the eastern edge of the Spanish town, where the most fearsome assault took place, forty or fifty soldiers lost their nerve and turned to run from the enemy. Captain Nuno Tovar ran after them shouting, "Where are you running? Do you think that the walls of Córdoba or Seville are here to shelter you?" (Maynard 1969, 223) Even in their desperation these soldiers realized their only chance of survival was to return to the fight. Cut off, hundreds of miles from the coast, in a land heavily populated by hostile forces, they knew that if they turned and fought they might die in battle, but if they ran it meant certain death. There was no other choice. A decade before, as a young captain with the expedition of Francisco Pizzaro, de Soto learned how in Pizzaro's second attempt for the reputed wealth of the Incas, he had most of his army sail away rather than face such hardships. After landing on the coast of Mexico a decade before that, Hernando Cortez secretly had his ships burned at anchor for that reason. With no ships, there could be no retreat. Cortez told his soldiers they either conquered the Aztec Empire or they died. Those experiences must have clouded de Soto's thoughts in the desperate fall of 1540. If he had headed south to the coast and the ships waiting there, his men would have had a way out of their desperate situation. Most likely heading south meant mutiny or desertion by his men, the end of the expedition, and financial ruin for de Soto and many of his followers. Ironically, if de Soto's army had been more successful, if his men had not suffered such hardships, if they had not been so desperate for the supplies in the holds of his waiting ships, he would more likely have headed south instead of north to his ultimate death and the death of half his army. The problem with ships as means transport, in Hernando de Soto's situation and others before him, was that they sailed in two directions. Sailing in one direction, they brought needed provisions and equipment, but sailing in the other direction they could take a captain-general's army away.

A problem of an even wider scope for ships as means of transport and supply was that Spanish ships were relegated to the margins of an extremely large continent. The conquistadors found no straits, inland seas, or other mythical water passages to carry their ships into that land. And the wealth of gold and silver they searched for had never been found along any coast of the Americas. Decades before, Cortez and Pizarro had traveled deep in to the territory of the Aztec and Inca to discover the treasure hidden there, and inland is where Coronado and de Soto thought they had to go too. To do that some alternative means of transporting the large quantities of equipment and provisions required by a Spanish army had to be found.

One alternative employed by early Spanish expeditions was native transport—human bearers or porters. Native bearers could be members of a tribe specifically trained to carry heavy loads, or slaves captured from another tribe, or, if they considered it necessary, any native man or woman Spanish forces could capture. The number of native bearers taken was often in the hundreds and the loads they carried substantial. Provisioning large numbers of bearers could be a problem; they had to eat, too, especially when carrying heavy loads. Security was another problem. While in their home province, bearers had to be kept constantly under guard to prevent escape, even though many were kept in chains. With a lax guard, some slipped away during the march; others filed away their chains with flints and escaped in the night, sometimes taking their load of equipment or provisions with them. Recaptured escapees could count on death as an example to the others. Once beyond their native provinces, bearers were much less likely to attempt escape since neighboring tribes were often hostile, and capture by them usually meant enslavement or death as well. Spanish forces released more fortunate bearers as they entered a new province and were able to requisition fresh bearers. Others might be released as unnecessary mouths to feed when provisions ran low. Otherwise they starved or died of exposure along with their Spanish captors.

The method for procuring native bearers was tried and true, learned from experience in earlier conquests of Mexico and Peru. On entering a particular native province or territory, the Spanish captain-general sent messengers asking leaders of those provinces to meet with him. If they came, the captain-general made his "requests" for bearers to carry Spanish supplies and equipment—along with requests for food, guides, and sometimes women for the amusement of his soldiers. With native chiefs as guests—or, more accurately, hostages—along the march through their provinces,

PART 3 — MOUNTED CONQUISTADORS

Spanish requests were usually met. A member of de Soto's expedition described the process as follows:

> *It was the practice to keep watch over the Caciques [native chiefs] that none should absent themselves, they being taken along with the Governor [de Soto] until coming out of their territories; for by thus having them the inhabitants would await their arrival in the towns, give a guide, and men to carry the loads, who before leaving their country would have liberty to return to their homes, as sometimes would the tamemes [bearers], so soon as they came to the domain of any chief where others could be got (Milanich 1991, 97).*

If the chiefs refused to meet Spanish demands, they would be made prisoners, along with enough of their subjects to fill the needs of the expedition. If that were not possible, pillaging, setting fire to towns, destroying crops, and creating general havoc usually brought the chiefs to sue for peace. It needs to be mentioned that in more than a few cases, native chiefs willingly gave bearers, although that may have been partially due to the Spaniards' reputation having preceded them. And at least one chief, believing that Hernando de Soto and his army were on their way to make war on his tribe's enemies, gladly gave eight hundred bearers to help deliver the bearded strangers to the land of his foe (Milanich 1991, 238).

Spanish explorers also introduced to the Americas a new means of overland transport, large, burden-bearing livestock: horses, mules, and burros. In time, these animals would revolutionize native culture. For the Spanish themselves, the importance of livestock in the colonization of the Americas was recognized from the very beginning. On his second voyage, in 1493, Columbus shipped sheep, goats, cattle, and hogs to the Caribbean island the Spanish called La Española, now Haiti and the Dominican Republic. Ranching and livestock breeding later spread to the islands of Puerto Rico, Jamaica, Cuba, and Trinidad (Wentworth 1948, 21). As colonization of the Caribbean increased and land became scarce, the need to expand operations helped push Spanish explorers toward new horizons. After the conquest of Mexico, stock breeding and ranching moved westward to larger quarters. Limited at first by the lure of gold, more astute colonists eventually realized that ranching was a much surer and safer way to riches. Several factors made this so. First, losses were high when shipping livestock from Spain, with a mortality rate of 50 percent or more. This was particularly so for large animals like horses and cattle. Too big to be housed in a ship's cramped lower decks, they spent the two- to three-month sea voyage on exposed upper decks (Wentworth 1948, 22). If delays caused water supplies to run low, endangering the lives of the human contingent, livestock were dumped over the side to drown. Restrictive Spanish economic policies added to the problem. Spanish officials, alarmed at the rate at which domestic livestock were being siphoned off for adventures abroad, placed limits on their exportation. And finally livestock raised in Spain just didn't survive well in the Americas. These conditions eventually made Spanish livestock breeding and ranching in the Americas a major industry. It grew at such a rate that profits from ranching operations provided a major source of funding for many Spanish expeditions. In the less than fifty years that elapsed between the introduction of livestock to the Americas and the first major Spanish exploration of the American West, horses, burros, mules, cattle, sheep, goats, and pigs had become plentiful and cheap.

But Spanish horses played a much larger role than that of a means of transportation. In the early battles for the Americas, horses were the terror weapons of the sixteenth century. From the moment these animals first landed in the Caribbean in 1495, Spanish forces played on the fear that horses instilled in native populations. Horses were huge, snorting, pawing beasts like nothing that had ever been seen before in the Americas. In the beginning native people believed horse and rider were all one animal that could run as fast as the wind, spreading death everywhere they went. Rumors passed from tribe to tribe that these beasts ate human flesh. To add to the clamor of a mounted charge, Spanish soldiers tied large bells to their horses' breastplates and smaller hawk bells to their tails. It was a sight and sound that might turn all but the bravest warrior. In Europe cavalry charges were broken up with massed pikes, but in the New World opposing native warriors caught in the open never had a chance; they had no effective defense against cavalry. Until native forces learned to find cover where horses couldn't move freely, mounted Spanish soldiers galloped among them, killing at will with lance and sword.

Pedro de Castaneda, traveling with Coronado's army through the American Southwest, wrote, "For after God, we owed the victory to the horses." These were sentiments echoed by all who participated in the early Spanish conquests. When winter floods mired travel along the Mississippi River, a soldier with de Soto's army wrote,

> The horses could no longer be used. Without them we were unable to contend, the Indians being so numerous; besides, man to man on foot, whether in the water or on dry ground, they were superior, being more skillful and active, and the conditions of the country more favorable to the practice of their warfare. (Bourne 1973, 188).

Horses were such feared and effective weapons that, for many years, any captured by natives were immediately killed as dangerous beasts and hated tools of the Spanish oppressors. A little too late, native people found that the beast much preferred grass to human flesh and that a horse could carry anyone along at what seemed like unimaginable speeds.

And that speed gave Spanish forces another important advantage. A large expedition on foot might cover, on average, five Spanish leagues (about twelve miles) in a day. A troop of mounted soldiers under the same conditions could cover twenty-five leagues a day (Graham 1949, 126). Relay riders, driving spare mounts in front of them, could travel even farther and faster (Denhardt 1975, 305). For that reason advanced parties of mounted soldiers often traveled well ahead of the main body of an army. On horseback they could explore large swaths of territory quickly, searching for provisions, water, native settlements, or routes to travel, then rapidly communicate that information to the main army moving slowly behind.

An important, if somewhat less romantic, addition to overland travel in the Americas was the introduction of large pack animals. Before the arrival of the Spanish, the only pack animal north of the Andes was the dog. Coronado's expedition into the American Southwest was reported to have taken up to six hundred pack animals, "including mules" (Hammond 1940, 7). The ratio of packhorses to mules wasn't mentioned. Both large-boned packhorses and mules were available from Spanish colonies throughout the Caribbean and Mexico by the midsixteenth century. Since mules are sterile offspring of a horse and donkey, ranchers kept large breeding herds of both. The breed of the horse mated with the donkey determined the type of mule produced, ranging in size from the smaller riding mule to the pack mule and the heavy draft mule. Generally, female mules were preferred for riding and males used as pack animals. In most cases mules would have been preferred over horses as beasts of burden, given the choice. Mules were stronger, had greater endurance, and were surprisingly good jumpers, even when loaded. A Spanish muleteer could jump a string of pack mules over obstacles on a trail that would have to be cleared or detoured around by other animals. An estimate of the load capacity of a mule, traveling long distances, might range between 150 to 250 pounds, depending on a variety of factors, including the size and condition of the animal, the length of the journey, how fast and how long the animals had to travel in a day, the quantity and quality of forage available, and the type of land and number of obstacles over which they had to travel.

Had some idle spectator made the calculations as they watched Coronado's formidable army head north along the western coast of Mexico, he might have been impressed by the transport capacity of a train of pack mules. Departing from the dusty little frontier outpost of Culicán in the spring of 1540, and well behind mounted Spanish hidalgos, were some six hundred pack animals, goaded on by their muleteer's cries of "anda mulo!" Estimating two hundred pounds per animal, these animals packed roughly sixty tons of equipment and provisions up the native trade trail, hopefully on its way to untold riches of the fabled Seven Cities of Gold.

The cost of all this baggage and provisions was that the horses and mules that packed them had to be cared for too. Keeping pack trains moving meant forage had to be found for all these many animals every day. Where grass didn't grow, expeditions could not travel unless hay was also added to the load of the pack animals. Where it was plentiful, horses and mules were feed corn, "on which they can do a hard day's work" (Graham 1949, 47). But in most cases time had to be allowed for grazing animals to feed, and this could significantly reduce the distance traveled during a day. A most onerous chore was the daily loading and unloading of tons of supplies from pack animals. One small advanced party lead by Coronado included pack animals but no packers. It seems mounted Spanish hidalgos didn't relish the lowly chores required of the pack train. In a letter to Viceroy Mendoza, Coronado complained of the tiresome loading and unloading of pack animals, "like so many muleteers" (Winship 1892–93, 564).

The effects of the unnaturally heavy weights carried by horses and mules, whether ridden or packed, also had to be dealt with. Without the protection of horseshoes, hooves under such weight soon wore down to the point at which animals became lame. A cavalry mount might carry as heavy a load as a pack animal. The weight of a rider, saddle, weapons, armor, rations, and other equipment resting on a horse's back could top 225 pounds. Horses and mules had to be strong, and they had to be kept shod (Graham 1949, 91). This was particularly so when traveling over the rocky ground that Coronado's army often had to contend with. In areas of heavy rain, like those traveled by de Soto, moisture softened horse's hooves, and shoes were lost. Enough extra heavy iron horseshoes and nails to keep all the mounts and pack animals shod during the entire journey added to transported supplies. Also included would be hammers, tools for paring hooves, and portable anvils and bellows for working the metal. When iron ran out, metal workers melted down cinch rings, stirrups, and buckles to make horseshoes and nails. Keeping mounts shod and serviceable was of such importance that when the conquistadors of Peru ran out of iron, they melted down the treasures of the Incas to make horseshoes of gold and silver (Denhardt 1975, 80). The expedition of de Soto, finding no treasure to melt down as a substitute for iron horseshoes and having lost most of their equipment in an early battle, traveled the majority of their time with many lame horses. And with this they lost their greatest advantage over native forces. These conquistadors would surely have agreed with a sentiment published centuries later in Benjamin Franklin's 1758 issue of *Poor Richard's Almanac*: "For the want of a nail, the shoe was lost; for the want of a shoe the horse was lost; and for the want of a horse the rider was lost, being overtaken and slain by the enemy, all for the want of care about a horseshoe nail."

Carrying enough provisions to feed a thousand or more Spanish soldiers and native allies for any length of time was beyond the means of even large pack trains. Feeding a mobile Spanish army

PART 3 — MOUNTED CONQUISTADORS

was always a problem, but there were provisions Spanish forces brought with them that didn't have to be carried.

Across the Atlantic, and at least as far back in time as ancient Rome, armies drove livestock along as a food supplies for soldiers. Livestock fulfilled two of any army's requirements at once, transport and provisions. Herded livestock were a reliable and self-propelled source of fresh meat. When Spanish armies entered the Americas, they trailed along herds of cattle, sheep, and even pigs in great quantities.

But a large army on the move could consume even sizable herds of livestock in a short amount of time. This was a fact that captain-generals of expeditions lasting several years would have been keenly aware of. Coronado, crossing the Great Plains in 1541 with a force of seventeen hundred Spanish soldiers and native allies, was reported to have herds of five hundred cattle and five thousand sheep (Hammond 1940, 278–279). Using an average daily consumption of beef by a marching army from a later era (Wentworth 1948, 122), Coronado's seventeen hundred men could have consumed about fifty cattle per day. Relying solely on the cattle as a food source, they had about a ten-day supply. Accordingly, leaders usually considered herded livestock a reserve food source for the sick and injured or as emergency rations when all other sources failed. De Soto only allowed the slaughter of some of the pigs herded along with his army when his men were starving.

As a reserve food source, livestock were invaluable, but again, like most solutions, while it solved one problem it created others. The Spanish introduction of horses and mules into the American West increased the speed and ease of travel and transport considerably; on the other hand, herding livestock along on an expedition slowed explorers considerably. How slowly they moved depended on the type of livestock herded. The speed of herded animals depended, not only on how fast they could move, but how long they could travel in a given day. Cattle were the fastest, able to move at the speed of a walking man while they were on the trail. But cattle didn't feed as they traveled, so four to six hours of grazing time had to be allowed at the end of the day, as well as time to rest after grazing. This necessity limited the amount of time cattle could be trailed in a day and therefore the daily distance traveled.

Sheep moved slower than cattle, but they grazed as they traveled. So sheep could be trailed longer and bedded down at the end of the day without the necessity of allowing time to feed. Under average conditions, a large flock of sheep might cover about eight to ten miles a day (Wentworth 1948, 272). What sheep Spanish armies took was stock useless for breeding; ranchers saved good breeding stock for themselves. Yeld ewes (barren females) and wethers (castrated males) were cheaper and served the purpose just as well. Sheep—wethers in particular—could survive under harsher conditions than cattle and on lower quality forage (Wentworth 1948, 21).

Mention the word conquistador and the image that most likely comes to mind is proud Spanish caballeros mounted on prancing horses, wearing plumed helmets and glittering armor. The prancing, plumes, and glitter didn't last long, and behind an advanced party of mounted soldiers, there often followed droves of rooting, snorting pigs. Coronado did not take pigs on his 1540 entrada into the Southwest, but many Spanish explorers, including Hernando de Soto, did. Pigs had the disadvantage of being the slowest of all livestock herded through the wilderness, probably averaging about five miles in a day's travel (Galloway 1997, 239–40). However, they were the most adaptable of all livestock introduced to the Americas. Pigs accompanying the conquistadors bore little resemblance to today's waddling balls of flesh. They were thin, rangy, long legged, tough, and able to feed on almost anything—plant or animal. Pigs bred and multiplied under the harshest of conditions. In less than four months, from conception to birth, a pregnant sow could add

PART 3 — MOUNTED CONQUISTADORS

a litter of a dozen or more pigs to the drove. De Soto's expedition landed on the west coast of Florida in May of 1539 with over six hundred soldiers, plus camp followers, bearers, religious, and other personnel. At times the ranks swelled to over a thousand. They brought a small drove of thirteen pigs as a reserve food source. In the three years that elapsed from that time to de Soto's death on the Mississippi River in 1542, the herd had grown to seven hundred (Milanich 1991, 168). But those numbers don't tell the whole story. For three years the drove was on the move, from Florida, north through Georgia, South Carolina, North Carolina, and Tennessee then turning southwest crossing Alabama, the State of Mississippi and the river, and wandering through much of Arkansas before finally returning to the Mississippi River by May of 1542. During that period Spanish journals record at least two major losses due to native attacks. The first occurred in the fall 1540, when four hundred pigs were killed in a battle at Mauvilla in central Alabama (Milanich 1991, 117). The following spring three hundred more died in an attack on de Soto's camp at Chicaza in northeastern Mississippi (Milanich 1991, 267). Considering that from the original thirteen a drove of seven hundred pigs grew, plus the seven hundred that were killed during the two reported attacks, plus the many that were eaten when needed for provisions, plus those lost as strays, plus those given as gifts to native people or where stolen by them, it's easy to understand why droves of pigs often followed the conquistadors.

Under certain conditions—like mountain trails and river crossings—movement of livestock of any kind could be extremely difficult. Traveling along a native trade trail in Northern Mexico's rugged Sierra Madre Mountains, an advance party under Captain-General Coronado found itself delayed by slow moving sheep. He left four horsemen behind to bring the herd along at a slower pace. After arriving in the native pueblo of Cibola, Coronado sent a letter to Viceroy Mendoza in Mexico City describing the terrain he had covered.

> *It was so bad that a large number of the animals...sent as provisions for the army were lost along this part of the way, on account of the roughness of the rocks. The lambs and wethers lost their hoofs along the way, and I left the greater part of those which I brought...because they were unable to travel and in order that they might proceed more slowly. Four horsemen who have just arrived remained with them. They brought only twenty-four lambs and four wethers; the rest had died from the toil, although they did not travel more than two leagues daily. (Hammond 1940, 164)*

The narrow and rocky trails through mountains were made for human travel, not routes for herding animals. Even at the much slower rate of two Spanish leagues, five to six miles a day, few of the original herd survived the trip. Coronado also told Mendoza, "If you are thinking of sending cattle, you should know that it will be necessary for them to spend at least a year on the road, because they can not come in any other way, nor any quicker" (Hammond 1940, 176). This was a remarkable statement in that the distance between the two was about nine hundred miles, and that distance, spread over a year's travel, would mean an average day's travel of less than two and a half miles, a single Spanish league. Finding a better trail for livestock would become an important objective for later Spanish explorers.

Mountain trails weren't the only obstacles for herding animals; river crossings also slowed the movement of Spanish forces herding livestock. Although most livestock, even pigs, could swim, care was usually taken not to lose animals by drowning in river crossings. Mounted soldiers ferried smaller animals, like sheep and pigs, across rivers one at a time, thrown across their saddles. When

PART 3 ~ MOUNTED CONQUISTADORS

necessary, large animals such as horses and cattle could be ferried across a river using dugout canoes. Two of these craft lashed together made a stable platform. A horse, mule, or cow, with front legs in one canoe and rear legs in the other, was poled, paddled, or pulled by rope across a deep river (Graham 1949, 40). Along the western bank of the Pecos River in Northern New Mexico, Coronado found his progress stalled by what was described as "a deep river carrying a large volume of water flowing from the direction of Cicuye [Pecos Pueblo]" (Hammond 1940, 235). There, he spent four days building a bridge to move his cattle and sheep safely across the river. Some years later an expedition under the command of Don Juan de Onate built an ingenious makeshift bridge to move his livestock across a river. On that trip Onate's party included a number of Spanish carretas, two-wheeled carts. When the expedition arrived at a river's edge, they removed all of the large, solid wood cartwheels, tied them together in a string, and pulled them across the water. Onate's men securely fastened the floating platform to the banks of the river then covered it with logs, brush, and dirt. After the livestock crossed over, his men took the bridge apart, remounted the cartwheels, and continued on their way (Wentworth 1948, 27). Further east, where timber was plentiful along river bottoms, de Soto's men built barge-like vessels they called piraguas, made from handsawn planks fastened together with iron spikes. Each piragua was large enough to carry four horses and their riders across the more than mile wide Mississippi River. After all the army had landed on the western shore, each of the piraguas was taken apart and the valuable iron spikes salvaged.

River crossings, mountain trails, delays, and dust were the inconveniences Spanish expeditions accepted for a reliable food source herded along in the rear, their insurance against hunger and starvation. In a freak accident, one man, at least, paid the supreme price for his livestock.

SUPPLYING AN ARMY IN A NEW WORLD

Although not born a gentleman like most Spanish officers, Melchior Diaz was one of Coronado's most able captains and the leader of a small force that searched northward along the Gulf of California and up the Colorado River in a vain attempt to make contact with Coronado's supply ships. After finding a note that told of the supply ships return south, his party continued exploring westward across the Sonoran Desert in an attempt to locate the Pacific coast. In that desolate country,

> *One day a greyhound belonging to one of the soldiers chased some sheep which they were taking along for food. When the Captain noticed this he threw his lance at the dog while his horse was running, so that it stuck up in the ground, and not being able to stop his horse went over the lance so that it nailed him through the thighs and the iron came out behind, rupturing his bladder (Winship 1892–93, 501).*

His soldiers carried the mortally wounded Diaz, "with extreme difficulty," for twenty days before he died.

With transported provisions, including livestock, limited on long journeys, armies often had to rely on the resources of the land or the people who lived on it. In this case Spanish travelers had the same options as the native people. They could forage for edible wild plants and hunt for game, grow their own food, trade for food, or plunder the resources of other tribes.

Foraging for food—living off the land by gathering wild plant foods and hunting game—was unreliable for a mobile army, and it would take a mess of pine nuts to make a meal for a thousand men. Foraging was something done to add variety to diet or when there were no other food sources available and they were literally starving. Although one of the stated goals of both the Coronado and de Soto expeditions was to settle the land for farming and ranching,

PART 3 — MOUNTED CONQUISTADORS

the effects of the "gold sickness" kept them constantly on the move in search of the mythical treasures that lay just beyond the next horizon. Growing provisions themselves was never an option. The last option, and one which early Spanish explorers relied heavily on, was food produced by native people. Settled tribes who grew the usual staples of corn, beans, and squash also developed means of storing their excess production for future consumption. So when Spanish forces traveled, their strategy was to move from one settled town to another, relying on access to native stored food by one means or another. And so, culturally, those who bore the brunt of the Spanish burden were the settled tribes. Migratory hunter-gatherers carried very little, including excess provisions. In lands where native provisions were unavailable—unsettled areas or those populated only by migrating hunter-gatherers—Spanish forces had to carry their food with them. These were areas to be avoided when traveling, if at all possible.

There were many examples of first contact between Spanish and Native peoples where provisions were willingly supplied to Spanish forces. There are also some examples of Spanish sensitivity to the ill will created by taking provisions by force. Coronado specifically instructed one of his captains to use trade goods to buy provisions because he "did not wish to disturb by force" the native people (Winship 1892–93, 554). In the majority of cases, however, if provisions were not freely offered, they were taken by coercion or force.

A rather odd Spanish legal procedure codified in the *Requerimiento* justified seizure by force. Developed during Spain's seven hundred–year effort to rid itself from Moorish invaders, the *Requerimiento* was required to be read before open conflict between Spanish forces and any people they considered part of "barbarous nations." In brief, the *Requerimiento* gave the history of the population of the world in a paragraph or two, explaining how the Catholic God had given authority over all nations, including "Christians, Moors, Jews, and all other sects," to a man called the pope. The document explained how the pope had given the land they were now standing on, and everything in it, to the Spanish king and queen. The *Requerimiento* proclaimed the barbarous nation should then be given the chance to swear allegiance to the Catholic God and the Spanish king as their lord and master, "without any resistance, immediately, without delay." For those who declined the honor, the *Requerimineto* promised the seizure of all their goods, enslavement for women and children, and the same or death for men. It also pointed out that these actions were not the fault of the conquerors but the fault of the barbarous nation since it was they who refused to recognize the one true God and his representatives here on earth, the pope, and the king and queen of Spain. The receivers of this speech, unfortunately for them, had the disadvantage of thousands of years of their own religious and cultural beliefs. In most cases they were not willing to give up these beliefs immediately, without some resistance, even assuming that they understood the Latin or Spanish languages in which the *Requerimiento* was read.

The ceremony of the reading of the *Requerimiento* began on the arrival of the Spanish force at some native town. Once the army was drawn up in front of the town, the Spanish leader marched forward with a few soldiers, the appropriate banners, and a priest or two for added authority. On the other side, people of the barbarous nation, to whom the proceedings were so much gibberish, watched as the document was read. When their patience ran out, warriors might send a shower of arrows toward the Spanish reader and his accomplices, and most likely that would be the only point of complete understanding between the native people and the Spanish army. Many resisted, but in the end it was usually the Spanish who took the field and the plunder.

Besides the obvious harm to native populations, plundering as a source of provisions could have disadvantages for Spanish

PART 3 — MOUNTED CONQUISTADORS

explorers too. Plundering took time, created considerable hostility, and when native forces were armed, it could lead to Spanish loss of life and property. A classic example of the downside of plundering occurred after the death of Hernando de Soto on the Mississippi River. The survivors of this expedition considered two options. First, they could build boats and sail down the Mississippi and then possibly along the Gulf Coast to Spanish settlements in Mexico. Second, they could march overland from the river to Mexico. Because of the uncertainty of where the Mississippi actually flowed, and for other reasons, the second option was taken. The Spanish force traveled, with difficulty, as far west as the Texas plains, which they described as a "wretched country." Starving in this unpopulated and barren land, the decision was made to return to their former camp on the Mississippi, where provisions were plentiful, and to over winter there. Unfortunately, on their way west, the Spanish army had seized native provisions and burned many settlements. Fearing the return of the Spanish, native people abandoned their villages, too afraid to replant their fields. One Spanish survivor remembered, "As they returned over the way, with great difficulty could they find maize to eat; for, wheresoever they had passed, the country lay devastated, and the little that was left, the Indians had now hidden" (Bourne 1973, 182). Victims of their own actions, the Spanish force suffered considerable hunger and hardship as they retreated back to the Mississippi, over the land they themselves had laid waste.

Chapter 7

Spanish Land Navigation

As Spanish explorers made their way inland and across the Americas, they carried with them a few basic navigational instruments to help chart the way. In unknown territory, however, a compass couldn't point the way to water, to the location of native settlements for food and shelter, to the correct trail to take, where to find a river ford, or, most importantly in Spanish eyes, to the rumored wealth of the Americas. A compass only told them which direction they were going, not which direction they should be going. That kind of information only came from people who lived on the land, whose ancestors had traveled over it for thousands of years. Without a doubt the most effective navigational aid available to any Spanish explorer was a reliable native guide.

But for the Spanish there were several potential obstacles to discovering what any native guide might know about the unknown land that lay before them. The first was language. The guide and the Spaniard had to be able to communicate either directly or more often through an interpreter or even a series of interpreters.

PART 3 ~ MOUNTED CONQUISTADORS

Because the need to communicate was so vital to the success of any expedition, captured natives, usually young men or older boys, were trained as interpreters. Spanish officers assigned captives to individual soldiers whose duty it was to teach them their language. Confounding the communication problem, North America was no single country of native people with a common language. It was a collection of hundreds of different native provinces, the people of which spoke several hundred different and distinct native languages (Kopper 1986, 57).

As an example, a Spanish force stepping ashore in the Americas might capture a native who spoke the language of the first province they entered and train him to speak Spanish. Then, moving inland to the next native province, a second interpreter would have to be found who spoke the language of the first province as well as his own. There, a Spaniard's question would be translated from Spanish into the native language of the first interpreter, who in turn translated the question from his language to the language of the second interpreter. Moving on into a third province, a third interpreter would be added and so on. Each additional step in passing information from one language to another added to the likelihood of information being translated into misinformation: like a yellow clay plate morph into a plate of gold. A Spanish soldier with de Soto recorded what travel was like without the ability to effectively communicate in the native language. On the Arkansas side of the Mississippi River, the army was attempting to make their way south, to the Gulf of Mexico, when their interpreter suddenly died.

> *The death was so great a hindrance to our going, whether on discovery or out of country, that to learn of the Indians what would have been rendered in four words, it became necessary now to have the whole day: and oftener than otherwise the very opposite was understood of what was asked; so that many times it happened*

the road that we traveled one day, or sometimes two or three days, would have to be returned over, wandering up and down, lost in thickets (Milanich 1991, 134–35).

A second problem with native guides was the reliability of the information they gave. Considering the fact that they faced an invading army, native people had little incentive to pass on information to Spanish forces. In spite of this, many did offer help and guidance to the Spanish. Sometimes these were simple acts of kindness. Often they acted through fear and sometimes for less noble reasons. Spanish forces entering a new territory usually treated natives relatively well, if they showed complete submission. Those who resisted were treated severely. This Spanish reputation often preceded them, and to keep the peace some native people gave them what they wanted, hoping they would move on—and soon. Others hoped to ally themselves with the power of the Spanish army and thereby settle old grudges with neighboring provinces. Only from this latter group could Spanish forces count on extremely accurate information on how to reach the land of their enemies.

Information from native people who resisted the Spanish invasion, and suffered the harsh consequences, could prove to be much less reliable. In this case native strategy usually followed one of two forms. Inspired by the Spanish lust for gold, native sources invented stories of great wealth in far-off lands to trick the Spanish into leaving. Another strategy involved leading the oppressors into uninhabited lands with little food or water then abandoning them to their fate. Combining both these elements, one recorded plot involved a guide Coronado's soldiers called "the Turk, because he looked like one." At the Rio Grande pueblos in Northern New Mexico, the Turk spread fantastic rumors among Spanish soldiers about his homeland, Quivira, far to the east. In this land, he said, there was a river two leagues wide in which swam fish as big as horses. The Turk said a great lord ruled there who took his nap, "under a large tree from which hung numerous golden jingle bells, and he is pleased as they play in the wind. He added that the common table service of all was generally of wrought silver, and that the pitchers, dishes, and bowls were made of gold" (Hammond 1940, 221).

This was the kind of news that Coronado and his soldiers—having marched, fought, and suffered much hardship for a year without reward—wanted to hear. The Turk gladly offered to lead the Spanish to Quivira, and the entire army headed east. The farther they marched, the more inhospitable the terrain became, until the Spanish army found itself on the desolate plains of what is now West Texas, with little food or water. Under questioning, including torture, the Turk admitted that he had been part of a plot by the pueblo people to lead the Spanish out on to the treeless, waterless, unbroken land of the Llano Estacado. There, the plotters concluded, Spanish soldiers would die, or those that did return would be in such a weakened condition they would be easily destroyed (Winship 1892–93, 583). In hindsight, one Spaniard remembered, "When the army left Tiguex [on the Rio Grande], the Turk asked them why they loaded their horses with so many provisions, saying that they would get tired and not be able to load so much gold and silver later, which showed plainly the deceit" (Hammond 1940, 246).

But the Turk, even after torture, continued to insist that the riches of Quivira were real. Coronado's advance party headed north to central Kansas, where they found nothing but a village of vermin-ridden grass huts. There, because of his original deceit and his secret attempt to incite the natives of Quivira to rise up against the Spanish, he was executed.

False guides under de Soto and, after his death, his successor, Luys Moscoso de Alvarado, suffered the similar fate more often and for lesser offenses. Near the Red River in Texas,

> *Two days' journey on the way, the Indians who guided the Governor [Moscoso], in place of taking him to the west, would lead him to the east, and at times they went through heavy thickets, out of the road; in consequence, he ordered that they should be hanged upon a tree. A woman, taken in Nissohone, served as a guide, who went back to find the road (Gentleman of Elvas 1907, 242).*

Even simply refusing to provide information could mean a horrible death. In one notorious episode, de Soto's scouts captured four or five native men. They were asked to guide the Spanish to their home village. When they refused, one was burned alive in front of his companions. Each survivor in turn was asked to act as a guide, each refused, and each in turn was burned alive down to the last man (Bourne 1973, 97). Although acts like these were meant to instill fear and set an example, being deliberately led astray by native guides was a constant problem for Spanish expeditions.

Without native guides, a most basic means of discovery in unknown territory was what one twentieth-century explorer labeled "home-center reference" (Gatty 1958, 52–53). A useful means of exploration by any culture, it required no fancy navigation aids or instruments, only patience and careful observation. How home-center reference worked, in microcosm, was demonstrated by a curious incident on the Great Plains in 1541. While Coronado's army rested in a sheltered ravine (barranca), parties were sent out to the surrounding plains to hunt buffalo.

> *During this time many of the men who went hunting got lost and were unable to return to camp for two or three days. They wandered from place to place not knowing how to find their way back... The best method for them to find their way was to go back to the place where they had slaughtered the cattle [buffalo] and to march in one direction and then in another until they came to the barranca or*

PART 3 — MOUNTED CONQUISTADORS

> *until they met someone who could direct them...This could be done only by experienced men...(Hammond 1940, 241).*

Lost and without any point of reference, the inexperienced wandered aimlessly, while the experienced men maintained contact with their one known point of reference, the buffalo carcass. From that point they systematically explored the land around it. Moving off in one direction, they traveled as far as they dared, without losing contact with their center point. If they found nothing they returned to the buffalo as reference and then started off in another direction. By the time they had made a complete circuit around the center point, experienced hunters would be familiar with their immediate surroundings, and, if necessary, they would be able to extend the search further out into unknown territory. A slow and tedious process for sure but one that was much more likely to bring the hunter back to camp than aimless wandering. This was a procedure as applicable to large parties of exploration as to a lost hunter. Starting from a fixed point, like a Spanish settlement or outpost, parties of exploration set out in all directions to gather information on the unknown territory that surrounded them. As they became familiar with their immediate surroundings, the exploring parties increased their range, relative to the fixed starting point, without losing their way.

How far a party of explorers could travel from their starting point and safely return was extended over even greater distances using a type of navigation now called dead reckoning. This was the kind of navigation that took Columbus across the unknown Atlantic and safely back home. All that was required for dead reckoning navigation, at sea or on land, was a means of direction finding and of measuring distance traveled. Finding direction was easy enough, night or day, using a most ancient navigational aid, the compass. Coronado's party carried at least one, as recorded in a soldier's journal: "The general sent Captain Diego Lopez ahead with ten companions, lightly equipped. He traced his direction toward the rising sun by means of a sea-compass, for he instructed him to travel with all speed for two days, to find Haxa, and to rejoin the army" (Hammond 1940, 236).

The European sea compass Captain Lopez carried would have been marked differently than a modern compass. Instead of 360 degrees, his would have had only thirty-two points on its compass card, each separated by 11¼ degrees to make a full circle. The origination of the thirty-two-point compass has several explanations. Before the introduction of the compass, early European sailors, like Native Americans, categorized directions by prevailing winds. Some say that when the compass came into use, these wind directions were incorporated into the thirty-two sailing points on a compass card, beginning with the four cardinal points or winds—north, south, east, and west. Others maintain that the original thirty-two points came from the Arab compass that marked the rising and setting positions along the horizon of fifteen tracked stars, plus north and south. Regardless of the origin, a possible source of error for all compasses was magnetic declination, the amount of variation between the earth's magnetic lines and true north, which, in places, was up to twenty-five degrees. A rough calculation of magnetic variation was easy enough to determine. The navigator faced the North Star at night and gave what was called "the pilot's blessing." Holding the flat of his hand, edge on, to his nose and lined up with the North Star, he then dropped his hand straight down to the compass face to find the difference between his sighting and the north reading on the compass, and that gave local magnetic variation (Fisher 1995, 88). Magnetic variation was added to the compass reading if the variation was east of true north or subtracted if the variation was west of true north, and this eliminated the compass's magnetic variation error. As a navigational tool, the introduction of the compass was a major advance in travel through the Americas.

PART 3 — MOUNTED CONQUISTADORS

With a means of direction finding available, dead-reckoning navigation only needed a way to measure distance traveled. Spanish forces sometimes measured distances from one point to another in units of time—days of travel—in a manner similar to the custom of native people. But this was not as useful for Spanish travel because of the possible variations in the distance a day's travel could cover. Native travelers had one basic mode of transportation—walking. For the Spanish, however, a day's travel on foot was different than that covered by a horse and rider or when traveling with herded animals. Each moved along at different speeds, and therefore a day's travel meant something different in each circumstance. Spanish travel distances were more often given in a specific unit of distance, the Spanish league. Given the number of leagues in a journey, a traveler on foot or mounted could calculate how long a journey would take, based on the estimated speed of his particular means of travel.

An idea of how far a Spanish force could travel overland in one day comes from a report by Nuno de Guzman, governor of New Spain in the 1530s. Referring to the mythical Seven Cities of Gold, Guzman wrote, "Since Tejo had said that it would be found after forty day's travel, they thought that they would cross the land upon traveling two hundred leagues" (Hammond 1940, 195). Guzman's native servant, Tejo, regaled the governor with stories of the great wealth he had seen as a boy at the native trade center near what is now Zuni, New Mexico, which Spanish imagination translated that into Cites of Gold. Tejo estimated the journey in native terms, days of travel, which Guzman converted into Spanish leagues. Based on this entry, an average day's march by Spanish forces large enough to venture into unknown, and possibly hostile, territory with mounted and foot soldiers as well as herded livestock, was considered to be five leagues, or about twelve miles. An overland march by such a force of six or seven leagues (fifteen to eighteen miles) per day was considered a hard day's travel.

A confounding factor in using reported distances in leagues to estimate Spanish travel, both then and now, was the fact that there was more than one Spanish league. Distances were most often given in "legal" leagues (approximately 2.6 miles), but "common" leagues (3.4 miles) could be substituted without being labeled as such. Because measurements were not standardized in Spain itself, varying from province to province, the standard used in the Americas in the early days of exploration varied according to which Spanish province the one who made the measurements came from (Haggard 1941, 68).

The accuracy of distances in leagues also varied greatly depending on whether they were actually measured or were estimated. Estimated distances were subject to considerable error. Estimates of travel distances looking uphill were usually underestimated and downhill overestimated. Travel on an unknown trail, or a meandering trail, always seemed longer than traveling a straight one (Galloway 1997, 242). Simply making an estimate at the end of the day was the least accurate method of reporting distances traveled.

A bit more reliable were leagues calculated from measured times of travel multiplied by an estimated speed of travel. Spanish journals of the day had many entries with periods of time measured "by the clock," or mentioned events at specific hours of the day. In one example, a Spanish soldier remembered an attempt to move their mounts across a cold and swift-running river: "For more than three hours by the clock, the Spaniards continued to belabor the horses..." (Varner 1951, 217).

The most likely timekeeper may have been the forerunner of the pocket watch, what was actually a pocket sundial. There were a variety of these small and portable instruments, but they all shared some common characteristics. Each used the position of the sun to tell time and required a compass to orient them in

PART 3 — MOUNTED CONQUISTADORS

the proper direction. They needed to have adjustments to correct for the seasonal changes in the sun's angle. Pocket dials could be made for a specific latitude, or they could be adjustable for use at any latitude. One type of dial looked like a pocket watch, and, when opened, a string attached to each half of the case was pulled taut. Inside the dial case was a small compass that oriented the dial to north then the shadow cast by the string showed the time of day (Decker 1999, 109).

Timekeeping wasn't only limited to the daylight hours, however. At night the Spanish could make use of a lightweight and portable instrument appropriately named the nocturnal (figure 5). Physically, a nocturnal consisted of two calibrated disks and a pointer arm mounted on a circular base. A small hole, used to sight the North Star, passed through the center of the device. Following the rotation of stars around the stationary North Star, the nocturnal was based on the same principle used by native peoples to measure time at night. Viewed from the earth, stars close to the North Star, like those in the Big Dipper, appear to make a complete circle of 360 degrees around the North Star every twenty-four hours. Careful observation would show, however, that the circling stars move slightly faster than that, slightly more than one degree of rotation every day. So a star viewed at 9:00 p.m. one night would have moved about one degree farther around its circle of rotation relative to that same star's position at 9:00 p.m. the night before. Shifting its position by about one degree in rotation per night, relative to a specific time at night, that star will return to exactly the same position, at exactly the same time, only once every year. European mathematicians and astronomers calculated the predictable daily position of a star circling the North Star, versus time, and then used that data to calibrate the circular disks of the nocturnal. But most Spanish observers would have little regard, or need, for theory to check the time at night. When darkness fell, and the North Star was visible, measuring time was quite simple. Figure 5 shows the proper alignment of the nocturnal to measure time relative to rotation of the Big Dipper (Great Bear, or "GB," on the inner disk) around the North Star. The GB nub on the inner disk was rotated to the appropriate date marked on the outer dial and the instrument held at arm's length. Then, sighting on the North Star through the center aperture, the observer rotated the long pointer arm until it was parallel to the outer most, "guard stars" of the Big Dipper. Where the pointer arm crossed the inner disk, the observer read the time. The nocturnal's rather surprising accuracy of about fifteen minutes (or better) per day was the most accurate portable timekeeper of that period. As a practical timekeeping device for travelers and mariners, the nocturnal had already been in use for three centuries when the Spanish army first entered the American West, and it would remain the instrument of choice for many timekeepers for another two hundred years.

With a timepiece, day or night, Spanish expeditions could calculate daily travel distances by multiplying hours of travel by an estimated speed per hour. Besides guessing a day's travel or calculating travel distance from estimated speed multiplied by the hours traveled, there was one other, more accurate, means of measuring distances. A clue of how this was done comes from the journal of one of Coronado's followers:

The army rested many days at this barranca in order to explore the country. They had traveled thirty-seven days of from six to seven leagues each to this point. A man had been detailed to make the calculations and even to count the steps. They said that the distance to the settlements was 250 leagues (Hammond 1940, 239–240).

The man detailed to "make the calculations and even count the steps" used an ancient method of measuring distance that went back in time, at least as far as Alexander the Great, and is still taught in schools of forestry today. Counting the steps, or *pacing*, was a simple means of measuring distance.

Using either foot, a pace was counted for each time the same foot struck the ground. In most cases the length of a pace was about five feet. In the time of Alexander the Great, surveyors measured roads in units of a thousand paces, a standard that would later become the basis for the English mile (Taylor 1971, 52). The Romans labeled their thousand-pace distance as one *milla*. The number of paces allowed for a Spanish league was likely to have been around three thousand (Haggard 1941, 68). Keeping track of the fifteen thousand paces in an average day's march of five leagues was no mean trick. One method would be to carry ten pebbles or large seeds, each representing one hundred paces (or a little over five hundred feet). When the traveler finished the hundredth pace, a pebble was shifted from one pocket to another. When all ten pebbles were moved from one pocket to another, a pebble representing one thousand paces would go in a third pocket, and the process started over again. Counting the pebbles at the end of the day gave the distance, in paces, traveled during that day. Knotting a cord, with each added knot representing a predetermined number of paces, was another means of tracking paces. Paced distances, as recorded in journals of Coronado's expedition, were often quite close to the mark. With a little practice, accuracies of one hundred feet or less, in a measured mile, are possible.

The most accurate type of dead reckoning—using compass and pacing together—made it possible to plot a reasonably accurate overland course of travel. With this method of navigation, Spanish explorers could estimate their current position relative to a known starting point, no matter where they traveled, and they could calculate which direction to travel to return to that starting point. Unfortunately the majority of early Spanish explorations, including that of de Soto, relied simply on inaccurate guesswork. Or they didn't bother to keep track of where they had been at all. Garcilasco de la Vega, who wrote a history of the de Soto expedition based on conversations with its survivors, gave a reason for this inattention to navigation. He wrote that after landing in Florida, de Soto's party headed northeast:

> *This direction and any other that you will find in the course of this history, I must warn you not to take precisely lest you blame me if contrary information should appear after...The first idea in the minds of these cavaliers was to conquer that kingdom and seek gold and silver, and they paid no attention to anything that did not pertain to these metals. Thus they failed to accomplish other things of more import such as tracing out the limits of the land (Varner 1951, 103).*

Besides dead reckoning, Spanish explorers also brought a rudimentary, early-sixteenth-century form of celestial navigation to the Americas. A celestial navigator had three requirements. First, there had to be some means of measuring the angle between the position of a celestial object—the sun, moon, or a star—relative to the position of the traveler. Second a navigator's almanac that gave the position of those celestial objects relative to some given point on earth. And, third, the navigator needed a working knowledge of a system for mapping the earth proposed by the Greek astronomer Ptolemy.

Originally proposed in the second century, Ptolemy's *Geographia* wasn't discovered by Europeans until the early fifteenth century. His method of mapping used a grid system of imaginary lines running north-south (longitude lines) to measure east-west position, and east-west lines (latitude lines) to measure north-south position. Using east-west lines to measure north-south position is a concept that can be a bit confusing. But imagine a huge, curved ladder with its feet resting on the equator (zero degrees latitude) and its top resting on the North Pole (ninety degrees north latitude). The rungs of the ladder (lines of latitude) are then oriented east-west, and if the ladder has ninety evenly spaced rungs, each could represent one degree of latitude. For each step the traveler takes up or down the east-west oriented rungs, he changes position one degree, north or south, in latitude. Likewise, if the ladder is laid on its side, its rungs then represent lines of longitude, oriented north and south, and a traveler moving along the ladder would be changing his longitude, or east-west position. Simply put, lines of latitude or longitude run perpendicular to the direction they measure.

Using Ptolemy's grid system, it was possible, theoretically at least, to plot the position of a traveler anywhere in the world. In practice though, celestial navigation of the early sixteenth century could only measure latitude—how far north or south a traveler moved. Longitude, east-west position, still had to be estimated by dead reckoning.

With the world conveniently divided into a measured grid system, the sixteenth-century traveler needed a fixed star and some means measuring its angle relative to his position on earth. From this he calculated his latitude, or north-south position, on that grid. The two stars most often used were the North Star and the sun. Sighting the North Star was the least complicated because the angle measured gave a direct reading of the observer's latitude, and a sighting could be taken any time at night as long as the weather was clear. Calculations were more complicated for a sun sighting. Unlike the relatively stable North Star, the sun's angle varies with the seasons, being low in the sky relative to the equator in the winter and high in the sky during the summer. That varying angle was the sun's declination. Added to that, the sun constantly changed position, moving in an arc across the sky. Astronomers predicted the sun's exact angle at noon, day by day, in published tables of declination—*Regimientos de Navegació*—the final requirement needed by all navigators. Determining latitude by sun sight meant a copy of the *Regimiento* had to be packed along on each expedition. But even with its added calculations, measurement of latitude by sun sight was the preferred method because it was the most accurate. When it came to instruments to calculate latitude, mariners had the greatest variety to choose from. Unfortunately, some of the most reliable at sea were useless on land.

The cross-staff fell in that category. It was a simple instrument consisting of a stick or staff calibrated with numbers and a smaller crosspiece that slid along the staff at right angles. One end of the staff was held to the observer's eye and the crosspiece moved to a position where the bottom of the cross piece aligned with the horizon and the top aligned with the sun or a star. When it was in that position, the observer read the angle marked on the staff between the celestial object and the horizon. From that he calculated latitude. Since this instrument had to be aligned with a perfectly flat horizon like the sea, it couldn't be used on land, where mountains, forests, and other obstacles blocked the true horizon. What could be used for land navigation were gravity-aligned (self-leveling) instruments like the astrolabe and the quadrant.

The astrolabe was circular and hung from mountings that allowed it to swing freely in any direction, and so it aligned itself by gravity with the plane of the horizon. Astronomers' astrolabes were solid plates with multiple interchangeable disks that made this instrument a mechanical computer able to determine the position of a variety of celestial bodies at any given moment in time. A mariner's astrolabe, also useable by land travelers because it was self-leveling, was a simple affair compared to one employed by astronomers. The mariner's astrolabe looked like a small, four-spoked wheel, the upper half engraved with a semicircular degree scale running from zero degrees on each side to ninety degrees at the top. Able to swing free, the instrument self-adjusted by gravity so that the two zero-degree points aligned parallel with the true horizon. An arm with two attached sighting vanes pivoted around the center of the astrolabe. Astrolabes varied in size from about six inches in diameter and an accuracy of one degree of latitude to two-foot-wide instruments with an accuracy of one-quarter of a degree. At sea, stability was a problem when sighting these instruments, so mariners' astrolabes were made of heavy brass with more weight at the bottom than the top to dampen the effect of swaying in the wind, while hollow spaces between the spoked-wheel design helped to reduce wind resistance of the instrument. But still, on a swaying deck, astrolabes were hard to hold steady long enough to align the sights on a speck as small as a star. For accuracy mariners tried to find an island or some other land where the astrolabe could be hung from a tree or tripod to make star sights.

On land, taking a sun sight with the astrolabe was relatively easy. Figure 6 shows a navigator kneeling, his arm resting on his knee to steady the free-swinging astrolabe. Turning the suspended instrument toward the sun, he rotated the sighting arm until a tiny sun spot appeared on the ground from light passing directly through the hole in the upper sighting vane and the hole in the lower sighting vane. When the sunspot appeared, the instrument was properly aligned and the land navigator had the sun's angle, relative to his position that he needed to calculate latitude.

Spanish land navigators had one other gravity-adjusted instrument with which to measure latitude: the quadrant. In the shape of quarter circle and usually made of brass, the quadrant had two straight sides coming together at a right angle, or apex, and a third side forming a quarter of a circle, on which were engraved degrees from zero to ninety. To sight a star, the observer held the quadrant to the eye until it was visible in the two sights mounted on one of the straight sides of the instrument. A string attached to the apex was weighted with a small plumb, and when it crossed the degree scale on the rounded side, the observer read the angle to the sighted object. Sun sights were usually taken with the astrolabe, as it was considered the most accurate instrument for that job, but if latitude was determined from the North Star, a quadrant would be the preferred instrument. The dim light of the North Star was easier to sight through a quadrant than an astrolabe.

In the realm of accuracy, large astrolabes could measure angles within one quarter of a degree. Since each degree of latitude covers roughly seventy (statute) miles, an accuracy of a quarter of a degree could, theoretically, give a position within about seventeen miles of its true north-south location. Relative to the size of the earth, that wasn't bad for a sixteenth-century navigator. Examples of typical latitude errors found in the letters and journals of Coronado's expedition, however, show measurements well off that mark. Consider three recorded latitude readings—34.5 degrees north latitude at the confluence of the Gila and Colorado River, thirty-seven degrees north at the pueblos near present-day Zuni, New Mexico, and forty degrees north at the native village of Quivira in central Kansas. Each of these calculated latitudes had an error of about two degrees, locating each of the three points approximately 140 miles too far north (Bandelier 1893, 235; Hammond 1940, 286). Since the error was constant, one possible source may have been inaccuracies in sixteenth-century tables of declinations used to calculate latitude. While such a large error would produce a poor map, those erroneous latitude readings were still useful. As long as the same error was made in each calculation, the relative distance between each location could give a fairly accurate measure of north-south distance between two locations. For instance, the calculated five-and-a-half-degree latitude (385-mile) difference between Quivira and the Gila River, or the two-degree (140-mile) difference between Quivira and the Zuni Pueblos, is a relatively accurate measurement of the north-south distance between these locations.

PART 3 — MOUNTED CONQUISTADORS

There was another recorded method of way-finding, a remarkable but not unusual one among the religious who often lead later Spanish explorations. It might be labeled navigation by divine intervention, and it was a method still applied centuries after the time of Coronado and de Soto. In the year Jefferson penned the Declaration of Independence, a small party under the leadership of Fray Francisco Atanasio Domínguez departed Santa Fe, New Mexico, with the task of exploring an overland route to Monterey on the Pacific coast. Moving across the high plains of southwestern Colorado, Dominguez's mounted travelers made good time until they descended into the austerely beautiful, and still remote, valley of the Dolores River, near what is now Slick Rock, Colorado. Traveling north and downriver, the valley narrowed and entered a labyrinth of rocky canyons and mesas. After they'd followed the river's rugged, meandering course approximately fourteen miles, and covering only half that distance in straight-line travel, the decision was made to leave the river valley for higher, more passable ground. At that point the party had two choices: follow a trail heading southwest or backtrack upriver to a trail heading northeast. Neither appeared to be a good option, and there was little agreement on which route to take, as recorded in the expedition's journal:

> *We put our trust in God and our will in that of His most holy Majesty; then, after begging the intercession of our thrice-holy patron saints that God might direct us through where it would be more conducive to His most holy service, we cast lots between those two trails...(Escalante 1995, 22).*

These travelers, being true believers, felt God would show them the way, not by the chance of cast lots but by manipulating the outcome as a demonstration of his will. And on the human scale, as a means of quieting dissent, it would be harder to argue with the will of a divine leader than a mortal one.

Leaving aside faith-based navigation, the identities of many of those who applied sixteenth-century science to a navigator's skills have long since faded into the past. The information on land navigation for the armies of Coronado and de Soto is a prime example of the fickleness of recorded history. With regard to Coronado's expedition, where distances and directions traveled were carefully measured and recorded, nothing is known of the navigators who made those measurements. On the other hand, a great deal is known of Juan de Anãsco, the self-appointed navigator for the de Soto expedition, who apparently kept no records.

The role of Juan de Añasco in the de Soto expedition is a story in itself. Añasco joined de Soto's inner circle sometime after de Soto returned to Spain from his part in the conquest of Peru. Añasco was a man of property and influence in the Spanish court. With his help the Spanish crown granted de Soto the right to make his attempt at discovery and conquest of La Florida. At the same time Añasco also arranged to have himself appointed as the royal comptroller of the expedition. Añasco was reportedly the most educated man in de Soto's army, but how he received his education in navigation is a mystery. He had never been to sea before the trip from Spain to Cuba. From Cuba he commanded the ships that twice sailed to the gulf coast of Florida scouting for a landing site for the main army waiting in Havana. Possibly he learned the mariner's art from one of the pilots during the Atlantic crossing or during his initial trips to Florida. Within a short period after the army landed on the mainland, however, he was piloting ships himself, north from the Tampa Bay area to the gulf coast below Tallahassee. On land Añasco was a captain of cavalry and as such would have been constantly in the thick of battle. He was a favorite officer of de Soto, and when there was a difficult task, Anãsco was the officer most likely called by his captain-general. But not all the men of the expedition held Anāsco in such high regard. In one instance Añasco commanded a detachment of thirty mounted cavaliers attempting to make a difficult river crossing in hostile territory, far from any possibility of reinforcement. Under such circumstances, river crossings were always dangerous maneuvers. At any moment a hostile force might catch them with their small party split, some crossing, others scattered on either side of the river. On this particular day the weather was so cold that Anāsco's men couldn't get their horses to cross. After hours of ferrying equipment and trying to coax the horses into the water, only two horses had been forced across. Losing patience, Captain Añasco swore at his soldiers, and one, Gómez Arias, replied,

> *Cursed be you and the lewd bitch prostitute who whelped you! You sit there on your horse finely dressed and wrapped up in your coat, taking no note of the fact that we have been in the water more than four hours, frozen with cold, and doing what we can. Get down off your horse, confound you, and come here; then we shall see if you are worth any more than we are (Varner 1951, 217–218).*

According to the witness on whose memory these words were based, Añasco made no reply because he realized he had spoken without reason, and he "found himself humiliated and his reputation diminished because of his failure to consider first what he should say in such cases" (Varner 1951, 217–218).

Others showed Añasco in a little brighter light. He "was a very cautious man" who had the foresight to rescue a brass astrolabe from the ashes of the great fire that destroyed most of the army's supplies during the battle of Mauvila (Varner 1951, 600). With this instrument, a homemade cross-staff, and sea chart, he was able to guide the survivors of de Soto's expedition from the mouth of the Mississippi River westward to the safety of New Spain. Even this feat didn't go without criticism. During the long sea journey with the approximately three hundred survivors distributed in seven small boats, Añasco, in one, heard men in another boat ridiculing what they considered his pretensions as a navigator:

> *The mariners and others with them, having pondered the fact that this man was not a seaman, and indeed he had never embarked in his life except for this expedition, ridiculed him. Then when he learned that they were making fun of him, he threw all of these things into the sea except the astrolabe. But they were rescued by another brigantine which came behind, for the chart and the forestaff were bound together. Thus we traveled, or better said, navigated, seven or eight days, when a storm coming up, we took shelter in a cove (Varner 1951, 600).*

The incident provides another telling comment on the character of Juan de Añasco. Even in his anger, he only threw overboard the navigational aids that would float long enough to be rescued, not the heavy brass astrolabe that would have immediately sunk and been lost forever.

The survivors of the de Soto expedition spent three years wandering over much of what are now the southeastern United States searching for the instant wealth of gold and silver. When self-preservation finally overcame greed, they spent another year and a half attempting to escape from that land, traveling overland as far as Texas before retreating to the Mississippi to take the water route to New Spain. By then all had long forgotten the goal of establishing settlements in the new territories. After more than two months in open boats, sailing and rowing down the Mississippi River and across the Gulf of Mexico, what was left of the de Soto expedition reached the Spanish outpost at Panuco, near present-day Tampico, Mexico. What the survivors saw at this shabby little Spanish settlement had a profound effect on how

PART 3 — MOUNTED CONQUISTADORS

they would view their four-and-a-half-year ordeal in La Florida. At Panuco, settlers, including Spanish gentlemen, lived in hovels and worked unproductive fields like peasants. Only then did the survivors realize what they had left behind in La Florida: fertile lands for farming and ranching, a land teeming with game—a source of hides and pelts that would bring a high price back in New Spain. Most had invested everything they had to join the expedition, and at the end of their travel and hardships, they had nothing left but the ragged animal skins they were dressed in. Feelings ran so high that discipline completely broke down. Soldiers attacked officers who had counseled for the flight from La Florida.

The expedition of Coronado ended with similar results. No gold or other wealth was discovered. After the fact, Coronado, too, was bitterly denounced because he had failed to establish Spanish settlements in the new land. But with the usual twist of human nature, none of the survivors of either expedition, when given the chance to return, took the offer. Some gave up the New World to return to Spain. The more adventurous headed south to Peru, once again dazzled by the lure of gold and instant riches. By the end of these two expeditions, Spanish explorers had traveled over most of the southern half of what would be the continental United States, from the Atlantic to the Pacific Ocean, and had done it eighty years before the first English pilgrim stepped ashore at Plymouth Rock. But without the lure of gold and silver, there would be no permanent Spanish settlement founded in the American West for another half century.

ILLUSTRATIONS

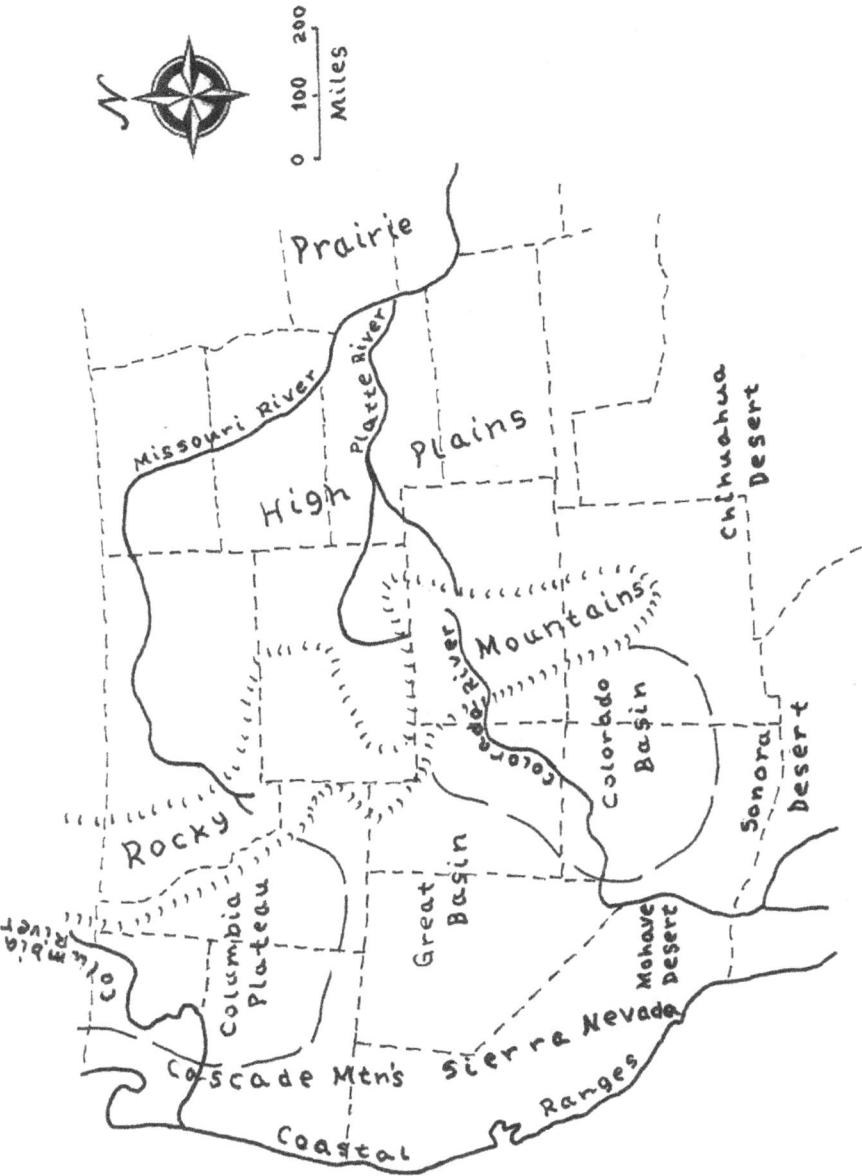

Figure 1. Geographical features of the American West. Author's Image.

ILLUSTRATIONS

Figure 2. George Catlin, Buffalo hunt on snowshoes." Buffalo Bill Center of the West/The Art Archive at Art Resource, New York.

ILLUSTRATIONS

Figure 3. Karl Bodmer, "Mih-Tutta-Hangjusch; A Mandan Village." Bullboats in the foreground. The New York Public Library/Art Resource, New York.

Figure 4. "Jackson Staircase," Chaco Canyon, New Mexico. Author's Image.

ILLUSTRATIONS

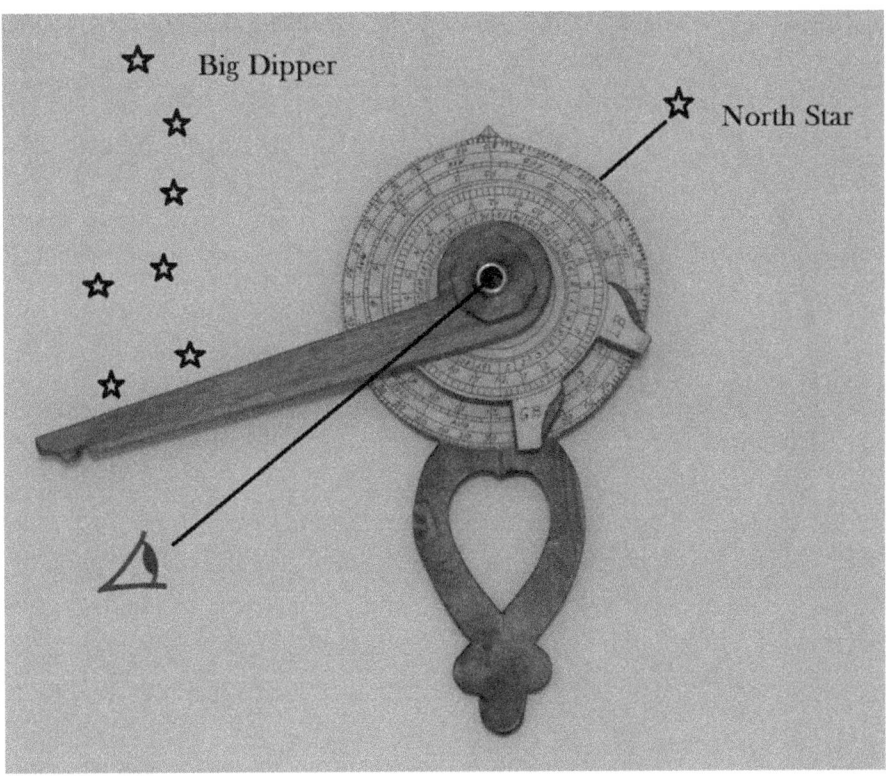

Figure 5. Sighting a Nocturnal. Author's Image.

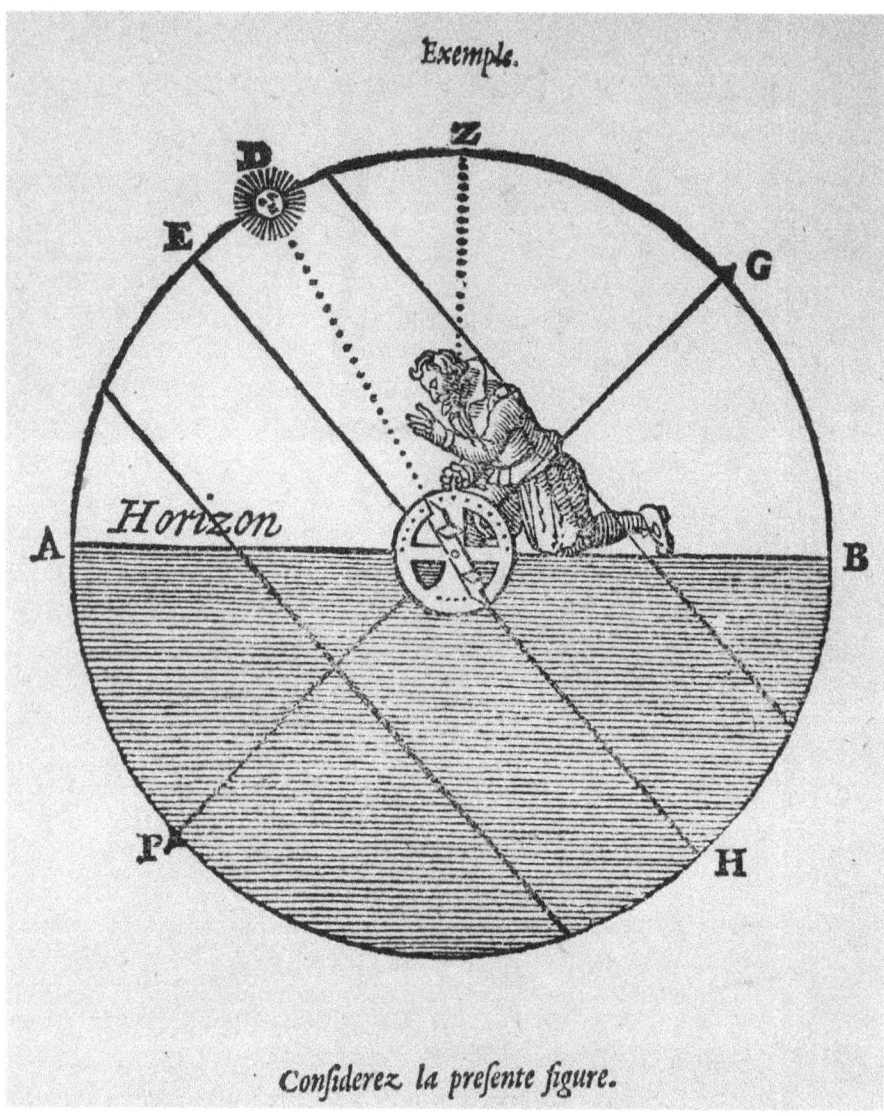

Figure 6. Navigator kneeling with astrolabe, 1635. The Mariner's Museum, Newport News, VA.

ILLUSTRATIONS

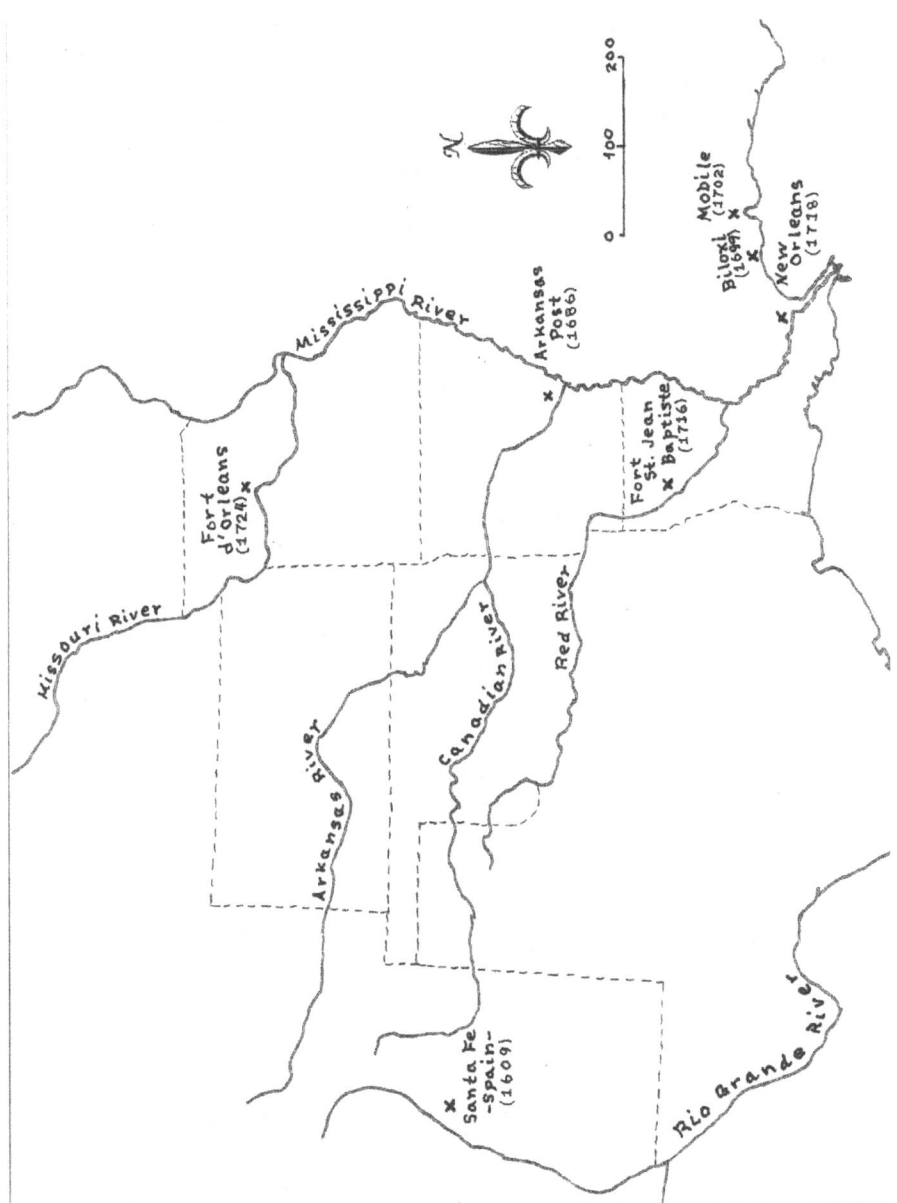

Figure 7. French rivers of commerce, from the Gulf of Mexico to the Great Plains. Fort and post settlement dates in parentheses. Author's Image.

ILLUSTRATIONS

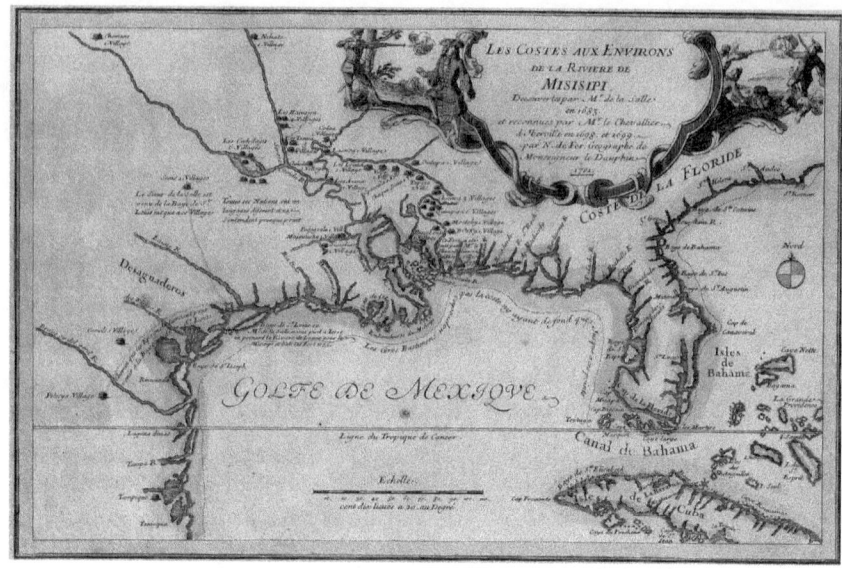

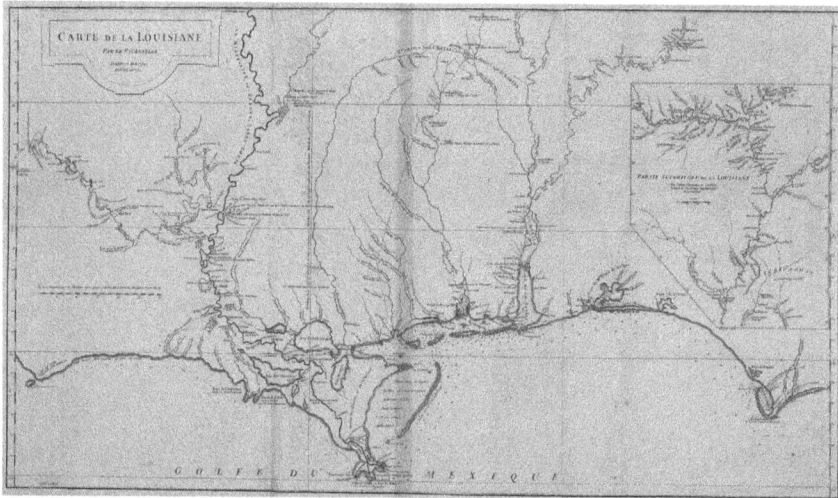

Figure 8. Top: Nicolas de Fer, "Les Costes Aux Environs de la Riviere de Misisipi, Decouvertes par Mr. de la Salle en 1683 et reconnues par Mr. Le Chevallier d'Iberville en 1698." Bequest of Richard Koch, Courtesy of the Historical New Orleans Collection. Bottom: Jean-Baptiste Bourguignon d'Anville, "Carte de la Louisiane." Gift of Richard Koch, Courtesy of the Historical New Orleans Collection.

Figure 9. Mid nineteenth-century English sextant. The Art Archive at Art Resource, New York.

ILLUSTRATIONS

Figure 10. J. Goldsborough Bruff, "Ferriage of the Platte above Deer Creek." This item reproduced by permission of the Huntington Library, San Marino, California.

Part 4

French Watermen

Chapter 8

Prelude—Down the Mississippi

By the mid sixteenth century, Spanish exploration had stalled in the American West. But far to the north and east, along Canada's Atlantic coast, French explorers made their first tentative steps toward what would become the next great chapter in western travel. Sailing along the North Atlantic coast, ships under the command of Jacques Cartier discovered an immense inlet, what would later come to be known as the Gulf of Saint Lawrence. Crossing the Gulf at its narrowest point, a sixty-mile gap of open water, Cartier landed on the southern shore, where natives informed him they were at the mouth of a great river flowing from deep within the country. It was the best news Cartier and his men could hope for. French explorers, like their Spanish counterparts, had dreams of a water route west across the unknown land of the Americas, an opening to the rich trade of China and the Indies. With instructions to search for the Northwest Passage, the French king Francois I agreed to help finance Cartier's first voyage. And this, Cartier hoped, might be that fabled passage.

PART 4 — FRENCH WATERMEN

Over the next century and a half, that dream carried them up the Saint Lawrence River and into a land of lakes and rivers, the land the French called the *Pays Haute*: the Canadian high country. It was a country of waterways, one quarter of the total area covered by lakes strung together like pearls on a necklace by innumerable rivers and streams. Along this extensive web of inland water trails, French explorers traveled hundreds and sometimes thousands of miles, across what are now Canada and the northern latitudes of the United States, with never more than a short portage between them. But no matter how far they traveled, rumors of the western passage drifted ahead like smoke in the wind.

By the final quarter of the seventeenth century, French forts and trading posts across the Great Lakes were inundated with reports of a great river to the south that native sources along Lake Superior called *Mes-che-ce-be* (Chappell 1905, 40). To test these rumors, a small party of seven explorers, led by Louis Joliet, left Green Bay, on the northwest shore of Lake Michigan, in the spring of 1673. From Green Bay they traveled south, ascending the Fox River to a portage that brought them to the Wisconsin then down that river to the Mississippi. The first known white men to travel this route, they discovered a river system so vast that when reports later reached cartographers in France, they were dismissed as exaggeration. Making their way downriver, Joliet's party was also the first Europeans to discover the Illinois, the Missouri, and the Ohio Rivers. Further south, somewhere below the confluence of the Arkansas and Mississippi Rivers, they were the first white men to paddle over the grave of Hernando de Soto, his body secretly committed to the river more than 130 years before. After two months of travel, Joliet was informed by native sources that they were within ten days' journey of the Gulf of Mexico. This information established the fact that the Mississippi did not flow west toward China, as they had hoped, nor east toward the English colony of Virginia, as they feared (Coulter 1971, 47).

Aware of the possibility of capture by Spanish forces if they continued downriver, Joliet and his small party of explorers turned north, ascending the Mississippi. Upriver, native sources advised Joliet of a much shorter route home. Ascending the Illinois and Des Plaines Rivers, the French explorers made a short portage to a small river emptying into the southern tip of Lake Michigan. Near the northern terminus of this second water trail between the Mississippi River and the Great Lakes, Joliet's party passed the tiny native fishing village they called *Che-cau-go.*

Almost a decade passed before the French traveled the Mississippi all the way to the Gulf of Mexico. Heading down river in the spring of 1682, René Robert Cavelier, Sieur de la Salle, finally reached that ephemeral margin between land and sea, the Mississippi River Delta. There he set up a cross, buried an inscribed lead tablet, and declared,

> *Possession of this country of Louisiana, the seas, harbors, ports, bays and adjacent straits; and all nations, people, provinces, cities, towns, villages, mines, minerals, fisheries, streams, and rivers, comprised in the extent of said Louisiana, from the mouth of the great river St. Louis, otherwise called the Ohio...as also along the Mississippi, and the rivers which discharge themselves therein, from its source beyond the country of the [Sioux]...as far as its mouth at the sea, or Gulf of Mexico (Coulter 1971, 65).*

With that pronouncement, La Salle, in the name of Louis XIV of France, laid claim to a territory of 1.2 million square miles, more than one third the land area of what would become the continental United States. Included within its boundaries were the Mississippi River, every river, stream, and creek that drained into it, and all the land that surrounded these waterways. La Salle's claim extended from the Ohio River, near what is now Pittsburgh, west to the headwaters of the Missouri in western Montana, north almost

PART 4 — FRENCH WATERMEN

to the present-day US-Canadian border, and south to the Gulf of Mexico. It was a giant land wedge centered between Spanish claims to the west and the English colonies to the east. Through it all ran a French controlled system of water highways connecting Canada's Atlantic coast to the Gulf of Mexico. In honor of the French king, La Salle called the territory Louisiana.

By the end of the seventeenth century, French settlements, forts, trading posts, and Jesuit missions had sprung up along the Mississippi. Often located near the mouth of a major tributary of the Mississippi, many played a role in future exploration and travel into the Great Plains of the American West. The first was Arkansas Post, a fur-trading settlement established by Henri Tonti near the confluence of the Arkansas and the Mississippi Rivers in 1686. Further north, Jesuit priests founded a mission at the confluence of the Missouri and Mississippi Rivers on the site of the long-abandoned native city of Cahokia. There, the French constructed huts on a native temple mound whose base area rivaled those of the pyramids of Egypt.

French settlements along the Gulf Coast at Biloxi and Mobile made it possible to supply explorers and settlers by ship from those ports rather than the more distant sites in Canada. By the dawn of the eighteenth century, the Mississippi River had already become an important water road for the French descending from Canada in the north and moving up river from the Gulf of Mexico (Chappell 1905, 20). With this great river reasonably explored, mapped, forted, and secure, French interests headed west.

What French explorers found as they moved westward across the Great Plains was just as subject to speculation, misinformation, and geographical wishful thinking as the Spanish imagination had been capable of inventing in the American Southwest. After a century and a half of coastal exploration, however, the hope for an easy shipping channel through the Americas to the wealth of the

Indies had waned somewhat, but the idea of a water passage to the Pacific via western rivers was very much alive.

Symmetrical geography, a popular theory proposed by French geographers of the period, prophesied such a passage. Using eastern experiences to predict western landforms and waterways, proponents of symmetrical geography argued that landforms of North America were like the matched grain of a split plank, the two halves laid side by side with the Mississippi River flowing between. What would be discovered in the West should mirror what had been found in the East. And based on what was known at the time, the idea wasn't as strange as it sounds to modern ears. A traveler standing on the banks of the Upper Mississippi, above the current city of Saint Louis, would see prairies stretching to the horizon, both east and west. Below that city, forestlands stretched hundreds of miles on both sides of the river. To the east lay the known Appalachian Mountains and to the west the rumored Rocky Mountains. From both sides of the Mississippi, major tributaries emptied into that great central funnel of a waterway flowing south to the Gulf of Mexico. Theoretically then, the fabled Rocky Mountains would be low, weathered mountains like the Appalachians. If it were possible to travel upriver from the Mississippi to the Appalachians and cross overland by a short portage to a river flowing to the Atlantic then it should also be possible to take a similar route westward to the Pacific. In the early eighteenth century, Englishman Daniel Coxe described the Rocky Mountains as a "ridge of hills, passable by a horse, foot, or wagon, in less than half a day, some what north of Mexico. On the other side are rivers which run into a great lake that empties itself by another navigable river into the South Sea [Pacific Ocean]" (Chappell 1905, 38).

Coxe's advice—unhindered by personal experience—also touched on another popular speculation of the day, the "Western Sea." According to this variation in the concept of an inland water passage from the Mississippi to the Pacific, a traveler would ascend one of the rivers of the Great Plains to a great inland sea. Crossing the sea, the traveler would then discover other rivers flowing west into the Pacific Ocean. These waterway myths prospered well beyond the time of the French, into the American era, when those explorers struggled over the not-so-trifling Rockies only to find vast desert lands and even more formidable mountain ranges blocking their path to the Pacific.

Trained on the rivers and lakes of the Canadian Pays Haute, it was natural for the French to look to waterways as their means of entry into the unknown West. As rivermen in the east, French voyageurs had honed their skills over many generations. But traveling westward, out of the Mississippi River valley and on to the Great Plains, they would have to replace eastern experience, and eastern-based theory and myth, with the reality of the West.

Jesuit priest Jacque Marquette, accompanying the first French party to navigate the Mississippi River, recorded one of the earliest impressions of a major western river. Descending the Upper Mississippi in 1673, this small band approached the mouth of the Missouri near what would later become the city of Saint Louis:

> *As we were gently sailing down the still clear water, we heard a noise of a rapid into which we were about to fall. I have seen nothing more frightful, a mass of large trees entire with branches, real floating islands came from the Pekitanoui [Missouri], so impetuous that we could not without great danger expose ourselves to pass across. The agitation was so great that the water was all muddy, and could not clear (Vestal 1996, 11).*

What Marquette saw in the great surge of water flowing out of the Missouri was a hint of what future French explorers would deal with, decades later, when serious exploration of the western tributaries of the Mississippi began. What altered the form and flow of these waterways, relative to eastern rivers, were differences in geography and climate, and the further west they went, the greater the differences they found.

In the East, relatively constant supplies of water from rain or melting snow kept those rivers flowing year round. In the West, river levels varied dramatically; some stopped flowing altogether in the late summer and early fall. The difference between East and West was rainfall; most of the West got very little. Mountain barriers like the Sierra/Cascades and Rockies caused weather fronts, moving in from the Pacific, to rise in elevation to the point where moisture-laden clouds released their burden as rainfall along the western slopes. Barren clouds crested the mountain peaks, leaving the opposite slope and the lands to the east dry, in what is called a rain shadow. A more fitting descriptor might be "lack of rain shadow." With limited rainfall, the few rivers that drain the dry land between the mountains and the parched grasslands east of the Rockies rely primarily on winter snowmelt for water. Before the era of massive dams and irrigation canals, when western rivers did flow, it came in a great seasonal surge.

Snow packs built up along the slopes of the Rockies all winter and melted in the spring to send torrents of water racing down mountain streams and out across the rivers that etched the Great Plains. How high and fast the rivers flowed depended on how much winter snow fell in the mountains and how fast it melted in the spring. Traveling in a broad wave, this great surge of water beginning in the Rockies could take months to reach the Mississippi River Delta. As the seasons progressed into summer, mountain snow packs gradually dwindled and the spring surge subsided. With little rainfall to augment river flow, streams dried up and larger rivers grew shallow, making travel by water haphazard.

PART 4 — FRENCH WATERMEN

While low water often made western rivers unnavigable, high water carried Marquette's "frightful mass of large trees entire with branches, real floating islands...so impetuous that we could not without great danger expose ourselves to pass across." Trees, of course, end up in all rivers, but it was the magnitude of these floating hazards that distinguished the West from the East.

Rivers flowing across the flatlands of the Great Plains meandered, snaking from side to side, forming alternating loops and bends. Around the outside of these meandering bends, river currents flowed fastest, scouring the banks and dredging the deepest part of the channel. The resulting wedge-shaped bottom of a meander bend gave river flow a spiraling motion, and this action, along with the faster speed of water around the outside bend, acted like a giant liquid auger undercutting riverbanks. Water flow gnawing its way outward from the river bend exposed roots of the trees growing along the bank; in time the overhanging soil collapsed with whole trees swept away downriver. This action, multiplied by thousands of river bends, sent untold numbers of trees floating down western rivers.

Moving downriver, these floating battering rams played havoc with anyone attempting to navigate the river. Some waterlogged trees sank to the bottom to form snags, jagged branches cutting the water's surface. Known to rivermen as sawyers, other trees sank trunk first with their roots hinged to the river bottom. Bobbing up and down ominously with the current, a sawyer could appear suddenly at the surface, too late to save a doomed watercraft from disaster (Burchardt 1978, 31).

What didn't sink—floating whole trees, logs, branches, and other debris—piled up along the first river obstruction they met—the head of an island, point bars, or around snags. Rising river levels, from spring snowmelt or the occasional downpour, picked up these floating debris piles and moved them farther downriver until river levels again dropped and deposited the debris to form ever-larger floating river obstructions. In places, concentrations of logs, tree trunks, brush, rocks, and even buffalo carcasses formed wing dams, partial river obstructions that jutted out from one or both sides of the river. These obstructions channeled river flow into a narrow passage of strong and dangerous currents (Bundy and Hall 1978, 116). In some locations debris completely covered a channel, forcing river flow underneath the pile along with the canoes of unwary travelers foolish enough to get too close. On larger rivers, floating debris formed piles, called rafts, up to several square miles, and some so old they had live trees growing on top (Russell 1898, 243).

The Great River Raft of the Red clogged 165 miles of that river with its mass of driftwood, logs, and trees (Burchardt 1978, 31). French cartographer Jacques Nicolas Bellin's 1764 map of the lower reaches of the Red labeled the head of this great river raft as an *Embaras de Arbes* (Bellin 2003, 113). From just above the current city of Natchitoches, Louisiana, where the single river channel of the Red braided into a maze of waterways and islands, this mass of floating *arbes* extended upriver, through northwestern Louisiana and the southwestern corner of Arkansas, and although the river still flowed beneath, as far as water travel was concerned, it plugged the Red like a cork in a bottle.

Whatever went into its tributaries eventually made its way into the Mississippi River. In the same year as Bellin's Red River map, British hydrographers published a large-scale map of the Mississippi Delta. On it they detailed "heaps of trees" that had been swept downriver and piled along the riverbanks, on mud banks, and on the scattered islands of the Mississippi River Delta (Royal Navy 2003, 89). In fact, perhaps symbolically, it wasn't long after La Salle set up his monument to the French claim of the Louisiana territory at the mouth of the Mississippi that a flood of logs and trees destroyed it. Descending the Mississippi in search of his leader, Henri de Tonti, La Salle's most trusted lieutenant, found the downed marker and left a letter in a prominent tree: "Sir: Having found the posts on which you had set up the Kings arms, thrown down by driftwood, I have planted another further in, about seven leagues from the sea…" (Charlevoix 1962, 123).

—⚉—

Chapter 9

Across the Mississippi and onto the Plains

Few western rivers were navigable year round. River obstructions jammed some; many had water levels too shallow even for canoes or ceased to flow at all during the dry season. Within the limited circle of navigable western rivers, those most widely traveled were the Red, the Arkansas, and the Missouri (figure 7).

Most southern of the three, the Red rose on the featureless plain of the Llano Estacado, near the current Texas-New Mexico border. From there the river flowed through land Coronado's army had crossed heading northeast to the Kansas prairie a century and a half before the first French trader passed that way. From its source the Red cut thirteen hundred miles eastward along what is now the border between Texas and Oklahoma, around the Great Bend of the Red near the borders of Texas, Oklahoma, and Arkansas then diagonally across Louisiana to its confluence with the Mississippi River. The Great River Raft of the Red closed the river to water travel above present-day Natchitoches, Louisiana.

PART 4 — FRENCH WATERMEN

It was at that point, traveling west to Mexico in 1714, that Louis Jurchereau de Saint Denis stopped long enough to build two huts to store trade goods in a village of friendly Natchitoches Indians. In the years that followed, what came to be known as Fort Saint Jean Baptiste grew to include a regular garrison with warehouses, barracks, cannons, and a church. Fort Saint Jean Baptiste became a focal point for most travelers in the lower Louisiana territory, an important center for trade with the local natives, and a place of flourishing but illicit—from the standpoint of the Spanish government—trade with the nearby Spanish fort Los Adaes. Besides its importance as a waterway, the Red was also generally regarded as one of the boundaries between the French and Spanish claims in North America.

North and west of the Red, the headwaters of the Arkansas River cascaded out of the Rocky Mountains onto the high plains of eastern Colorado. As a second river road across the southern Great Plains, the Arkansas flowed through Kansas before dipping south into Oklahoma, where it, along with the Canadian and Neosho Rivers, formed an important landmark, the Three Forks of the Arkansas, near Muskogee, Oklahoma. Below the Forks, the river cut its way through the Ozark Mountains of Arkansas, entering the Mississippi River just below the only French settlement along this waterway, Arkansas Post. Established in 1686 by Henri de Tonti as a fur-trading center, Arkansas Post was the first French settlement west of the Mississippi. Although the settlement was strategically located, its fortunes were as irregular as the river that flowed past it. Arkansas Post was repeatedly abandoned and resettled until it finally passed into history following the American Civil War. But in the first half of the eighteenth century, Arkansas Post, on the Arkansas, and Fort Saint Jean Baptiste, on the Red, were the two most important French trade and supply posts west of the Mississippi.

How far up the Arkansas a traveler could paddle was as variable as the weather. The Arkansas was navigable from its confluence with the Mississippi upriver to the Forks, near Muskogee. From there a water-bound traveler heading for Santa Fe could usually count on taking a tributary, the Canadian River, at least as far west as the meridian of present-day Oklahoma City. At that point, if river levels were too low, the French traveler might wait, hoping a lucky upriver rainstorm would allow him to continue by water, or he could start searching for native horses for sale and then take the overland route. Failing that, he could turn around and go home.

As western waterways, the Red and Arkansas had several things in common. Both rivers shared a similar physical geography. Unlike other western rivers, about one third of the lower reaches of the Red and Arkansas flowed through lands whose vegetation was indistinguishable from that found on the other side of the Mississippi. Deep forests and heavily wooded uplands of the East extended west of the Mississippi up to three or four hundred miles in a grand arc from where Saint Louis now stands, south through Oklahoma City, Dallas, and Houston. Along its western border, forestland graded into a savanna-like band of scrub oak and patches of mixed grass prairie called the Cross Timbers. It was a hard place to travel overland. A century after the French crossed this land, writer Washington Irving explored the same area with a company of American Rangers. In *A Tour of the Prairies*, Irving recorded his impression of travel in the Cross Timbers:

> *The fires made on the prairies by the Indian hunters had frequently penetrated these forests…calcining the lower twigs and branches of the trees, leaving them black and hard, so as to tear the flesh of man and horse…I shall not easily forget the mortal toil, and the vexations of the flesh and spirit that we underwent occasionally, in our wanderings through the cross timber. It was like struggling through forests of cast iron (Irving 2004, 96).*

PART 4 — FRENCH WATERMEN

Both the Red and the Arkansas Rivers were considered part of potential trade routes, either to the Spanish settlements of New Mexico or possibly to the "Western Sea," that mythical route to the Pacific. Although a transcontinental water route was never discovered, French traders did find their way to the Spanish settlements of New Mexico. This had little practical value, however, as their trade goods were usually confiscated and the men themselves arrested or sent packing. The Spanish government vehemently opposed trade or anything else that would support what they considered French intrusions along their eastern boundaries.

Surprisingly, the Missouri, the most northern and the greatest of the western river roads, was also considered for many years to be a route to Mexico. Twice the length of the Red and Arkansas Rivers, the Missouri rose in the Rocky Mountains of far western Montana. From there its course arched northward, at one point flowing within fifty miles of the Canadian border. The river crossed North Dakota then turned southeast through South Dakota. It ran along the eastern border of Nebraska and Kansas then east, cutting the center of what would become the state of Missouri, to the river's confluence with the Mississippi, just north of the present-day city of Saint Louis. And it was there, in 1673, that the French party under command of Louis Joliet first heard a claim from local natives that by ascending the Missouri they would come to the land of the Spanish. It was a story repeated for almost seventy years. Early Missouri River explorer Etienne Véniard de Bourgmont wrote in his 1714 report, *Description of Louisiana,*

> *By way of the Missouri one can also reach the place to trade with the Spanish, where they have many mines, according to all the information one has been able to gather. They [Spanish] are not far from these rivers, according to the Indians who go to their homes and who trade with them (Norall 1988, 108).*

In 1724 Bourgmont established the only major French post on the Missouri River, Fort New Orleans, at the confluence of the Missouri and Grand Rivers in what is now north-central Missouri. Later, in the spring of 1739, a party lead by two French Canadian brothers, Pierre and Paul Mallet, ascended the Missouri, still understood to be the trade route to the Spanish settlements in northern New Mexico. On what was then considered the Upper Missouri, other natives finally, and correctly, informed the Mallets that what they sought lay far to the south and west. Abandoning their canoes for packhorses, the Mallets made their objective via an overland route, ending the myth of the Missouri as a potential trade route to Mexico. Traveling westward from Lake Superior in 1743, by water and then overland, the Vérendrye family, father and sons, struck the Missouri where it flows through central North Dakota. Although no permanent French post resulted, the French Canadians did establish direct relations with the most important native trade center of the upper plains. This might have been the limit to official French exploration of the greatest of western river roads. Within the limits of their exploration, French travelers found the river navigable year round, and time would show that even steamboats could make their way many hundreds of miles further west on the Missouri.

The common characteristics shared by these important western waterways, ephemeral flow and dangerous river obstacles, required adaptations to long-standing water-transport practices as French explorers and traders made their way out onto the Great Plains.

In the East, French voyageurs of the Canadian High Country had perfected a water-transportation system based on the native bark canoe. Rivers and lakes were so numerous that travelers could cover hundreds of miles with no more than short portages between waterways. In its day the bark canoe that cruised eastern

PART 4 — FRENCH WATERMEN

waterways served every modern purpose, from passenger car to semi-trailer truck.

French trading companies often contracted the job of canoe building to native craftsmen. Their bark canoes began with a frame constructed from light, soft wood of the cedar tree. It was easy to work, and resins in cedar made it resistant to rot. The bark covering, on average only about an eighth of an inch thick, came from the paper birch tree that grew across southern Canada and the Great Lakes region (Adney and Chappelle 1983, 3). Birch bark was harvested when it began to "slip," or separate from the inner wood, making it easy to peel from the tree in large sheets. Normally, bark slipping and harvesting occurred during the spring and fall when trees were actively growing. But in an emergency, winter bark could be tricked into slipping by pouring hot water down the trunk of the tree. A fast canoe had to have as smooth an outer surface as possible to create less drag, so canoe builders carefully cut and fitted sheets of birch bark then sewed them to the canoe's cedar frame with spruce roots. A mixture of spruce gum, charcoal, and animal fat sealed and waterproofed the joints. A course of small fir or spruce poles laid along the bottom of the canoe helped distribute the weight of the cargo and protect the thin bark covering from clumsy-footed watermen (McCaig 1978, 7). And in the Canadian High Country, a plentiful supply of birch bark trees assured a quick patch for any damaged hull.

Bark canoes varied in size, but most canoes used by French voyageurs were either the large canots maitre—running thirty-six feet in length, five and a half feet wide at the beam, and about two and a half feet deep—or the smaller, twenty-five-foot canots nord. Outbound, across the Great Lakes and deeper rivers, Frenchmen in a canot maitre could freight eight thousand pounds of cargo in a single canoe. Where the water grew too shallow for the big canoes, voyageurs transferred goods to smaller canots nord for transport up the rivers and streams of the backcountry. On the return trip each large-freight canoe brought home its four-ton cargo of hides and pelts in tightly pressed bales (McCaig 1978, 6).

References to the durability of bark canoes cover a confusing range from frail to tough and sturdy. The reasons for these divergent opinions might be that canoes, like eggshells, could be both. A marvel of natural engineering, the eggshell is a sturdy container for its weight and construction, as long as it isn't given a sharp blow. Similarly, the bark canoe, given its weight and construction, was a sturdy container for carrying great quantities of cargo and passengers, as long as it wasn't given a sharp blow. In a letter to his brother, Jesuit missionary Sébastian Rasles described his experiences with bark canoes in the early eighteenth century. Rasles wrote that he had made many journeys on Canada's rivers and had crossed lakes four to five hundred leagues in circumference "without having run any risk." But he wrote this of his experience on the Saint Lawrence:

> *Crossing the river...I suddenly found myself surrounded by masses of ice of an enormous size; the canoe was cracked by them. The two savages who were piloting me immediately cried out: "We are dead men; all is over; we must perish!" Notwithstanding, they made an effort, and jumped upon one of those floating cakes of ice. I did likewise; and, after having drawn the canoe out of the water, we carried it to the very edge of the ice. There we were obliged to again enter the canoe, in order to reach another cake of ice; and thus by jumping from cake to cake we at last came to the bank of the river, without other inconvenience than being very wet and benumbed with cold (Thwaites 1900, 139).*

A short time in those icy waters and they would, no doubt, have been dead men. Raseles, later reassigned to a more southerly mission in the Illinois country, left the Great Lakes region by canoe traveling along shallower inland rivers. On one he wrote, "We ran greater hazards on the rivers, especially in places where they flow with extreme rapidity. Then the canoe flies like an arrow; and if it happens to touch any of the rocks, which are numerous there, it is broken into a thousand pieces" (Thwaites 1900, 151). So traveling by bark canoe was reasonably safe, as long as it didn't hit anything. And for its size and carrying capacity, the bark canoe was extremely light in weight. In the water it had a draft that could navigate the shallowest of rivers, and it was highly maneuverable. Out of the water even a large thirty-six-foot freight canoe could be carried on the shoulders of four men in portage. In camp, bark canoes easily flipped over to provide shelter from rain, snow, or blowing winds.

As French watermen moved from Canada down the Mississippi River and into its western tributaries, the probability of hitting things increased dramatically. On western rivers, bark canoes smashed into snags and floating river debris, broke on exposed rocks when water levels fell, and were worn to shreds from constant hauling over shallow gravel beds and exposed sand bars.

A different type of river required a different kind of watercraft. French watermen soon recognized the need to abandon bark canoes for the more durable water transport of western natives, the dugout canoe. The native dugout became the French pirogue. The dugout had none of the advantages of the bark canoe. Cut and hacked from a single log, dugouts were much heavier than bark canoes. Their greater weight gave them a deeper draft, so dugouts couldn't navigate as far upriver as the lighter-draft bark canoe. Heavy, water-soaked, hollowed-out logs, dugouts were difficult to portage. They were clumsy, hard to control, and slower than their bark counterparts. But dugouts had the one advantage lacking in bark canoes—they were nearly indestructible. And on western rivers, that was by far the most important requirement.

An average dugout was much smaller than the large birch bark freight canoes used by French voyagers in the East, ranging in length from fifteen to twenty-five feet and two to three feet in width. Two dugouts fastened eight to ten feet apart with poles and with the space between decked over allowed for a greater carrying capacity of equipment and supplies (Vestal 1996, 15). Twin hulls made more stable watercraft in rough water and rapids than a single dugout.

Dugout construction depended primarily on what was available in a particular region. In southern Louisiana Territory, cypress, with its rot resistant wood, made a durable craft. Dugouts cut from solid walnut came from the Mississippi and lower Missouri Rivers where large trees of that species were once plentiful. Westward, along the narrow forested galleries that lined riverbanks of the Great Plains, cottonwood trees became the source for most dugout canoes. While native people followed the custom of shaping and hollowing their dugouts by laborious burning and scraping, the French, with the advantage of metal tools, could make one much faster—though not necessarily better. Jean-Baptiste LeMoyne de Bienville, exploring overland in the spring of 1700 with a party of twenty, after slogging through back swamps north of the Red for twenty-five days, used the term "wretched" several times in describing the land they crossed. And these were men who would surely set the bar higher when defining *wretched* than those of a more modern era. On reaching the banks of the Red, he wrote, "I immediately set my men the task of digging out a pirogue [dugout] with our hatchets. It was finished in five hours, big enough to carry six men..." (Iberville 1981, 151). It couldn't have been much of a dugout in that time, but it did fulfill its purpose—to send men a few miles downriver where they were told they would find three native-built dugouts to continue their journey.

Besides the canoe, d'Bienville's men had to carve their own paddles, and those they made would have narrower blades than modern canoe paddles. Although the stroke of a narrower paddle blade had less power, it also took less force to pull through

PART 4 — FRENCH WATERMEN

the water. Narrow-bladed paddles were less tiring than those with wide blades—an important consideration for men who spent long hours, day after day, on the water. Where a stream was too shallow for a paddling, voyageurs stood, pushing their canoes along with long setting poles. Water too shallow to pole meant dragging canoes over exposed sandbars, gravel beds, and rocks. As a last resort French voyageurs made a portage, unloading and carrying the cargo overland around shallows, rapids, or falls. Along with the cargo, the heavy, waterlogged dugouts had to be dragged overland too. With numerous or long portages, average daily canoe travel, upriver, of ten to fifteen miles might be cut to two or three miles a day or even less.

But French watermen never entirely abandoned bark canoes in the West. Returning eastbound in 1740, after their first successful journey from French Louisiana to the Spanish colonies of New Mexico, a party led by the Mallet brothers crossed the plains with a string of fifteen horses. Striking a river, the Mallets followed it downstream, hoping it to be a tributary of the Red or Arkansas Rivers and therefore a route to the French settlements at Natchitoches or Arkansas Post. In the Cross Timbers area that separated the plains from the forestlands of the East, their packhorses gave out. Although the Mallets were unsure of their position, they were in fact on the Canadian River, south of present-day Oklahoma City. There the river being deep enough for a canoe, the voyagers decided to abandon their worn-out horses for river travel. In only five days they scouted the river, held a council to decide their course of action, and with only two knives that remained as tools, built several elm bark canoes that would eventually carry them over five hundred miles downriver to Arkansas Post near the Mississippi.

The speed with which they accomplished the task suggests that Mallets may have relied on a method of constructing temporary bark canoes used by native people when their journeys began with overland travel then switched to river travel. Crudely built to save time and labor, these temporary watercraft started with a single sheet of bark stripped from trees large enough to cover a canoe frame. Instead of the time-consuming cutting and sewing fitted pieces of bark to make a smooth hull, the single sheet of bark was folded and crimped to a rough frame (Adney and Chappelle 1983, 212). A crimped bark hull created more drag than one carefully fitted and sewn, but the craft was serviceable.

In the year following the successful conclusion of the original Mallet expedition, the two brothers were once again on the Canadian River, this time as members of a party lead by André Fabry de la Bruyére. The French government authorized Fabry to retrace and map the route of the Mallets in hopes of establishing a viable trade route to the Spanish colonies in New Mexico. From Arkansas Post the party ascended the Arkansas and the Canadian Rivers in five dugouts. They didn't get far up the Canadian, however, before low water made the river too shallow to continue. Unable to procure horses from native sources for overland travel, Pierre Mallet suggested they build bark canoes. With shallower drafts than their dugouts, Mallet believed it possible to continue upriver toward their goal of New Mexico. Fabry rejected this plan, and with much dissension the party turned back downriver. At the conclusion of the journey, the Mallets and others in the failed party of exploration made bitter accusations against Fabry, as recorded in an official French government report along with Fabry's replies. In it Fabry's reasons for rejecting the bark canoe option, suggested by Pierre Mallet, highlight many of the weaknesses of these craft in western river travel:

> *Bark canoes require a great deal of attention, and they would be damaged by exposure to the sun and would be worn out quickly by dragging them across the sand. He [Fabry] argued further that Mallet should realize that soldiers are not accustomed to using such*

> canoes, and that they would break one every day; that while sailing in hot weather, it would be impossible to protect them from the sun; that since they would be obliged to drag the canoes, which was a virtual certainty, the canoes would not last long; that they would find themselves in the prairies where there would be no bark with which to build others, and they would be placed in a very difficult situation (Blakeslee 1995, 237).

Fabry's reference to protecting the canoes from the sun may have been due to the fact that only elm bark was available for canoes at their latitude. Elm bark wasn't as pliable as northern birch bark and dried and cracked more quickly. And as Fabry correctly pointed out at the time of the confrontation, they were near the boundary between woodlands and plains and would have soon crossed into territory where even elm bark was no longer available to repair damaged canoes. It was ironic that according to Fabry's testimony, he was only repeating remarks Mallet himself had made concerning bark canoes earlier in their journey.

Whatever watercraft was used moving upriver against the current, experienced watermen knew it was better to take several small craft, with less resistance to river flow, than a single, large watercraft. Moving downriver with the current, the situation was reversed. At the end of a successful trading venture, French voyageurs often relied on large, flat-bottomed *bateaus* to carry their cargo of furs downriver. On deeper rivers these craft could range in size from fifty to seventy-five feet with a beam of ten to twelve feet (Chappell 1905, 56). Bateaus were crudely made from hand sawn planks cut lengthwise from a log suspended over a pit. One man stood on top of the log, another less fortunate in the pit, each alternately pushing and pulling on a two-man saw. Knocked together, these craft with straight sides, a flat bottom, square stern, and raked bow looked more like a huge floating crate than a river craft. How fast the bateau moved was determined by the speed of the downriver current. Two large sweeps, one forward, one aft, kept the craft headed in the right direction. At the end of the downriver journey, crews broke up their bateaus and sold the planks as lumber.

With any western river travel, timing was everything. During the spring snowmelt, river levels ran high and fast. That was the time to move downriver quickly, with flood waters covering rocks and sandbars that would be obstacles when river levels dropped. And it was a time of moving upriver only with difficulty, fighting strong currents all the way. When that spring surge of melt water occurred depended on where along a river a traveler happened to be. Close to the Rockies, torrents of water began cascading down mountain streams in March and April. Several thousand miles downstream, that spring surge became the summer high water of June or July on the Lower Mississippi. As the seasons progressed, river levels dropped through late summer or early fall, when water levels were lowest and slowest. Paddling upriver with less current to fight made late summer/early fall the easiest time to ascend western waterways—if there was still enough water left to float a canoe. But upriver travelers had to also take into consideration where on the river system they were and how far they intended to travel. Planning an upriver journey on western rivers was a balance between waiting for slow current along the lower reaches versus the need to arrive at the upper reaches before water levels fell to a point that made them unnavigable, even by dugout.

At the opening of the eighteenth century, most official French river journeys to the West began not only downriver but across the Gulf of Mexico, near present-day Biloxi, Mississippi, or, later, Mobile, Alabama. Outfitting in one of these early French ports, voyageurs in canoes paddled westward, along what is now the Intracoastal Waterway—between the mainland and the scattered barrier islands strung along the Gulf Coast. Starting from Mobile, this sea leg of the voyageurs' journey took five days to reach the Rigolets, the eastern channel from the Gulf into Lake Pontchartrain and the beginning of an alternate water route to the Mississippi River, avoiding the confusing maze of shifting channels in the Mississippi Delta. Entering Lake Pontchartrain, voyageurs followed a well-established native route to Lake Maurepas, up the Amite River, and westward along Bayou Manchac into the Mississippi River, just below the current city of Baton Rouge. From there the great river road led north to the Red, Arkansas, or Missouri Rivers, gateways to the western plains. A French party leaving Mobile could expect to travel upriver for about two months before arriving at the French settlement of Arkansas Post—near the confluence of the Mississippi and Arkansas Rivers. The return voyage downriver took less than half the time.

On long river journeys, travelers often lacked the luxury of waiting for optimal water flow to begin a voyage upriver. But it was possible to travel up the Mississippi, even during spring floodwaters when river currents flowed fastest. For most of the year, the Mississippi River channeled between natural levees formed along the riverbanks by annual sediment deposits. But high waters of the spring surge breached levees, flooding the river valley outside the main channel. In the slower-moving water of these back swamps, upriver canoe travelers had a much easier go of it. The sheer size of the flooded Mississippi River valley, in some places over a hundred miles wide, however, caused other problems for the river traveler. Paul du Poisson, a Jesuit priest on his way north to the Arkansas in 1727, gave an account of what it was like to travel the Mississippi River in flood:

> *We set out at the time of highest water; the river had risen more than 40 feet higher than usual; nearly all the country is lowland, consequently it was inundated. Thus we were exposed to the danger of finding no cabanage,—that is to say, no land where we could cook or sleep. When we do find it, this is the way we spend the night:*

If the ground be still muddy, which happens when the water begins to recede, we begin by making a bed of boughs so that the mattress may not sink into the mud; then we spread upon it a skin,—or a mattress and sheets, if we have them. We bend three or four canes in semicircles, the ends of which we fix in the ground, and separate them from one another according to the length of the mattress; across these we fasten three others; then we spread over this frail structure our baire,—that is to say, a large canvass, the ends of which we carefully fold beneath the mattress. In these tombs, stifling with heat, we are compelled to sleep. The first thing we do on landing is to make our baires with all possible haste; otherwise, the mosquitoes would not permit us to use them. If we could sleep in the open air, we would enjoy the coolness of the night, and would be very happy. We are much more to be pitied when we have no camping-ground; then we fasten the pirogue to a tree, and if we find an embarras of trees [floating log raft] we prepare our meals on it; if we do not find one, we go to bed without supper,—or rather, we have no supper, and we do not go to bed; we remain still in the same position that we kept during the day, exposed through the whole night to the furry of the mosquitoes (Thwaites 1900, 287).

Poisson had more to say about that scourge of all river travelers, the insect that could drive man and beast insane and try the most saintly soul. "This little creature has caused more swearing since the French came to the Mississippi, than had been done before that time in all the rest of the world" (Thwaites 1900, 293).

If Poisson was lucky enough to find his embarras of trees on which to prepare supper, the meal, at least at the beginning of the journey, would likely include European rations like cheese, biscuits, and brandy. Over time and distance the voyageur's diet became that of the native people that surrounded them. Dried corn, beans, jerked meat or pemmican, and grease provided the staple diet of soups or stews, to which might be added fresh game or fish and local herbs or roots for flavor (McCaig 1978, 7). When time and opportunity allowed, berries, wild grapes, plums, persimmons, walnuts, and pecans gathered along the wooded banks that galleried the river valleys supplemented such a tiresome diet. As a beverage, spirits like brandy were more than just a pleasantry. An evening ration of brandy made mosquitoes and companions more tolerable and the ground a little softer. Experienced leaders were particularly mindful of this provision, making sure it lasted at least to the point of no return. After the brandy ran out, travelers had little to drink other than muddy, sediment-filled river water. Journals recorded with a bit of surprise that it didn't seem to do travelers any harm. In support, Father Louis Vivier, traveling the river in 1750, declared that the clear water of the Upper Mississippi "before its alliance with the Missouri, is not the best. On the contrary, the water of the Missouri is the best in the world" (Chappell 1905, 41).

The reason given for the greater purity of muddy, versus clear, water was the absorption of pollutants by fine particles in the sediment-laden river water. When a bucket of muddy river water was allowed to settle overnight, the sediment, along with pollutants, ended up on the bottom. It was also considered good practice to take drinking water from well below the surface of the river to avoid floating contaminants. The Jesuit Poisson mentioned the voyageurs' curious practice of using hollow reeds like straws to drink from the river (Thwaites 1900, 291).

Once upriver there was a point in many a journey west where French watermen had to morph into French plainsmen. One motivation for such a change could be the convenience of distance. Rivers were not highways moving in a straightest possible line from one destination to another. Their valleys cut the land following the path most convenient for them, not the traveler. When rivers did flow to or from a desired destination, it was often by a roundabout course. Within a river valley, channels wandered from side to side, covering many river miles and few in a straight line. The path of a river's meanders alone could easily double the distance traveled from one point to another relative to the same journey made overland. Sometimes it made more sense to travel overland.

Another, more common reason for the switch from water to land travel wasn't a matter of choice. In the well-watered east, where rivers and streams were more plentiful and flowed year round, it was possible to cover great distances by water, moving upriver until its flow became too shallow for canoe travel then overland in short portages to another river. Western waterways were fewer and farther apart. The amount of river flow at any given location, or point in time, was difficult to predict—changing from year to year, season to season, and sometimes on a daily basis. How far a canoe traveled on the upper reaches of a river could vary by hundreds of miles from one journey to the next. Unexpectedly stranded due to low water, voyageurs sometimes sat and waited for an upstream rainstorm, and the resulting temporary increase in water flow, to carry them on. Sometimes they were lucky, and sometimes they got stuck, like André Fabry and the Mallet brothers, halfway to Santa Fe without means of transport.

Wherever the river journey ended, and for whatever reason, for travelers stranded with large amounts of equipment, supplies, and trade goods, continuing on foot wasn't an option. The only real option, if they were available, was horses. The French themselves were not ranchers or stock raisers in the New World and imported few horses from the old one. Even if they had had horses it wouldn't have been practical to herd them upriver, some unknown distance, to some unpredictable location where the river journey became an overland journey. The choices were to find horses or turn around and go home.

A plentiful supply of horses and pack animals could be found far to the southwest, in the Spanish stock ranches scattered throughout New and Old Mexico. Spanish ranches were the primary source of horse flesh for native populations and, indirectly, for the French. Sometimes purchased, more often stolen by native raiders, Spanish horses, over time, made their way north and east onto the plains. With luck, French voyageurs ascending a river might procure horses if they could find the roving native bands that owned them. One accepted means of establishing communications was to set the plains on fire. Anyone in the area who might be interested followed the path of the fire to its source to find out whom, and for what reason, the blaze was started. Once contact was established, hard trading followed. In parts of the early-eighteenth-century Great Plains, horses were still a scarce commodity, being most numerous closer to the Spanish ranches of the Southwest and fewer in number to the north. Those natives who had them didn't give them up easily or cheaply.

The French, however, had several things going for them. First, according to one French trader who had traveled both sides of the Mississippi River, natives west of the river were more "peaceable, showing kindness and goodwill toward whites." And, he wrote, the difference between natives of the east and west was "as night and day" (Nasatir 1952, 382). Native peoples of the Great Plains were not as warlike as those in the East, and they were well aware of the importance of trade and the potential for gain, for themselves and for their tribes. A tribe clever enough to maneuver itself into a position of trade middleman between the French and surrounding tribes could count on riches and power. The desire for trade with the French was strong. Native people were eager to give up stone axes for metal ones, cooking baskets and hot stones for brass kettles, and all the other marvels of European technology. On the French side, although trading was not without risk as a business venture, it could return a financial backer twenty times the original investment (McCaig 1978, 7). All that was necessary were conditions acceptable to both sides. And the French, after many generations of contact in the East, had developed a trading system and rapport with the native people that was the envy of other European powers. In the East, while the English established posts on the frontiers waiting for native trade to come to them, the French, traveling in small groups, took their trade goods to native villages. With this close contact, over time, Frenchmen learned the languages, culture, and wilderness skills of the native people. Many became members of the different tribes they allied themselves with through marriage and adoption. They brought the same successful trading system and approach to native relations in the West.

The journey of trade and exploration by Etienne Véniard de Bourgmont in 1724 provides an example of the contrast of French policy toward native people versus the earlier Spanish approach. A surviving journal, most likely written by Philippe de La Renaudiére, a mining engineer who accompanied Bourgmont, recorded that expedition. Ascending the Missouri River, Bourgmount split his party, one group going overland and one upriver. They were to meet at a native (Kansa) settlement in what is now eastern Kansas. Bourgmount's overland party reached the village first, only to find the river party, with most of their supplies, delayed by low water. In the journal entry of Saturday, July 8, 1724, La Renaudiére records Bourgmont's concerns over the delay. It mentions messengers sent to the leader of the river party, advising them "to make haste, not only to arrive in order to hasten his voyage to the Padoucas [Plains Apaches]" but also pointed out that Bourgmont had 160 Indians to feed and "that it was necessary to trade European goods every day for their subsistence" (Norall 1988, 128).

Depending heavily on the goodwill of their Kansa hosts, Bourgmont's overland party of about a half dozen Frenchmen and 160 native allies, members of the Missouri and Osage tribes, would have been a considerable drain on the resources of the Kansa village. As he waited for the river party to arrive, Bourgmont's limited trade goods slipped through his fingers as payment for Kansa hospitality. The fact that it was an extremely hot summer didn't make the wait any easier.

It was the general policy of Bourgmont's party, as well as most other French traders and explorers, to pay for supplies or services rendered by native hosts. This was in sharp contrast to the native policy of the Spanish, as represented in the *Requerimiento*, that Spanish explorers had a divine right to take by force, if necessary, anything they needed.

French native policy had a direct effect on their ability to travel throughout the West. As an example, consider the party of seven Frenchmen under Louis Joliet, including a priest, traveling in relative safety and without loss of life from northern Lake Michigan to within ten days of the Gulf of Mexico and back again. Almost a century and a half earlier, the armies of Hernando de Soto and Francisco Vasquez de Coronado had battled their way into the American West. Behind them they left many hundreds of fallen comrades before their retreat to Spanish settlements in Mexico. Without the cooperation of the native people, French traders and explorers venturing in small, isolated parties out of the familiar Eastern Woodlands and into the unknown of the Great Plains would have suffered a similar fate.

Chapter 10

Navigating the Rivers and Plains

The waterways French voyageurs followed into the West—the Red, Canadian, Arkansas, Kansas, Platte, Niobrara, Missouri, and Yellowstone Rivers among others—even when unnavigable by canoe, remained important navigational aids. A traveler ascending a waterway could be certain that by turning around and following it downstream, he would always return to where he started.

Where French pirogues couldn't float and voyageurs had to resort to overland travel—like those before them and those who followed—French travelers relied heavily on native guides for wayfinding. Natives lead the French over ancient plains trails meandering along dividing ridges, the high ground between river drainage systems that cut the prairies and plains. They interpreted the piles of rock and sod that served as signposts for trails, water holes, and river fords. Native sources provided information on travel time, terrain, where and what kind of game could be hunted along the route, which tribes might be hostile, and where friendly settlements could be found for food, shelter, or horses for transportation.

But although native navigational skills and information were critical in early exploration of the Great Plains, as competition heated among England, France, and Spain for New World territory, the need for accurate maps to record that information became critical not only for navigation and military purposes but as instruments of political power to consolidate territorial claims. Unfortunately, the navigational instruments used to collect data for map making had changed very little since the days of de Soto and Coronado. During early French exploration of the Great Plains, the two mainstays of land navigation remained the magnetic compass, to provide direction, and the astrolabe, to calculate latitude or north-south position. The only means of calculating east-west position or longitude was still by dead reckoning. However, the accuracy of these instruments had improved through advances in other sciences and better education. One important step, the first nautical almanac published by the French National Observatory in 1696, provided improved tables of the sun's declinations. Used with the astrolabe to calculate latitude, they were more accurate and easier to understand and therefore less prone to error. A few years later, work on magnetic variation by Englishman Edmund Halley gave explorers a better understanding of another source of error in the use of the magnetic compass.

Accuracy came not only in improvements of mathematical tables and scientific theories but also in those who had to apply them—and do so under the rigorous conditions of frontier travel in the first half of eighteenth century. In that era French explorers themselves were more likely to be competent navigators, trained in such skills as mathematics, geography, map making, free drawing, astronomy, and other allied navigational sciences. Religious orders, particularly the Jesuits, often provided the training for their own missionaries and secular students. The two great explorers of the Mississippi River, René-Robert Cavelier, Sieur de la Salle and Louis Joliet, were both educated in Jesuit Colleges, La Salle in La Fléche, France, and Joliet at the Jesuit College in Quebec (Coulter 1971, 21 and 40).

One suspect exception to the educated explorer theme, at least according to official Spanish records, might have been Frenchman Juchereau Saint Denis. In 1714 Saint Denis led a party from what is now Mobile, Alabama, across the Gulf of Mexico, up the Mississippi to the Red River, and from there overland, crossing the Rio Grande near present-day Eagle Pass, Texas, to the Spanish settlement at San Juan Batista in Old Mexico. Sent by the French government in the Louisiana Country, his mission was to establish trade with the Spanish colonies, something the Spanish government had no interest in whatsoever. The Spanish were particularly concerned that Saint Denis may have mapped his route to Mexico that could be used by a flood of his countrymen to find their way into the Spanish colonies and their trade. From San Juan Bautista, Saint Denis was sent to Mexico City for questioning by Spanish authorities. According to Saint Denis's recorded declaration, when asked about maps, he said he made no maps of the route to San Juan Bautista. He said that he did not note latitude and longitude of important points because he didn't know how. He further testified that he calculated his position by computing the number of leagues he traveled from morning to midday and midday to night and by the direction of the winds. The interrogation continued with questions unrelated to Saint Denis's navigational skills. Spanish authorities then returned to the mapping question. Asked for a second time if he took latitudes of important places he passed through between Mobile and the Rio Grande and the Rio Grande to Mexico, he replied that he did not because he didn't "understand the taking of bearings" (Shelby 1923, 172–174). Spanish authorities must have wondered why the French government would go to the expense

PART 4 — FRENCH WATERMEN

of sending an exploring party headed by such an incompetent explorer (born near Quebec, Saint Denis was sent as a youth to Paris to be educated, possibly at the Collége Royal).

Leaving the Spanish impression of Saint Denis aside, highly trained explorers, providing more accurate field data along with advances in the art and science of mapping and mapmaking, led to one of the most significant improvements in aids to travel and navigation during the period of French exploration of the Great Plains. A graphic example of the improvements can be seen in a comparison of two maps of the upper Gulf Coast region, the 1701 map of Nicholas de Fer and Jean Baptiste Bourguignon de Anvile's "Carte de Louisiana," originally drawn in 1732 (figure 8).

With the advent of printing in fifteenth-century Europe, scarce, hand-drawn maps, could be reproduced quickly and in large numbers. Later, the development of copper engraving allowed for the rapid reproduction of more finely detailed map images. New attitudes toward the collecting and representation of geographical information also evolved. French cartographers led the way, establishing the "Académie des Sciences" in 1668, whose primary purpose was to improve the accuracy of mapping and mapmaking (Linklater 2002, 91). Prior to the late seventeenth century, geographical information was often based on hearsay evidence or misinterpreted information gathered from native sources. Cartographers, who shamelessly copied each other's work, helped perpetuate those errors long after they were first printed. Substituting fantasy for facts, earlier mapmakers ornately decorated large areas of unknown territory with sea monsters, weird land animals, or sensational depictions of native life. As the French school of cartography evolved, decorations disappeared and fear of the unknown was replaced with fact. Where no reliable information was available, map space was left blank, a distinctive trait of French maps of the era (Cohen 2002, 40). Mapmakers like Guillaume Delisle and others insisted on scientific accuracy in the gathering of geographical data. Information that hadn't been made by direct observation was considered unreliable (Cohen 2002, 50). Information from native sources, or hearsay, had to be actually seen and verified by an explorer to be included on a Delisle map. French cartographers' passion for accuracy, as well as government pressure, necessitated more detailed record keeping from French explorers. The government mandate given to Fabry de la Bruyére for his exploration of the Arkansas River would be a common theme. Fabry's instructions required that:

Along his route he will make all observations appropriate to geography, astronomy, botany, and to the knowledge of the location and quality of the lands he travels through, so that we may be well informed upon his return. He will assess and draw roads, giving consideration to the distances in order to provide an approximately correct map (Blakeslee 1995, 228).

Early exploration into unknown territory yielded preliminary or reconnaissance maps. Even then French explorers were required to keep meticulous travel information, as in the surviving navigational log, *Route to be taken to ascend the Missouri River*, of Etienne Verníard de Bourgmont. Bourgmont kept a day-by-day journal of useful navigational information in the spring of 1714 as he made his 635-mile ascent up the Missouri, from its mouth to its confluence with the Platte (Norall 1988, 25). One day's entry, April 11, the day Bourgmont's party passed the Osage River about a hundred miles up the Missouri from current-day Saint Louis, is given below:

Wednesday 11. Advanced a league and a quarter; at the beginning, an island half a league in length; another one opposite, a quarter of a league long, with little trees; farther up, a succession of hills.— West a league and a half; the hills continue; farther up above some

> rocky outcroppings, a river; to the east, rocks, an island of a quarter of a league.—West half a league, with an island on the same side, an eighth of a league in length.—Southwest a quarter of a league, with an island of half a league in the middle of the river.—West-southwest a quarter of a league with rock outcrops for the same distance, and at the end of those, the Osage River, with an island of about 15 arpents; farther upriver, a cape and a little low point (Norall 1988, 115).

While not the most enthralling of literary endeavors, Bourgmont's navigational log was pure poetry to cartographers back in Paris, providing information for the first accurate map of the lower Missouri. Bourgmont's entry cites the longer distances in French leagues of about 2.4 miles and shorter distances in *arpents*, a distance of about two hundred feet. He gives distances traveled down to one eighth of a league, or roughly one third of an English mile. His directions of travel are points of the compass, west, northwest, etc. But his estimates of distances traveled were usually too high, possibly because they were calculated from an estimate of speed multiplied by the time of travel. Wind and current influence estimates of river travel. Moving upstream, as in the case of Bourgmont's party, a strong head wind or river current, or both, gave the sensation of speeds greater than what were actually being made. Explorers like Bourgmont included in their journals all the major landmarks they saw as they moved up or downriver: hills, bluffs, rock out crops, confluence of other rivers and creeks, islands, general vegetation like forest lands or prairies, location of native villages, and trails. They would, most likely, have left the river on occasion to find a high point for a better perspective of the surrounding area. From there they could sketch or make notes of significant landmarks at a distance—the general outline of the horizon, the mountains or other recognizable silhouettes—and note the relative position and distances of travel between the landmarks they saw. They would record directions of mountain ranges and valleys to be used as natural travel guides (Gatty 1958, 31).

After preliminary exploration of a territory, those areas considered of interest by authorities, such as future trade trails, water highways, locations of potential natural resources, and so on, were revisited for more accurate exploration and mapping. These higher-level exploring parties might include surveyors, topographical engineers, hydrological engineers, or mining engineers. Since the Gulf Coast was the starting point for most inland exploration and where French ships offloaded supplies and trade goods, accurate coastal charts were a necessity. Along the Gulf of Mexico, hydrological engineers made soundings for the depth of the sea and charted coastal inlets, potential harbors and ports, hazards, barrier islands, navigable channels, and inland waterways. Inland, surveyors and topographical engineers mapped the major rivers and their tributaries and filled in the land features that separated them. The more accurate maps included lines of latitude, longitude, and map scale. Some included *hachures*, parallel lines used to signify contour—representations of topographical features like hills and valleys. Besides the normal landmarks, maps showed positions of forts and French settlements and included the location of as many native villages and territories as possible. Some native tribes were friendly, and some were not, and it was important to know where each was located.

French surveyors and engineers had a powerful method for accurately measuring distances that were beyond the skills of the average explorer: triangulation. Triangulation, applied to land surveying, allowed the calculation of distances over large areas from a single measured "baseline" distance. From a baseline a surveyor could find the distance to any object he could see, as close as the opposite bank of a river or as far as a distant mountain peak. All he needed was the known baseline distance and some means of measuring angles. A compass or even an astrolabe laid on its side would do the trick. But for greater accuracy surveyors and engineers carried a simple device called a plane table, which consisted of a flat board set on a tripod or single pole. The top of the board, scribed with a circle graduated in quarters of degrees, had a centered, movable sighting vane to make angular measurements.

For an example of the simplest form of triangulation, picture someone standing on a riverbank with a current too strong to cross. To measure its width he would find some visible object close to the opposite bank. Keeping the object in sight, he'd pace off a distance down his side of the river until he reached a point where the angle measured back to the object on the opposite bank was exactly forty-five degrees. At that point the baseline he just paced would form one side of an equilateral triangle, and the distance across the river formed the other side of the same imaginary triangle. Since the adjacent sides of an equilateral triangle are equal, the baseline distance paced down the bank is equal to the distance across the river—and that distance was calculated without ever making the trip across the river.

The same simple procedure could, theoretically, be used to measure long distances, to a far-off mountain range, for instance, without actually having to travel to it. But if the mountain were, for example, twenty miles away, the surveyor would have to walk twenty miles along one leg of the imaginary equilateral triangle (baseline) to make that measurement. It would hardly be worth the effort unless his line of travel happened to be in that direction anyway. But it was possible to measure distances with triangles of unequal sides, measuring a relatively short baseline, to calculate the distance to an object far away. The Dutch mathematician Gemma Friscius developed such a system in 1533. However, the complicated mathematical skills needed to solve those kinds of triangulations were beyond the average surveyor until the late seventeenth century, when tables of logarithms became readily available (Linklater 2002, 14). As aids to calculation, tables of logarithms reduced the more complex operations of multiplication and division to simpler additions and subtractions. With the advent of logarithms, calculations for triangulation problems were much simpler, and therefore triangulation was more widely usable as a powerful method of measuring distances. From one central point a surveyor could measure distances to every prominent landmark within his sight, or the sight of his telescope, without actually having to travel to them. Knowing the angles and distances to two far-off landmarks, the surveyor could also calculate the relative distance between those landmarks. With a few strategically placed survey points, surveyors now had the ability to gather information over large amounts of territory in a relatively short amount of time. Measuring distance by triangulation, along with the introduction of logarithm tables, made possible major advances in map making during the era of French exploration of the plains. Together they helped transform maps from ornate, expensive, and often inaccurate objets d'art, decorating the palaces of the rich, to practical tools of navigation carried in a pirogue up the Arkansas or stored on a pack horse crossing the plains.

Officially, the era of the French on the western plains ended in 1762 by secret treaty. At that date, with the outcome of its war with the English in doubt, the French government ceded a large part of their American territories to Spain. At the end of the French and Indian War in the following year, French claims east of the Mississippi became English (and, within a few decades, American) territory. French Louisiana, west of the great river, belonged to Spain. Unofficially, no one will ever know how far independent-minded French voyageurs traveled or the sights they saw. Based on the history of the Coureur de Bois that preceded them, it's likely that there were many who operated outside the bounds of official French authority, their exploits unrecorded and lost forever—a necessity for self-preservation. In all their travels, French voyageurs never found the mineral wealth they sought. They never found the hoped for inland waterway to the Pacific, always maintaining the myth that, just over the mountains, at the far edge of the Great Plains, there were westward-flowing rivers that ensured an easy passage to the Pacific Ocean. They had followed the rivers and overland trail to outposts of northern New Spain and never, officially, cracked the rigid Spanish policy against foreign trade. But under the Fleur de Lis, long-forgotten men like Saint Denis, Bourgmont, La Harpe, Du Tísne, Mallet, and Verendrye traveled and mapped much of the Great Plains, from the Mississippi to the foothills of the Rockies. They explored and recorded its rivers and its great trails beaten across the land for ages. In the end it was French voyagers who opened the Great Plains to travel by the hordes of Europeans and their descendants that followed—a flood of humanity across the plains to Santa Fe or up the Platte to the Rockies and, cresting those horizons, flowing on to the Pacific West.

Part 5

The Americans—Overland by Wagon

Chapter 11

The Way West

By the opening of the nineteenth century, English rebels who'd settled on the eastern seaboard had ousted the forces of King George III and formed a new country. These somewhat united states claimed a land bounded on the east by the Atlantic Ocean and on the west by the Mississippi River. Spanish authorities claimed much of the land west of the great river, although little had been done to settle it. Scattered Franciscan missions hugged the California coast from San Diego to San Francisco, and the Spanish government kept its tenuous hold on the pueblos of the Rio Grande Valley. Beyond those limits, native populations continued in the belief that the land was still theirs. But the advent of a new millennium would also mark the beginning of a new era in the history of the West. Across the Atlantic, representatives of the French and Spanish governments met once again to decide the fate of what was left of the Louisiana Country. Again, in secret agreement, the land drained by the Mississippi River west to the Rocky Mountains—claimed by France in the late seventeenth

PART 5 — THE AMERICANS—OVERLAND BY WAGON

century and ceded to Spain in the mid eighteenth century—reverted to French territory by the opening of the nineteenth century. As part of that agreement, the French government, under Napoleon Bonaparte, made assurances to the Spanish king that the Louisiana territory would never be sold to any foreign power. Bonaparte kept his word for about three years before offering Louisiana to the Americans. Overnight, the United States more than doubled its territory, and its western boundary leapt from the banks of the Mississippi, across the prairies of the Midwest and the Great Plains to the Rocky Mountains. And even before the purchase was made official, a US-government-sponsored party of exploration camped impatiently on the American side of the Mississippi. Immediately following the formalities of transferring the Louisiana Territory from French hands to the United States, Captains Lewis, Clark, and company began their historic trip up the western rivers and overland to the Pacific Ocean in the spring of 1803. Exploration parties under US Army Officers Zebulon Pike, Stephen Long, and others, followed: mapping the land and providing on-the-job training for future explorers, mountain men, and fur trappers who carried on after them.

The 1820s and 1830s were the heyday of the beaver trade for large, well-organized American fur companies. Moving into the Rockies, they vied with British trappers from the old-line Hudson Bay Company. Changing fashions and two decades of over trapping brought an end to the golden age of the mountain man, their last official rendezvous held in 1840. But knowledge gained by trappers and traders of western trails and travel became an important factor in one of the largest mass migrations in history. What began as a trickle of hardy souls in the early 1840s became the flood of the early 1850s. An estimated one-third to one-half million people traded their farms and businesses for wagons and provisions and headed west (Wight 1993, 53). They assembled at jumping-off places scattered up and down the Missouri River and left the "States" for the Oregon Country, valley of the Great Salt Lake, and California.

What got them rolling was economics, health, wanderlust, and hype. To encourage white settlement in the Oregon country, early missionaries sent back glowing reports of the region, particularly the Willamette Valley in what is now northwestern Oregon State. Land was free in Oregon Country. Each emigrant could claim 320 acres; a man and wife together could claim a whole section of land—640 acres. Then too, the sentiment of the day was that western air was purer, the climate healthier, with less disease. And Americans had a history as an itchy-footed people. Letters and journals from each wave of western emigrants published in Eastern newspapers—along with hucksters, land swindlers, and US congressmen—helped feed the fever. The word *fever* was one often spoken and written to describe the feeling in that era. In an Iowa farmhouse in the winter of 1847, a young wife recorded in her diary what she then considered the folly of the times: "The past winter there has been a strange fever raging here (it is the Oregon fever) it seems to be contagious and it is raging terribly, nothing seems to stop it but to tear up and take a six months trip across the plains with ox teams to the Pacific Ocean" (Belknap 1983, 209). She and her husband had moved to their farm only a few years before and, with some struggle, made it a prosperous one. But before the spring was out, she found herself, her family, and everything they owned jammed in a farm wagon, bumping their way over the prairie heading for the Oregon Country.

With the exception of Mormon emigrants to the valley of the Great Salt Lake, the majority of western travelers of the 1840s and '50s headed to the Pacific West of California and Oregon. The deciding factor on how to get to the Promised Land was usually money. Most made their way overland by wagon, but there were alternative routes by sea. A western emigrant could sail from the east coast of the United States, along the Atlantic Ocean,

PART 5 — THE AMERICANS—OVERLAND BY WAGON

rounding "The Horn" at the southern tip of South America then north along the Pacific coast to California or Oregon. This sea route covered about seventeen thousand miles, usually lasted six months or more, and cost six hundred dollars—a very expensive price for the day (Ware 1932, v–vi). An alternate sea route with a short but arduous overland journey had emigrants sailing from New York, Savannah, or New Orleans for the Chagres River, where the Panama Canal now crosses a narrow strip of land separating the Atlantic and Pacific Oceans. Native boatmen poled passengers and cargo up the Chagres by canoe to the small town of Cruces. From there pack trains carried travelers overland, twenty miles to Panama City on the Pacific coast. Ships sailing out of Panama City made their way up the coast to California and beyond, some entering the Columbia River from the Pacific and sailing nearly one hundred miles inland to where the city of Portland now stands. The combined sea and overland route from New Orleans to California via Panama could be made in a month, by far the fastest way west but at a cost of three hundred dollars per passenger, still out of range for most would-be western travelers. Another mark against the Panama route was a widely held fear of tropical travel and diseases. Although only fifty miles long, the trip by canoe across the Panama jungle then by mule over the Sierra de Veraguas could take up to a week in the rainy season. Later in the westward migration—February 1855—an American company cut a railroad across the isthmus shortening the journey to four hours by rail. The Panama Railroad hauled a traveler from the Atlantic Ocean to the Pacific for twenty-five dollars; the transport of his horse (at the owner's risk) cost forty dollars. If the traveler happened to be traveling back East after a lucky strike in California, he could freight his gold from the Pacific to the Atlantic at a reasonable quarter of a cent per pound.

Still, the cheapest way west, at one tenth the cost of a sea passage around The Horn, was overland travel from the Missouri

River to the Pacific. In his 1849 edition of *The Emigrants Guide to California*, Joseph Ware estimated the total cost per person, overland by wagon, to be about sixty dollars, with four partners sharing common expenses, wagon, teams, provisions, and equipment. From the Missouri via the Platte River route to California, the Overland Trail covered approximately two thousand miles and could take a wagon company up to six months to cross in the early years. By the late 1850s and the establishment of well-traveled wagon trails, skillful, and lucky, wagon travelers could make the trip in under three months. To lighten the load and speed their travel, emigrants with money could still take advantage of the sea routes west by sending supplies and equipment ahead by ship to ports like San Francisco. The trick was to have the shipboard supplies and the overland emigrant arrive in the same place somewhere close to the same time. Once offloaded and onshore, shipped goods that sat around too long were likely to be pilfered or stolen. One thoughtful soul, blessed with the euphonious appellation of Ledyard Frink, shipped an entire house to California.

Before heading west by wagon train in 1850, Mr. Frink learned from letters printed in a local newspaper that lumber prices were more than a hundred times higher in California than his hometown of Martinsville, Indiana. So he hired carpenters to build a prefabricated house. When completed, it was loaded on a flatboat and sent down the White River, to the Wabash, to the Ohio, to the Mississippi, to New Orleans. From there Mr. Frink's new California home was loaded on a ship that sailed to the southern tip of South America, north along Pacific coast as far as the Golden Gate, where it entered San Francisco Bay, then up the Sacramento River to the sprawling new city of the same name, "having just been one year on the journey." Mr. Frink and his wife arrived safe and sound, via the overland route, about six months ahead of the house.

The overland routes that Mr. Frink, and many thousands of other western emigrants, took west had been well-established

PART 5 — THE AMERICANS—OVERLAND BY WAGON

trails that native people traveled for countless millennia—on foot. Many were adaptable to horses and pack animals, but moving wagons across country—particularly over narrow, twisting mountain trails—was another story. It took time and considerable exploration to locate viable wagon roads from the Missouri River west to the Pacific.

In Mexico, following the revolution of 1821, new government policies opened trade with the Americans to the northeast. Eager traders established the Santa Fe Trail along the Arkansas River from Independence, Missouri, west to the Front Range of the Rockies then south rounding the tip of New Mexico's Sangre de Christo Range to Santa Fe. For the most part the Santa Fe Trail crossed relatively flat plains, and when the demand for trade goods increased, pack trains were readily replaced with supply wagons. Later, when settlers began moving west, the Santa Fe Trail became part of what was known as the Southern Route to California. After arriving in Santa Fe, emigrant wagons followed the Rio Grande south then west along the present-day border with Mexico, across the Sonoran and Mojave Deserts to California. Although this trail avoided crossing the Rocky and Sierra Nevada Mountains, at about twenty-eight hundred miles, it was considerably longer than what would become the most widely traveled route, the "Great Emigrant Thoro'fare," west along the Platte River to California and the Oregon Country.

From the opening years of the nineteenth century, and Lewis and Clark's trip up the Missouri, that river had been the highway west for trappers and traders. But the Missouri was a long and circuitous route—upriver, it trended north almost to what is now the Canadian border before heading west. As the trapping industry grew, the need for a more direct route grew, too, an overland route to carry supplies and trade goods west by pack train to the annual mountain man rendezvous and return east with bales of furs and pelts. By the mid-1820s, trappers located a viable overland route, an ancient native trail, rediscovered, following the Platte River through Wyoming's Great Divide Basin to the headwaters of the Sweetwater River. There, at the southern tip of the Wind River Range, the trail crossed the Continental Divide at a point described in a US government report from the fall of 1825 as "an easy passage across the Rocky Mountains, by approaching them due west, from the head waters of the River Platte; indeed so gentle in ascent, as to admit wagons taken over..." (Dale 1941, 115).

This was the mountain gateway later described in one emigrant guidebook as a "slightly undulating plain between mountains several miles apart" (Platt and Slater 1963, 14). Ascent and descent of what became known as South Pass was so gentle that travelers weren't aware, unless they were told, that they had crossed over the Continental Divide into lands draining west to the Pacific Ocean. As trade increased, the cargo capacity of pack trains couldn't keep up with demand. In the summer of 1830, a supply train led by William Sublette, "with ten wagons, two Dearborn buggies, four head of cattle, and a milch cow" (Dale 1941, 296), left Saint Louis heading for the trappers' rendezvous in southwestern Wyoming's Green River valley. Arriving at the Green, the wheel ruts Sublette's party left behind marked what would become the Platte River Road, the first half of the Oregon and California Trails. Trappers' supply trains continued along the trail and into the Rockies for another a decade until the collapse of the beaver market, when emigrant trains of the early 1840s gradually replaced them. In the mid-1840s, the true pioneers of the western emigrant movement established the second half of the way west to the Pacific, groping their way across deserts and over mountains, along native foot trails, literally hacking and scraping them into wagon trails as they went. From South Pass those new wagon trails split; one ran northwest to Idaho's Snake River Country then north to the Columbia and down that river to the Willamette Valley in present-day Oregon. The other trail ran southwest to the Humboldt River

PART 5 — THE AMERICANS—OVERLAND BY WAGON

in Nevada and across the Sierra Nevadas into California. With some justice, Edwin Bryant wrote in 1846,

> *Our government, doubtless, has been desirous of exploring and pointing out the most favorable routes to the Pacific, and has appropriated large sums of money for this purpose. But whatever has been accomplished in the way of exploration...has resulted from indomitable energy...of our hardy frontier men and pioneers, unaided directly or remotely by the patronage or even approving smiles and commendations of the government (Bryant 1967, 197).*

An example in favor of Bryant's point would be the party under command of US Army Lieutenant John C. Frémont, nicknamed "The Pathfinder." Surveying and mapping the Oregon Trail in 1843, Frémont actually followed almost one thousand emigrants who had started west along the trail earlier that spring.

Western trails were not always single trails; in places they split like a braided river, separating around geographical obstacles into many channels. And once an obstacle was passed, they became one channel again. Over flat lands of the Great Plains and the Intermountain West, trails tended to a narrow course following rivers whenever possible. In the mountainous country of the Rockies and Sierra Nevada, their course dispersed into a maze of trails, cutoffs, and alternates. Through these most difficult of obstacles to western migration, there was a constant search for a better mountain pass, an easier, faster, safer route across fearsome snowcapped peaks. Some trails were improvements, while others were figments of imagination, hyped by land promoters who sent agents east to lure wagon companies and settlers to their territory. Breaking trail through unknown territory in the early years of western emigrant travel required the most demanding way-finding skills. Once trails were established, the ability to determine position, or exactly where they were along the trail, became the most important navigational requisite. Distance traveled and distance left to travel, relative to the calendar, was always a subject of paramount importance. Time and the elements were not on the side of the emigrants, and they knew it. Travelers to the Pacific West needed to clear their last mountain pass by October, if not sooner, or face the horror of being snowbound for the winter with little hope of rescue or relief.

Moving from the Missouri River across the western half of North America to the Pacific, emigrant companies used navigational techniques that ranged from the most primitive to sophisticated celestial navigation taking hours of mathematical manipulations to compute. By the peak of emigrant travel in the early 1850s, travelers had a plethora of information—sometimes conflicting, sometimes false—to consider when choosing the best route west. There were ex-trappers as guides, maps, emigrant guidebooks, guideposts, river courses, landmarks, compasses, and sextants to navigate by. Some employed many of these resources; some simply followed the wagon tracks of those who had gone before them.

In the early 1840s a wagon company's best available navigational aid would have been an unemployed mountain man. Hiring an experienced trapper to show the way brought not only knowledge of western trails but also invaluable wilderness survival skills and the ability to deal with native people. And with the collapse of the market for beaver pelts, many former trappers made career changes to army scout, trading post operator, or wagon company guide. The Bidwell-Bartleson wagon company of 1841, first to attempt wagon travel to California, followed mountain man Thomas "Broken Hand" Fitzpatrick as far as Soda Springs, in what is now southeast Idaho. From there the party split. Fitzpatrick headed up the Snake River to Oregon Country, and the Bidwell-Bartleson wagon company, without a guide, headed southwest to California. Near the Ruby Mountains, in what is now northeastern Nevada, they abandoned their wagons, loaded what supplies they could on the backs of their draft animals, and made their way west through the desert lands along Nevada's Humboldt River to the awesome eastern flank Sierra Nevada Mountains. Late in the season, they groped their way across the mountains, devouring their pack animals as they went. With luck and plenty of fortitude, they all—thirty-one men and one woman with a baby—made it safely to the Mexican settlements in California. What was most remarkable about California's first wagon company was that they had almost nothing to guide them through the last half of their travel. Sources at Fort Hall in Idaho gave vague mention to a large salt lake and a western-flowing river beyond. Lack of communication limited information from native sources. They followed no maps and were guided for the most part simply by the one known fact that their destination lay somewhere to the west.

As wagon travel across the West increased, so did the supply of knowledgeable guides. Emigrants who successfully completed the trip west made their way back east to lead other wagon companies to California and Oregon. Many emigrants kept travel journals or diaries with the idea of having them published at trail's end; a few of these even became the basis for emigrant guides, written instructions and advice for western travelers. *The Daily Routine*, by Edwin Bryant (1846), was one style of emigrant guide, a day-to-day narration of the author's travel experiences with concluding advice for those who followed. The voluminous congressional reports of US Army Lieutenant John C. Fremont's first and second exploring trips into the west, published in 1843 and 1845 respectively, contained practical information for the would-be traveler but buried in a mountain of scientific data. *The Latter Day Saints' Emigrant's Guide*, by William Clayton (1848), was more in the style of a seaman's rutter, an ancient form of navigation that predated the sea chart. Rutters were written sailing instructions that guided mariners from port to port noting all the hazards and prominent coastal landmarks along the way. Like a seaman's rutter, Clayton's guide moved from one noticeable land feature to another, recording rivers, creeks, lakes, springs, significant rock formations, bluffs, hills, mountains, and forts. His guide gave distances between these features, distances from each feature back to the starting point on the Missouri River, and the distance left to travel from each point westward to the valley of the Great Salt Lake. Brief notes included travel conditions, locations of water, fuel, and forage as well as good campsites.

Published in early 1849, Joseph E. Ware's *The Emigrants' Guide to California* rode the crest of the oncoming wave of California gold seekers and those who followed. Ware himself had never been west, and he never claimed so. Emigrant guides, like maps, are simply distillations of travel experiences—one written, the other graphic. Few mapmakers ever travel the territory they describe; their maps derived from a compilation of the best information available. That's what Ware did for his guidebook, sifting through Fremont's cumbersome reports, taking information from Bryant's travelogue, "borrowing" heavily from Clayton's emigrant guide—and others—to publish the first complete travelers' guide to California. Although not without error, it remained for several years "the best book available" (Stewart 1962, 222) for those taking the trail to California. Soon after publication of his journal, Ware did decide to try his luck with the rest of the gold seekers of '49. He should have stayed home. While traveling west, Joseph Ware became, ill and his companions left him alone along the trail, without food or water, where he died.

One error in Ware's guide, the one his critics most often pointed out, was his estimated distance across a particularly dry section of what came to be called Sublette's Cutoff in Wyoming. Estimated distances across the desert, from multiple sources of the day, ranged between thirty-five and fifty-five miles. Ware's guide quoted the shorter distance. The usual method for making dry crossings was to cut grass as forage for livestock and take on extra

PART 5 — THE AMERICANS—OVERLAND BY WAGON

water, balancing need against added weight. If the traveler ran out of these extra supplies before clearing the desert, Ware got bad press. But the great variation in estimated distances across a defined section of the trail demonstrated one of the problems in land navigation at that time—one man's mile was not another's.

A sure way to start a heated argument in night camp would be to offer an opinion on how far to log the day's travel. And estimating distances was especially difficult on the flatlands of the plains. Edwin Bryant gave this interpretation in 1846:

> *It is very difficult to determine distances accurately on the plains. Your estimate is based upon the probable dimensions of the object, and unless you know what the object is, and its probable size, you are liable to great deception. The atmosphere seems frequently to act as a magnifier; so much so, that I have often seen a raven perched upon a low shrub or undulation of the plain, answering to the outlines of a man on horseback (Bryant 1967, 176).*

William Clayton's wagon company was the first reported to calculate distance traveled by making accurate instrument measurements along trail. Clayton's solution to the distance problem evolved from his duties as the wagon company's record keeper. In his first attempt to accurately measuring distance, Clayton tied a rag to a spoke of a wagon wheel. As the wagon moved forward, he counted each time the rag hit the ground. At the end of the day Clayton calculated the distance traveled by multiplying the number of wheel revolutions times the known circumference of the wheel.

If necessity is the mother of invention then tediously repetitive labor has to be a leading candidate for the father. Assuming a wagon wheel four feet tall, each revolution equaled about twelve and a half feet of travel. An ox team pulling the wagon would cover about two miles in an hour, and at the end of one hour, without stopping, the wagon wheel would have made about eight hundred-forty four revolutions—fourteen revolutions per minute. Keeping track of a flopping rag, in the dust of a wagon train, hour after hour, would certainly fall under the heading of a tediously repetitive task. No doubt William Clayton soon came to the conclusion that he had better things to do with his time. In early May of 1847, near the forks of the Platte River, another member of Clayton's wagon company, Orson Pratt, made the following entry in his journal:

> *For several days past, Mr. Clayton and several others have been thinking upon the best method of attaching some machinery to a wagon, to indicate the number of miles traveled daily...I proposed the following method:—Let a wagon wheel be of such circumference, that 360 revolutions make one mile. (It happens that one of the requisite dimensions is now in camp.) Let this wheel act upon a screw, in such a manner, that six revolutions of the wagon wheel shall give the screw one revolution. Let the threads of this screw act upon a wheel of sixty cogs, which will evidently perform one revolution per mile. Let this wheel of sixty cogs, be the head of another screw, acting upon another wheel of thirty cogs; it is evident that in the movements of this second wheel, each cog will represent one mile. Now, if the cogs were numbered from 0 to 30, the number of miles travelled will be indicated during every part of the day. Let every sixth cog of the first wheel, be numbered from 0 to 10, and this division will indicate the fractional parts of the mile, or tenths; while if any one should be desirous to ascertain still smaller divisional fractions; each cog between this division, will give five and one-third rods. This machinery (which may be called the double endless screw) will be simple in its construction, and of very small bulk, requiring scarcely any sensible additional power, and the knowledge obtained respecting distances in travelling, will certainly be very satisfactory to every traveler, especially in a country, but little known. The weight of this machinery need not exceed three pounds (Pratt 1975, 391).*

PART 5 — THE AMERICANS—OVERLAND BY WAGON

Pratt gave his design to Appleton Harmon, a mechanic, who built the mile machine from a wooden feed box and scrape iron in two days. The machine measured distances up to thirty miles with a theoretical accuracy of five and a third rods (eighty-eight feet). Later modifications extended the range of the mile machine to a thousand miles. Clayton's published emigrants' guide included measurements from the Clayton-Pratt-Harmon mile machine, giving accurate distances between each notable landmark—from Council Bluffs on the Missouri River to the valley of the Great Salt Lake. In following years the use of wagon devices to measure distances spread. Elisha Perkins met a friend named Chapin, leader of the Harmer Wagon Company, crossing Nevada's Great Basin in the summer of 1849. He wrote in his journal, "Chapin has calculated & put on his wagon a neat road meter & by it we find our estimates of one days travel & speed generally, is pretty correct. My notes of distances corresponding almost exactly with his own taken from his measurement" (Perkins 1967, 104).

Eventually the various segments of the California and Oregon trails were measured with these primitive odometers and distances incorporated into later emigrant guides like Platt and Slater's 1852 publication, *Travelers Guide across the Plains upon the Overland Route to California, showing distances from point to point, accurately measured by roadometer*...(Platt and Slater, 1963).

A month after installing their new mile machine at the forks of the Platte, the Mormon wagon company of 1847 made their way to Fort Laramie, just west of the present-day Wyoming/Nebraska border. From that point on, wrote Orson Pratt, "we have measured the road with our mile machine and placed mile boards every ten miles since we left Laramie" (Pratt 1975, 422). Manmade trail markers, as navigational aids, became more common as road use increased. Guide boards or guideposts, in addition to recording distances, also marked trail crossings and gave direction.

And western emigrants developed other unique means for leading wagon companies to pass on information to those that followed: on routes to take or avoid, dangers ahead, game, water sources, Indian troubles, or trail conditions. Edwin Bryant, crossing the plains in 1846 near present-day Grand Island, Nebraska, gave the following description:

> *A sort of post office communication is frequently established by the emigrant companies. The information which they desire to communicate is sometimes written on the skulls of buffalo—sometimes on smooth planks—and at others a stake or stick being driven into the ground, and split at the top, a manuscript note inserted in it. These are conspicuously placed at the side of the trail, and are seen and read by succeeding companies (Bryant 1967, 79).*

A member of the first Mormon emigrating company of 1847 detailed a more elaborate method of passing information to a wagon company a month behind:

> *The letter was carefully secured from the weather, by sawing five or six inches into a board, parallel to its surface. The board was about six inches wide, and eighteen inches long. The letter was deposited in the track made by the saw, and three cleats were respectively nailed upon the top and two sides, and after writing upon the board necessary directions, it was nailed to the end of a pole, four or five inches in diameter, and about 15 feet in length, this pole was firmly set about five feet in the ground, near our road (Pratt 1947?, 37).*

A pole four or five inches in diameter, about the size of a standard wooden fence post or a little bigger, towering ten feet above the prairie would have been conspicuous enough, but it's hard to

PART 5 — THE AMERICANS—OVERLAND BY WAGON

imagine how easily the necessary directions might be read on a small board at that height.

In a land where no government services were available, unofficial post offices sprang up along the trail, not only for wagon companies that followed but to serve as a means of communication with those back in the States and beyond. A barrel or cask left along the trail and marked "post office" was a place to leave messages, letters, and notices. Any sheltered place could fit the purpose. At Ash Hollow, a little west of the Forks of the Platte, one traveler wrote that an abandoned trapper's cabin "has been turned into a sort of general post office...inside, in a recess, there was a large number of letters deposited, addressed to persons in almost every quarter of the globe, with requests, that those who passed would convey them to the nearest post office in the States" (Bryant 1967, 98).

Eastbound supply trains, emigrants who turned back for home, and even native travelers carried letters, from hand to hand, until they crossed the Missouri for deposit in official government post offices. Elisha Perkins wrote in his diary of 1849 that neither natives nor whites molested letters or messages left on the trail:

> At the forks of the regular road & where Sublettes cutoff leaves by (passing) Ft. Bridger I saw some 40 or 50 notes stuck up in forked sticks with directions and news &c from those in advance to acquaintances behind... This kind of post office is very common at the different points on the road & I have never known an instance of any note or scrape of paper being disturbed or misplaced. Every person looks to see who they are from & goes on leaving all as he finds it (Perkins 1967, 77–78).

But further along in his journey, Perkins, traveling well ahead of his partners, left the trail for the night to find a suitable campsite. On the trail he left a note on a stick telling where he had gone.

To draw his partner's attention to the note, Perkins hung a saddle blanket on a bush. The next morning, still alone, Perkins returned to the trail to find the note torn down and the saddle blanket stolen. In his journal, Perkins referred to the thief as a "rare scamp" (Perkins 1967, 111–112).

For many emigrants, letters were the only connection they would ever have with friends and relatives once they left home. It's hard to imagine today the thrill of letters from loved ones back East or the agony without them. One unhappy husband, arriving at the end of the long trail to California, expected to find letters from his wife waiting there. Furious when he found none, he wrote her one: "Next time I marry it will be to some one that knows how to write letters and that <u>will do it</u>" (Dean 1979, 21). In his letter, he wondered if it was too much trouble for her to devote a few minutes, once in two weeks, to write. He asked if she was married to someone else, and he supposed she didn't even care to find out when he is coming home, otherwise she would write.

Besides information passed on from trappers, guidebooks, and the experiences of preceding wagon companies, western emigrants followed the most ancient of all navigational aids: land features. When travelers to Oregon or California reached the huge stone feature called Scott's Bluff, in what is now western Nebraska, they knew they had completed one third of their journey. At South Pass, below Wyoming's Wind River Range, they passed the half way mark. And, as in the past, the geographical features most often used for navigation were rivers. The majority of trails west followed some watercourse whenever possible. Rivers were life, the source of all that was needed to make successful journey west—water for man and beast, forage for livestock, game and fish to eat, and wood to burn for cooking and heat. And it was hard to get lost following a river.

While early western emigrants relied on more primitive means of navigation, those departing from the jumping-off points along the Missouri from the mid-1840s onward could add maps to their

PART 5 — THE AMERICANS—OVERLAND BY WAGON

repertoire of navigational aids. A federally funded party of exploration under Lieutenant John C. Frémont left Westport on the Missouri less than a year after Bidwell-Bartleson, the first wagon company to make the attempt, arrived in California. Fremont's succeeding official reports of exploration, published in 1843 and 1845, included, along with considerable scientific data, practical advice for western emigrants. Data from Fremont's explorations were the basis for Charles Preuss's 1846 *Topographical Map of the Road from Missouri to Oregon.* In seven sections, covering ten miles to the inch, Pruess's map laid out the Oregon Trail from Westport Landing near present Independence, Missouri, to the Columbia River. At the Dalles on the Columbia, Fremont considered his mission accomplished, and from there his party headed south to over winter in California. The rest of the 1846 map, west to the Pacific, was supplied courtesy of the US Navy.

In the late summer of 1838 a small flotilla of six ships—with a full complement of officers, seamen, scientists, and artists—weighed anchor in Hampton Roads, Virginia, heading for the Pacific Ocean. Officially known as the US Exploring Expedition—unofficially as the Ex.-Ex.—this party spent three years surveying and charting islands in the Pacific—primarily for the benefit of the American whaling fleet—before making for the Pacific Northwest in the spring of 1841. There, the Ex.-Ex. charted the area around the Puget Sound and the Columbia River inland to Fort Walla Walla below the mouth of the Snake River then sailed south to chart San Francisco Bay.

Like their land bound counterparts, these marine surveyors used triangulation to establish distance and position when charting coastlines but with one unique difference: they used cannon fire to measure their baseline distances. Arriving at a survey area, Ex.-Ex. ships anchored in a line along the coast. As one ship after another opened fire, officers on other decks measured the time between the visible flash and the sound of the guns. At the speed of sound, the time difference between cannon flash and the sound of the gun, for a ship a mile away, would have been about four and a half seconds. Each of these established distances between ships became a measured baseline for use in triangulation. Bearings taken from each ship to common prominent features visible along the coast completed the measurements needed to chart a given area. This type of survey continued on into the night by taking bearings on rockets fired from positions along the coast—a technique particularly useful over very long distances (on land or sea) since a rocket rising only a quarter of a mile (most went much higher) could be seen in darkness for a distance of forty-four miles (Gibson 1814, 221). Once all the necessary measurements were taken, the ships repositioned to another section of the coast and repeated the process.

After San Francisco the Ex.-Ex. headed east, circumnavigating the globe to arrive back in the States by the summer of 1842. Although delayed, data from the Ex.-Ex.'s Pacific coast and Columbia River surveys were made available in time to be combined with Fremont's western explorations and published in the Pruess map of 1846.

About the time Charles Preuss was preparing his map of the Oregon Trail for publication, T. H. Jefferson headed west via the overland route to California. Three years after, Jefferson published his *Map of the Emigrant Road from Independence, Missouri to San Francisco.* In four sections, Jefferson's map to California followed basically the same route as the Oregon Trail as far as Fort Hall in Idaho then split southwest to the infant settlement of Salt Lake City. From there the map crossed the Great Salt Lake Desert, followed Nevada's Humboldt River then went over the Sierras to San Francisco. There would be many more maps—adding roads, trails, and cutoffs to the way west.

Between the era of the French on the Great Plains and the first American wagon companies heading west, science had achieved

PART 5 — THE AMERICANS—OVERLAND BY WAGON

a monumental advance in land and sea navigation, and at long last what had been labeled the longitude problem—the ability to accurately measure east-west movement—was solved. Longitude measurements combined with latitude meant, for the first time, a traveler's position could be accurately determined anywhere in the world. But those with the ability to apply this most accurate means of navigation were rare in wagon companies heading west. One reason was that the instruments used to measure longitude were expensive. Another was that it took considerable knowledge and skill to collect accurate data. The calculations needed to determine longitude were complex and only possible for someone with advanced training in mathematics, particularly spherical trigonometry. Few outside official government mapping and surveying parties had those kinds of skills. Orson Pratt, the man who designed the mile machine, was one of the exceptions. His journal entries show how he, and others of that period with the necessary training, could accurately establish their exact position along the trail as they moved west. Before Pratt's wagon company left the Missouri near Council Bluffs in the spring of 1847, he wrote, "We prepared ourselves with astronomical instruments of English construction, viz.: One circle of reflection, two sextants, one quadrant, two artificial horizons, one large reflecting telescope, several smaller ones, two barometers, several thermometers, besides nautical almanacs, books, maps, etc" (Pratt 1947?, 82).

As suggested in Pratt's journal entry, "We prepared ourselves with astronomical instruments of English construction"; until the end of the nineteenth century, most scientific instruments used in the United States came from Europe: France, Germany, the Netherlands, and England. Of these, Pratt's choice isn't surprising considering English instrument makers' reputation for quality and workmanship dating back to the age of Elizabeth. During that period the burgeoning English navy's need for navigational instruments provided one incentive for the precision instrument trade. The other was Elizabeth's father Henry VIII's break with Rome a generation before. Taking control of the Catholic Church in England, Henry sold or gave away much of the Church's extensive land holdings. The demand for surveys spiked—along with the demand for surveyors equipped with accurate surveyor's instruments—as the tide of new landowners rushed to mark the boundaries of their holdings.

Even into the mid nineteenth century, with few domestic options, American dealers sold scientific instruments imported from England, along with English nautical and astronomical almanacs. In the case of the almanacs, American dealers used the revenue-enhancing "buy one, get all the rest free" business model of pirating English almanac data and publishing it under their own names.

Curiously, in Pratt's list of navigational equipment, there was no mention of the timepiece, his chronometer, without which there could be no calculation of longitude. The development of accurate chronometers had been the key to solving the problem of longitude. Although the use of a timepiece to measure longitude, in theory, dates back to the mid sixteenth century, it wasn't until two hundred years later that Englishmen John Harrison built the first marine clock rugged and accurate enough for seagoing navigators. At a hefty seventy-two pounds, however, Harrison's first effort was of little use to land bound navigators. Over time Harrison was able to miniaturize his clockwork mechanism to fit a five-inch-diameter case. Set in gimbals in a small wooden box and looking something like an oversized pocket watch, Harrison's marine chronometer was the prototype for all navigational timepieces carried on land or sea. Handmade and of intricate design, late-eighteenth-century chronometers were astronomically expensive. The price for one chronometer Captain James Cook took into the Pacific was five hundred English pounds, a quarter of the total price the Royal Navy paid for one of Cook's ships, *The Adventure*.

PART 5 — THE AMERICANS—OVERLAND BY WAGON

By the 1840s the cost of a marine chronometer had dropped to around forty English pounds—still dear enough to keep a middle-class English family comfortable for the better part of a year.

Astronomical observatories maintained accurate regulator clocks available to instrument makers for setting (regulating) their timepieces. Once set, the utility of a chronometer was not in its ability to keep perfect time but that any error be constant and predictable. That chronometer error was known as its "rate of going."

Of the instruments listed in Pratt's journal entry, the circle of reflection, sextant, and quadrant made the angular measurements between the earth and some celestial body, or two different celestial bodies, necessary for calculating a traveler's position in latitude and longitude.

What was recorded in Pratt's journal as a quadrant was not the same instrument Spanish conquistadors used to calculate latitude. Pratt's quadrant, sometimes referred to as a Hadley's quadrant, Davis quadrant, or quadrant of reflection, was what became more commonly known as an octant. The octant, like the sextant, was triangular in shape with curved bottom leg—an arc—marked in degrees and across which a movable index arm described a measured angle. The length of the arc at the bottom of the instrument determined its name—the octant with an arc of one eighth of a circle (forty-five degrees) and the sextant (figure 9) with an arc of one sixth of a circle (sixty degrees). Both instruments were double reflecting, employing two opposing mirrors—one fixed and one on the movable index arm—to make angular measurements. The double-reflecting nature of these instruments made them more accurate than the earlier quadrant and astrolabe and halved the distance needed along their arcs to record one degree. Octants, then, could actually measure angles up to ninety degrees and sextants up to 120 degrees along their natural arcs. Pratt's reflecting circle worked on the same principle as the sextant but was made in a complete circle that could measure larger angles. Reflecting circles had multiple (usually three) index arms that allowed the navigator to make multiple measurements on the same instrument at the same time and thereby minimize error.

The octant was the oldest of the three in common use by the eighteenth century. It was the cheapest, the early models made from wood. Octants were the least accurate but accurate enough to survive into the early twentieth century. Sextants and the reflecting circles appeared later in the eighteenth century, after the introduction of the lunar distances method of measuring longitude, which required instruments capable of measuring angles beyond the range of the octant. Less expensive than the reflecting circle, the sextant became the instrument of choice for both land and sea navigators. A miniaturized version called the pocket sextant, about three inches in diameter and rugged, was popular with land surveyors.

Unlike the ancient astrolabe and quadrant, however, these newer, more accurate instruments couldn't be used on land because they were not self-leveling. Designed for use at sea, octants, sextants, and reflecting circles had to be aligned with an absolutely level horizontal surface. At sea, water being self-leveling, navigators used the horizon as a reference. The irregular surface of the land, however, had no such level reference, and a sextant or octant alone was useless for land navigators unless, like Pratt, they carried an artificial horizon. An artificial horizon could be as simple as a small box filled with water. But because even the slightest breeze rippled the surface of water, distorting the reflected image, a thicker fluid like mercury made a better substitute. An artificial horizon had to be positioned so that its surface reflected whatever celestial object was to be sighted, the sun, moon, stars, or a planet. To take a sighting, the observer trained an octant or sextant on the surface of the artificial horizon, adjusting the mirrors of the instrument until they captured that object. Since the true horizon was halfway between the actual celestial object and its reflected image in the artificial horizon, the observer needed to halve his instrument reading to get the true angle to the object. And so, with the addition of an artificial horizon, overland travelers could make measurements of latitude and longitude with what would have otherwise been mariners' instruments.

Once the proper sightings had been made, the final item needed in calculating longitude was a navigational almanac. Almanacs contained tables predicting the position of the sun, moon, planets, and stars at given time intervals, relative to a predetermined east-west reference point, a prime meridian. The time given in the almanac for some specific celestial event at that prime meridian, compared to the time of the same event recorded along the trail, gave the traveler's east-west position.

The rub for a nineteenth century navigator was: which reference point? Where does an imaginary east-west line around a circular earth begin and end? Ptolemy, who proposed the original grid system for marking the earth, placed his prime meridian in the Canary Islands, then the edge of the known world. As technology advanced, each of the major countries established their own prime meridians. Spain had two, one for land and one for sea. The United States established its prime meridian passing through the Naval Observatory at Washington, DC. Lines of longitude on a Spanish map were completely different than one made in France. Then, too, each of the many different prime meridians required a published nautical almanac with timed calculations for the multitude of celestial events specifically calculated for that meridian. In a world of multiple prime meridians, any given longitude meant little unless the traveler knew the specific east-west point referenced as the prime meridian—and carried the appropriate charts and almanac for that meridian. The confusion ended late in the nineteenth century, when most countries agreed to use the English starting point at Greenwich as a universal prime meridian.

Orson Pratt's journal entry made while encamped along Iowa's Shoal Creek in 1846, points out his method for determining longitude: "March 31st. The day being pleasant, I obtained observations for true time, and regulated my watch. From observations, I determined the latitude of my encampment upon Shoal Creek to be 40 deg. 40 min. 7 sec. Longitude by lunar distance, 92 deg. 59 min. 15 sec." (Pratt 1975, 334).

Regulating a watch meant synchronizing it to local time. Most likely Pratt would have set his watch to exact local noon using the method of taking equal altitudes of the sun. Equal altitudes of the sun was also one of the methods used for determining latitude. The sun appears to rise quickly in the morning, slow to an imperceptible crawl with little apparent change in altitude as it approaches midday, then speed up as it sinks to the horizon. It's this midday motion that makes direct measurement of exact noon difficult. So to find the exact peak (noon) of the sun's daily arc, Pratt would record the time the sun reached a given height above the earth as it rose in the morning and at the same height as it set (equal altitudes). Then he would average the two to calculate the precise moment the sun reached its highest point in the sky: the exact local noon.

With his watch properly regulated, Pratt then waited for darkness to make a timed observation of some known celestial event that he could compare with an event recorded in his almanac. Although there were several methods for calculating longitude, the one commonly mentioned by Pratt and other observers of the era was by measuring lunar distances. Entries in the English *Nautical Almanac of the Royal Greenwich Observatory* predicted the position of nine easily identifiable and immobile stars, relative to the revolving moon. The moon's changing angle between it and each of the nine stars was given in three-hour intervals. Depending on weather and visibility, Pratt would pick one of these stars and measure its angle to the moon while recording the exact local time of

PART 5 — THE AMERICANS—OVERLAND BY WAGON

his reading. He'd compare his local time with the time given for the same observation at Greenwich in the English almanac. In essence, it was that time difference that gave Pratt's longitude, his east-west position.

On the rotating surface of the earth, time is directly related to distance—one complete 360-degree rotation occurs every twenty-four hours, a rotation distance of fifteen degrees of longitude per hour. If, for example, Pratt found seven hours' difference between his observation and the one recorded in the Greenwich almanac, his position would be (seven hours times fifteen degrees per hour rotation) 105 degrees from Greenwich—about as far west as Fort Laramie in what is now eastern Wyoming.

In theory this was simple, but in reality Pratt would spend several hours computing his exact position. But if, after a day of dealing with the day-to-day necessities of life on the trail, regulating his watch, and preparing for the evening's astronomical observation (while others rested), the sky clouded over, he'd have to start all over on another day.

The final two instruments in Pratt's list, the barometer and thermometer, also recorded useful information for mapmakers and navigators. They added the third dimension, the up and down of overland travel.

Moving along the North Platte River valley, Pratt wrote in his diary, "Today several of us visited the tops of some of these bluffs, and by a barometrical method, I ascertained the height of one of them to be 235 feet above the river, and 3590 feet above the level of the sea" (Pratt 1947?, 45).

Pratt measured elevation based on changing air pressure at different altitudes. Considering air as a column, air pressure is greatest at the bottom of the column, at sea level, and decreases with increasing elevation—roughly 4 percent for every thousand feet of elevation. Explorers and surveyors of the era used what were called mountain barometers to measure air pressure and from those measurements calculated changes in elevation. Although the process wasn't as easy as reading an altitude off a barometer scale—corrections had to be made for temperature, humidity, and latitude—barometers could measure the height of a mountain for anyone willing, and able, to climb to the top.

Chapter 12

Transport and Supplies

It does seem as though the whole world were going to California. Thousands of teams in every shape are going on their way & one man with a wheel barrow stopped here the other night he travels faster than the ox teams & carries his provisions...(Thaddeus Dean, crossing Iowa, spring 1852).

The means of transport used by western emigrants was as varied as the mind of man could invent. During the gold rush years, journals mentioned men heading west pushing their worldly goods in wheelbarrows or traveling on foot with only what equipment and provisions they could carry in a backpack. The lone individual making his way across two thousand miles of plains, deserts, and mountains is a colorful image, but without the kindness of strangers, the chance of a successful trip would have been slim. He couldn't have carried enough food to even make a fair start on the trip. With a pocket full of cash, he might hope to buy what he needed along the way but only in the later years of wagon travel when wagon roads were well established—along with a multitude of trading posts and forts. Traveling on foot limited his ability to hunt game. He could move faster than a wagon company, but traveling faster meant he had to be willing to travel alone. If he escaped all the other hazards of the trail he would have been easy prey for Indian raiders unless they thought him insane, and there might have been some cause for that conclusion.

Most successful emigrants traveled in groups, and they took beasts of burden to pack or pull the heavy weight of supplies and equipment needed to cross the American West. Westward emigrants that loaded their supplies on the back of animals were called packers. The burden of the pack would almost always have gone to a mule. Horses moved faster in the short haul, but they couldn't carry the load or survive the hardships of the long haul west as well as a mule. For safety, packers traveled in trains of pack animals. Pack trains had two advantages over wagon trains. The first was speed; pack trains moved faster than wagon companies. Over ground that a wagon company might make fifteen miles in a day, packers traveled twenty-five or thirty miles. Pack animals could also travel over narrow mountain trails and ground too difficult for wagon travel. For that reason, packers were most prevalent in the early days of western migration, before trails were fully developed.

In the late 1830s and the opening years of the 1840s, wagon companies heading for Oregon Country had to switch to pack trains on arrival at Fort Hall, in what is now southwestern Idaho. Travel beyond that point proved too rugged for wagons. Likewise, early travel over the Sierra Nevada had California emigrants converting from wagons to packing. Speed of travel made packing a popular means of travel during the gold rush years as would-be miners flooded westward, from 1849 through the early '50s. But packing was a hard way to travel. Each mule had to be loaded and unloaded every day; handling and packing mules took skill.

PART 5 — THE AMERICANS—OVERLAND BY WAGON

Mexican mules were considered the best, but a good Mexican mule would stop dead in its tracks if its load weren't properly balanced (Bryant 1967, 179). Options for dealing with sick or injured in pack trains were limited to either being strapped to a mule or left behind. Compared to wagons, cargo capacity of a pack animal was another disadvantage—a situation similar to native people's use of dogs as beasts of burden. For the same reason that a dog could pull a much greater load along on a travois than it could carry directly on its back, a mule could pull a greater burden loaded in a wagon than it could packed on its back—between two and three times as much. Travel by pack train, relative to wagon travel, meant limiting supplies and equipment. Anyone who has camped for more than a few days can understand the importance of meals to a traveler—and on a trip that could last up to six months. Packers carried fewer heavy cooking utensils, limiting the types of meals that could be cooked. Weight considerations also limited the variety and quantities of provisions packers carried, relative to those carried by wagon companies. Their meals suffered for it. Elisha Perkins, a packer traveling along Nevada's Humboldt River in 1849, met friends in an ox-drawn wagon company. After taking a few good meals with them, he wrote in his diary,

> *By far the most comfortable way of traveling this road is with oxen. They can carry more comforts & luxuries, cooking apparatus, &c than any other means of conveyance, & hunters of the party can mount their horses in the morning & run to the hills at their leisure without fear of being left behind...and they always have game in abundance (Perkins 1967, 108).*

With their advantage of speed, Perkins's pack train soon left the wagon company behind, and he went back to his usual noon meal of crackers crumbled in sugar water. Because of the limitations and hardships involved with pack train travel, packers were usually men, and they had to be fit and healthy. As trails and roads improved through the late 1840s into the '50s, the numbers of wagon companies increased, while emigrant pack train travel declined. By the early 1850s one packer wrote that he thought his was the only pack train on the road. He wrote that when passing wagon companies, his pack train aroused "as much curiosity as an unchained monkey" (Dean 1979, 11).

For families—men, women, children, the elderly, and infirm—overland travel by wagon was a better option. Although slower and more difficult to manage at river crossings and along narrow mountain trails, wagons were a home on wheels. They provided shelter from spring rains or pounding hail and shade in the treeless plains and deserts of the West. Unlike pack animals, wagons didn't have to be loaded and unloaded every day. Wagons carried the sick and injured, pregnant women, and young children in relative comfort—at least compared to straddling a mule. Circled wagons made a corral for livestock or defense against attack. And, of course, any given number of animals hitched to a wagon could haul a much greater cargo than the sum of the individual loads that the same animals could pack on their backs.

The wagons that draft animals hauled to California and Oregon were not the familiar sway-backed Conestoga of the East—large freight wagons hitched to twelve to sixteen mules and hauling cargos up to three tons. Conestoga wagons might be found carrying supplies across the flat ground of the plains to trappers' posts and military forts or southwest along the Santa Fe Trail to capture the Mexican trade. But Conestoga's were much too large and heavy and, with so many teams, much too long to navigate narrow, twisting mountain trails across the Rockies, Sierra Nevada, or Cascade Mountains. Over that type of terrain, they were labeled ox killers. Emigrant wagons had to be smaller, more like farm wagons—three or four feet wide, nine to ten feet long, and a two-foot-deep wagon bed. Large, canvas-covered wooden hoops topped wagon beds to provide shelter and protect cargo. On average one of these "prairie schooners" carried enough equipment and provisions to take four adults from the Missouri River to the Pacific. Large families took several wagons if they could afford it. And at their starting point along the Missouri, emigrant wagons were nothing like the drab, weathered carcasses adorning the entrance of museums today. Their wagons brightly painted, both for protection and for looks, emigrant families were no less drawn to the glamour of a "shiny new set of wheels" than today's traveler. Some had wagon boxes painted navy blue with bright red wheels and undercarriage; others, described in one pioneer woman's journal as "gorgeous green and yellow wagons, with snowy white canvases" (Hunsaker 2003, 131). In those years spectators likened a wagon company starting out across the prairies to a circus train. But that was at the beginning of the trail.

Farm wagons were not the only means of conveyance used by emigrants. Emigrant journals also mention spring carriages and Dearborn buggies, whose primary use was to haul passengers. Traveling to California along the desert lands of the Southern Trail in 1849, Louisiana Strentzel offered this advice for those who followed: "To each family I would say one light strong carriage for women and children to ride in (two mules) and a woman can drive it anywhere; one strong wagon with six mules." She added, "some women rode horseback, but a carriage was best, especially in bad weather" (Strentzel 1983, 266–267). Passengers who rode in these covered carriages and buggies had the advantage, in bad weather, of curtains let down from the roof for protection from wind and rain. A carriage was a luxury for many emigrants who might otherwise spend considerable time on foot—walking beside a bouncing, bone-rattling farm wagon rather than in it. While women and younger children rode in the carriage, men or older boys drove the "strong wagon" loaded with the families' equipment and supplies. A man rode the mule closest the wagon—the wheel team—and guided his mules with a jerk line. With oxen, the driver walked alongside the team, guiding them by voice commands and a whip.

The draft animals western travelers chose for their wagons were a critical decision; most emigrants didn't fully understand how critical until long after they had left the banks of the Missouri. Poorly chosen draft animals could leave a family in desperate straits, stranded in a Nevada desert or high in the Sierras with snow in the air. Later in the westward movement, after trails had been established and improved, horses became more common as draft animals. But for much of the overland migration, there were only two reliable types of draft animals that could be counted on to make the long journey, oxen and mules. Which was best depended on the goals of the traveler, the type of land they traveled over, and money.

Measured on a day-by-day basis, oxen were slow—top speed, about two miles an hour. Ezra Meeker, heading for the Oregon country, estimated his ox team could make fifteen to twenty miles a day crossing the flat plains on a relatively good road (Meeker 1925, 23). Measured on a day-by-day basis, mule teams were faster. On the long haul, however, mule and ox teams were more evenly matched. A series of entries in the 1849 journal of Elisha Perkins demonstrates this fact. Perkins left Saint Joseph, on the Missouri River, in early June heading for the gold fields of California. He began the journey with mule-drawn wagons but later switched to packing near Independence Rock in present-day Wyoming. When his mule-drawn wagon company passed an ox train that left Saint Joseph ahead of them, he wrote,

> *Cattle [oxen] cannot travel anything like as fast as mules... The supposition that they will crawl up to their more speedy rivals every night, & so keep up with them is a notion or a story of those having them to dispose of, for they cannot travel as long or as many hours*

> *per day as mules... We heard so much about the relative merits of these two means of locomotion across these plains, that I have taken some pains to observe & inform myself & am satisfied that my above expressed opinion is entirely correct (Perkins 1967, 19).*

Three weeks later Perkins's wagon company approached Chimney Rock, near the present-day Nebraska-Wyoming border. There, the trail passed over soft, sandy ground, tough going for Perkins's wagon company. After noting that his mule teams had to stop to rest every quarter of a mile, he made this journal entry:

> *Traveling today has been heavy, deep sand of yesterday & same slow traveling. Passed today two large trains of ox teams plodding slowly on their weary way, although we pass oxen so easily I'm not sure we gain on them very much. They keep steadily on without stopping up hill & down & we have been several days passing and repassing the same train before finally losing sight of it (Perkins 1967, 45).*

With larger and wider hooves, oxen had the advantage over mules on sandy or muddy trails—the kind of travel most likely encountered crossing the plains in the spring. Oxen pulled slowly but steadily, while mule teams rested. Perkins was on the verge of an epiphany. By the time he reached Sacramento, his opinion of the merits of mules versus oxen had swung 180 degrees: "If I were going with a wagon I should take cattle [oxen] in preference to mules & they travel on a long journey nearly as fast & are much better for the steep hills & rough roads, pulling steadily & patiently..." (Perkins 1967, 141).

Still, the debate among partisan supporters of the ox or the mule was fierce. But the clinching argument for most was cost; on the Missouri an emigrant paid three times as much for mules as for oxen.

The number of such animals hitched to a single wagon was a balance between the number required to haul a given load and maneuverability. The more animals hitched to a wagon, the less strain each had to endure on the long journey. Santa Fe freight wagons, crossing relatively flat ground, had as many as eight teams of mules or eight yoke of oxen—sixteen draft animals—to haul their heavy loads. But such long rigs couldn't navigate the narrow, twisting mountain trails that emigrants bound for California or Oregon had to follow. At approximately forty feet in length, a wagon hitched to three yoke of oxen was about as long as most early mountain trails could handle. A total of six oxen or mules could haul a carefully loaded farm wagon without wearing themselves out under normal conditions. Later, when trails were improved, more animals could be hitched to a single wagon.

One curious means of western transport, relying solely on human power, was two-wheeled carts. These tiny conveyances, similar in design to handcarts used by porters and street sweepers in eastern cities (Hafen and Hafen 1960, 53), had an overall cargo area roughly half the size of today's standard front door. Loaded with provisions and equipment, weighing up to four or five hundred pounds, handcart companies pushed, pulled, and dragged their supplies and equipment across the country.

Although Mormon emigrants weren't the only ones to cross the West in handcarts, they were by far the largest users of this means of transport. By the mid-1850s, increasing numbers of Mormon converts overwhelmed the Church's ability to provide wagons and teams to carry them westward to the valley of the Great Salt Lake. Mormon leader Brigham Young proposed handcarts as a cheaper alternative. Ten handcart companies headed west for the roughly thousand-mile trip from the Missouri River to the Great Salt Lake between 1856 and 1860. The first two handcart companies made the trip in two months (Hafen and Hafen 1960, 251). Eight companies made the trip successfully, while two, starting late in the season, were caught in Wyoming snowstorms with considerable suffering and loss of life. Mormon handcart companies had the advantage of only traveling half the distance California and Oregon emigrants covered, and they were highly organized. Although the size of each company varied considerably, an average of the ten companies would be about three hundred people and sixty-five handcarts per company. With five people usually assigned to a single cart, each adult was allowed seventeen pounds of personal baggage, children ten pounds each (Hafen and Hafen 1960, 84). When it came time to weigh in, some attempted to thwart the limit by dressing in many layers of extra clothes that would later, and secretly, be added to the cart. Leaders thwarted the thwarters by conducting surprise weight inspections—after the company began its journey (Hafen and Hafen 1960, 59).

Mounting handcarts on large, four-foot-tall wheels made them easier to haul. To save weight, some early Mormon handcarts had no metal parts and weighed a total of about forty pounds. Instead of the standard iron rims—called tires in those days—wheels were rapped with rawhide. Later, practical experience and excessive wear from dust and sand lead to design changes. Iron tires replaced rawhide bindings, and cart builders added metal sheathing to protect axles (Hafen and Hafen 1960, 147).

Daniel Robinson, captain of the ninth Mormon handcart company (1860), described how the carts moved along the trail:

> *The people pushed the carts...The tongues of the carts had a crosspiece 2½ feet long fastened to the end. Against this crosspiece two persons would lean their weight, this they called pushing instead of pulling. It was very common to see young girls between the ages of 16 and 20 with a harness on their shoulders in the shape of a halter, a small chain fastened to that, and then fastened to the cart. There were some four or five to a cart, some pushing, some pulling*

all day long through the hot, dry sand, with hardly enough to eat to keep life in their bodies (Hafen and Hafen 1960, 182).

Even so, human-powered handcarts moved surprisingly fast, usually outdistancing the slower-moving freight wagons that followed behind with extra provisions and tents. But with the intense physical exertion required to move the handcarts, food rations, even with added freight wagons, were often not enough. Those who didn't have money to buy extra rations along the way had to scavenge for fish, game, or edible wild plants. Hunger was a common topic in the journals of handcart emigrants. Mormon handcart travel ended in 1861 with better economic conditions and the establishment of church-sponsored "down and back" wagon trains that left Utah with goods for eastern markets and returned with Mormon emigrants.

Regardless of the means of conveyance, what went on or in them was a major factor in the level of hardship faced on the trip west. On average, an emigrant wagon starting out from the Missouri River carried a load of from fifteen hundred pounds to a full ton. Wisely counseled emigrants took only the necessities of life, the most important of which were provisions. Food requirements, for an adult traveling the two thousand miles from the Missouri to the Pacific coast, ranged between three hundred and 350 pounds. Assuming four adults sharing one wagon, that meant three-fourths of the wagonload had to be food.

The majority of the provisions taken, about 60 percent, fell under the heading of breadstuffs or bacon. Breadstuffs consisted most often of flour but could also include cornmeal, crackers, and hardtack. The term bacon, as defined in that era, included much more of the hog than what today is considered as breakfast food. Other major food items carried by weight were beans or rice, dried fruit, sugar, salt, and coffee. Lesser in weight but important

PART 5 — THE AMERICANS—OVERLAND BY WAGON

for variety were tea, chocolate, lard, pepper, baking soda, vinegar, pickles, and whiskey. Some brought sour pickles and vinegar (referred to as "acid" in emigrant journals) to ward off scurvy. As for the final item on the list, and as in the past, travelers found an evening sip of "Oh Be Joyful" made the trip more agreeable. Some emigrants brought cows. Besides providing milk, in a pinch a milk cow could be hitched to a wagon to replace a missing ox.

The rest of the load consisted primarily of tents, bedding, cooking utensils, clothing, and a few essential tools. Under the unusual bedding category, one woman boasted of what may have been the first waterbed to head west: "We had an India Rubber mattress that could be filled with either air or water, making a very comfortable bed. During the day we could empty the air out, so that it took up but little room" (Frink 1983, 60).

In the beginning, heavy, "portable" cook stoves, sold to emigrants at many of the jumping-off points, cooked the meals. Soon discarded as unnecessary weight, women found a more practical means of cooking on the move.

> *We adopted a plan which was very fashionable on the Plains. We would excavate a narrow trench in the ground, a foot deep and three feet long, in which we built a fire. The cooking vessels were set over this, and upon trial, found it a very good substitute for a stove"* (Frink 1983, 97).

Western emigrants supplemented their diet by doing what all travelers before them had done, hunting and gathering. In the early years of westward migration, game was plentiful—buffalo, deer, and the elusive pronghorn antelope. Rivers provided freshwater mussels and fish. Western travelers gathered wild strawberries, gooseberries, currants, and rose hips, to name a few, to add variety to their fare. Native traders were another willing source for these items, plus some that most emigrants never considered. Edwin

Bryant, heading around the south end of the Great Salt Lake toward California, reported trading with natives for food. One item the fainter of heart passed up looked like hard, dried fruitcake. The fruitcake was made from serviceberries crushed into a jam then mixed with pulverized grasshoppers (Bryant 1967, 162). In the latter years of emigration, the increasing numbers of travelers stripped the country of its resources for many miles along the trails and drove away game. At the same time, however, increasing numbers of trading posts and forts established along emigrant routes to California and Oregon provided an alternate source for supplies and provisions—at a price.

Private American and British fur companies established trading posts in the West long before the first settler, in the first wagon, ever dreamed of that Promised Land. The proprietors of these early and remote supply points referred to them as forts. After the collapse of the beaver market in the early 1840s, traders abandoned some posts or switched to trade in buffalo hides, but those close to the developing emigrant trails took on that trade. Of the men who operated these posts, one emigrant wrote,

> *The emigrant trade is a very important one to the mountain merchants and trappers. The countenances and bearing of these men, who have made the wilderness their home, are generally expressive of a cool, cautious, but determined intrepidity. In a trade, they have no consciences, taking all the "advantages", but in a matter of hospitality or generosity they are open-handed-ready, many of them, to divide with the needy what they possess (Bryant 1967, 143).*

In the early years of emigrant travel, once beyond the Missouri, wagon companies crossed the Great Plains to the Front Range of the Rocky Mountains before they encountered their first major trading post at the confluence of the Laramie and North Platte

PART 5 — THE AMERICANS—OVERLAND BY WAGON

Rivers. It was an area that had served as a native trade center for thousands of years and where two major native trade trails met, one running north-south along eastern edge of the Rockies, the other east-west along the Platte through the Rockies via Wyoming's Great Divide Basin and points west. Under a variety of names—Fort William, Fort John, and finally Fort Laramie—this trading post began as a supply point for trappers' caravans heading west to the annual rendezvous near Wyoming's Green River (Robertson 1999, 144).

Later, on Blacks Fork of the Green River, in southwestern Wyoming, mountain man Jim Bridger and his partner, Louis Vasquez, built Fort Bridger. Situated in a wide valley surrounded by mountains, it provided the two most important requisites of wagon travel: plentiful grass and water. Bridger strategically located his trading post at the junction of the Cherokee, Oregon, and California trails. To the north, Fort Hall on the Snake River of southeastern Idaho switched from American hands to Britain's Hudson Bay Company then back again, becoming one of the most important parting of the ways along the California/Oregon Trail. From there, California-bound emigrants headed southwest for Nevada's Humboldt River and the High Sierras beyond, while Oregon-bound settlers followed the Snake River west then overland north to the Columbia. In these outposts, considered islands of civilization in a sea of wilderness, western emigrants hoped to find extra provisions, replacements for livestock, and blacksmiths shops to repair metal wagon parts.

Private trading posts catering to the emigrant trade had a very short season. Travelers to California and Oregon needed to get an early start to make it all the way from the Missouri through the Sierras or Cascades before winter snows blocked mountain passes. This restricted emigrant departure to a narrow period of time: leave too early, and there wouldn't be forage on the prairie for their teams; leave too late, and they might share the fate of the Donner party: trapped for the winter on some snowbound mountain. Only a limited window of opportunity remained, and in its peak years annual emigrant train migration moved from east to west like a huge wave, numbers quickly rising, cresting, and falling as they passed each point along the trail. From beginning to end, a trading post could count on emigrant trade that lasted about two months.

The mass movement of so many of its citizens prompted the American government to increase its presence in the West. The US Army established Fort Kearny in 1848 on the Platte River in what is now central Nebraska. There, many of the trails originating from jumping-off points along the Missouri came together to a single point. The year following the establishment of Fort Kearny, the US government bought out the private trading posts at Forts Laramie and Hall and later Fort Bridger, all becoming military posts. The military mission in the West was ostensibly to prevent native "depredations" against whites, protect natives from each other by discouraging intertribal warfare, and to protect natives from "illegal activities from whites" (Frazer 1965, xii). But emigrants also viewed military forts as stopping points were extra supplies and wagon repairs might be had. A government post's first priority, however, was the supply of its own troops, and conflicts between that duty and the needs of emigrants occasionally caused friction. Emigrants arriving at Fort Kearny were ordered not to camp closer than one mile from the fort because forage within that limit was reserved for government animals. In 1850 disappointed travelers of George Keller's California-bound wagon company arrived at Fort Hall to find no supplies available and the soldiers themselves on half rations (Keller 1955, 10). Fort Hall was eventually abandoned by the US military due to of lack of provisions for soldiers and scarcity of forage for government livestock.

Government forts and private trading posts of all sizes that sprang up along the trail to meet the demands of western emigrants

PART 5 — THE AMERICANS—OVERLAND BY WAGON

eliminated some of the hardships and risks of earlier trail travel. In June of 1853 Mary Burrell wrote in her journal, "Ferried Green River at $5.00 pr wagon & 50 cts a head for horses. Swam the stock; swift current; quite an establishment here; court house, groceries, pie & cakes. Beer. dwelling houses, black smiths shop & c." (Burrell 1986, 240–241).

Although she seemed impressed with "groceries, pie, and cakes," beer rated a whole sentence on its own. Mary's journal entry also illustrated another travel requirement, of even greater importance, as trails developed and more services became available. Travelers needed cash. A year before Mary arrived at the Green River, Oregon-bound Ezra Meeker wrote, "We had not dreamed that there would be use for money on the plains, where there were neither supplies nor people. But we soon found out our mistake" (Meeker 1925, 51). Some later emigrants who had sunk their fortune in supplies, wagon, and a team were caught short when they needed money to replace lost or stolen livestock, buy extra provisions, or pay for wagon repairs. Bridge and ferrying fees replaced the free but dangerous river fords of earlier years. Settlers along the trails charged grazing fees for each head of livestock turned out on their land. Toll roads appeared. Things that emigrants of the 1840s would never have dreamed of were available in the '50s and beyond—again at a price.

Chapter 13

Jumping Off

For the western emigrant poised on the banks of the Missouri River, life was excitement and anxiety, chaos and hope. Moving by wagon across Iowa or up the Missouri on steamboats, most emigrants had already traveled further from home than they had ever been in their lives. But their western migration wasn't considered to have begun until they reached their jumping-off point along the Missouri. From there they stepped off into the unknown, roughly two thousand miles across country as foreign to them as to any emigrant from the other side of the Atlantic. In the early years of the 1840s, crossing the Missouri River meant leaving "America" or "the States." Emigrants heading west along the California Trail traveled through Mexican territory in what are now the states of Wyoming, Utah, Nevada, and California. Those traveling to the Oregon Country entered an ill-defined and immense land covering present-day Oregon, Washington, Idaho, and parts of Wyoming and Montana as well as British Columbia. It was a land claimed and occupied by both the Americans and the British—and native

PART 5 — THE AMERICANS—OVERLAND BY WAGON

people. Before the end of the decade, a treaty with the British government and a war with Mexico gave all the Oregon Country, with the exception of British Columbia, and all the land crossed by the California Trail, and more, to the United States.

An exotic mixture of people from all over what were then the United States, along with emigrants from across the Atlantic, crowded the jumping-off points along the Missouri. Jumping-off points were a rendezvous for individuals to meet to form wagon companies and supply points to buy wagons, teams, provisions, and equipment for the long haul west. A good jumping-off point needed an operating ferry, or many ferries, to carry wagons and supplies safely across the Missouri River. As riverboat service extended up the Missouri, new jumping-off points sprang up, too, northward along the river. Although many jumping-off points developed through the decade of the 1840s, three were particularly significant. Independence, below present-day Kansas City, was the oldest and most established and the farthest south of the three. Independence had been the chief outfitting point on the eastern end of the Santa Fe Trail since 1828, well before the westward migration to California and Oregon began. Roughly fifty miles upriver—as the crow flies—Saint Joseph (Saint Jo), Missouri, established a reliable ferry by 1845. Starting from there instead of farther south at Independence, a wagon company avoided crossing the Kansas River (Stewart 1962, 85). Saint Jo was a favorite jumping-off point for early gold-rush emigrants. About a hundred miles northwest of Saint Jo, the area known as the Council Bluffs, on the Missouri River, became a third major rendezvous and jumping-off point. In the spring of 1852, Thaddeus Dean arrived in Council Bluffs at the peak of the westward migration. As he waited for his chance to ferry across the Missouri, he wrote to his wife back home:

I find this "Council Bluffs" a hard old hole—C. Bluffs is a general name for a whole country bordering on this river for some miles and not as I supposed it to be—a small city on the Missouri— Kanesville is the point all imigrants make, and it is a sight worth beholding to enter it. The town is very poorly built (mostly logs) and contains I should say two thousand inhabitants—every hole, crack & corner is crowded full of people, horses and cattle. I never saw its equal, it is with great difficulty one can move about, and such a clatter & mixed medley New York never saw! (Dean 1979, 7).

A full complement of idlers and loungers populated the Missouri riverfront towns, and amid the rush for last-minute supplies and livestock, they gladly provided newly arriving emigrants with dire rumors about what lay ahead. Robbery and murder was the usual fate prescribed for those foolish enough to head west. In 1846 one emigrant, after searching Saint Jo for extra mules, brought news back to his friends in camp. First, he heard, there was a large party of Mormons ahead on the trail who were lying in wait to rob and murder them. Then there was Indian trouble out on the plains, and a large party was lying in wait to rob and murder them. And finally there was gang of Englishmen ahead, who, in an effort to discourage Americans from settling the Oregon Country, were stirring up anyone who might be willing to lie in wait somewhere along the trail to rob and murder them (Bryant 1967, 16). It seems idlers and loungers, true to their calling, didn't waste much energy on variety in their dire rumors.

Once on the trail an emigrant's more likely enemy was monotony, not Englishmen, Mormons, Indians, or any combination thereof. The excitement and novelty of the experience began to fade after the first few days and life on the move settled into a familiar routine. Across unending plains to the front range of the

PART 5 — THE AMERICANS—OVERLAND BY WAGON

Rockies, emigrants saw the same landscape, ate the same meal, and lived in close quarters with the same people day after day. Then there was dust.

Emigrant companies—complete with teams, wagons, livestock, and people on foot—raised a considerable amount of dust. The further back in the line, the more there was. Each wagon's place in line rotated daily, so no one continuously had the worst of it in the rear. Alkali dust, raised crossing the dry lands of western Utah, Nevada, and southern Idaho, made throats sore and irritated eyes, sometimes to the point of temporary blindness. Along the Snake River in southern Idaho in 1847, Elizabeth Smith—unfettered by formalities of spelling, grammar, or punctuation—recorded her thoughts on the subject:

> *Aug 29 (Sunday) made 16 miles today camped on snake river plenty of grass and willows very dusty roads you in the states know nothing about dust it will fly so that you can hardly see the horns of your tongue yoke it often seems the cattle must die for want of breath and then in our wagons such a specticle bed cloths victuals and children all completely covered (Smith 1983, 131).*

Those walking could move away from the train to avoid the dust, but the teams and their drivers were in the thick of it. Team drivers fortunate enough to have them broke out their "false eyes"—leather goggles with glass eyepieces. Little could be done except pity choking teams of oxen or mules who inhaled great clouds of the fine powder. Fellow drivers laughed at one man who used precious water to clean the nostrils of his oxen at the end of a day's travel through an alkali desert. But his wife wrote in her diary that the animals truly seemed to appreciate it.

Common concerns of every wagon company, every day they were on the trail, were the three requisites of overland travel: wood, water, and grass. It would be hard to overemphasize the importance of these resources. The abundance, or lack thereof, of wood and water became a subject for comment in emigrant journals on a daily basis. The supply of water for man and beast, forage for livestock, and fuel to cook meals determined whether a day's travel was made with relative ease or became a grinding hardship. Wagon companies kept riders out in a constant search for water, grass, and cooking fuel. Of the three, water was by far the most important; where there was water, a traveler most likely found forage and fuel. Trails following rivers and streams provided a free-flowing, but often muddy, source of water. Sprinkling a handful of cornmeal in a bucket of muddy water settled it—river sediment bound to cornmeal and precipitated to the bottom of the bucket (Platt and Slater 1963, 5). But wagon roads often avoided the dense thickets and wet ground along river bottoms, so a night's camp might find a wagon company miles from a river. In that case digging a shallow well to provide one night's supply of seep water added to the chores at the end of a long day's travel. When thirsty enough, any source would do. Crossing the plains in 1849, one traveler wrote,

> *I would have given anything for a drink during the day, but no water was to be had for love or money, so on we jogged, mouths parched & throats cracking. Once we came to a puddle where the rain water had been standing till green on top & so muddy that if there had been hogs about I should have set it down at once as one of their wallowing places, yet this stuff which would have been rejected very suddenly by my stomach at home I drank with considerable relish, by shutting my eyes & holding my breath* (Perkins 1967, 21–22).

Without the readily available water supply of a river, emigrants had to rely on finding an elusive spring or carrying it with them. In drier areas, riders often spent considerable time and effort searching for

PART 5 — THE AMERICANS—OVERLAND BY WAGON

water. On the plains, what they looked for was a thin line of trees or shrubs, marking the course of a river, stream, or a spring. Willows, anywhere, were an indicator of water or at least wet ground where digging a shallow well might yield enough water to continue on. Without any sign of water on the plains, scouts headed for the closest mountain, a more likely place to find flowing springs than on flat ground. Because of the added weight, carrying water was a last resort. Wooden water casks or, better yet, lightweight, waterproof India rubber sacks supplied travelers across desert lands. Usually only enough water for human use could be carried for any distance. Wagon teams and livestock had to make it through dry lands by a long night drive or a series of these. In the cold deserts of western Utah, Nevada, and southern Idaho, alkali springs could sicken or even kill man or beast. Keeping thirsty wagon teams and livestock away from alkali water took considerable vigilance, and when that failed, knowledgeable owners dosed alkali-poisoned livestock with vinegar and molasses (Hunsaker 2003, 139). Vinegar, a weak acid, neutralized the basic alkali water. Adding molasses helped get the vinegar down a stubborn ox's throat.

After water, forage for wagon teams, pack animals, and livestock was the most important trail requirement. Wagon teams were the engines that powered western migration, and grass was the fuel that made them go. Without grass, nothing moved. It took healthy draft animals to haul up to the ton of supplies and provisions required to move a family overland to the Pacific West. Anxiety would be a mild term among travelers who couldn't find ample pasturage for their animals. And in places there was plenty to be anxious about. Moving from the Missouri River west to the Rocky Mountains, the land got drier. Luxurious tallgrass prairies of the east graded into scattered bunchgrass of the West; the further west an emigrant traveled, the scarcer forage became. Some desert stretches across the Intermountain West had no forage at all. Before crossing the most barren legs of a trail, emigrants cut grass and packed it in the empty spaces of their wagons to feed livestock. Most wagon companies, heading for the Far West, crossed the prairie in the spring when the grass was still green and the danger of loss of forage to fire was still low. But late stragglers, when the grass was dry, faced the added hardship of crossing thousands of acres of barren wasteland blackened by prairie fires from nature or man.

As trail travel surged in the early 1850s, greater numbers of livestock competed for a finite amount of grass. Pressure mounted on wagon companies to be the first out in the spring, to travel fast, and to get to forage before it was grazed over. Nature limited the starting time to early May, when grass was high enough to head west, but later emigrant guidebooks gave another option. George Keller's 1851 *Guide to California* advised, "Endeavor to make an early start—do not wait for grass, but carry along grain sufficient to supply your stock until 'grass comes.' Start from the Missouri River as early as the first of April…" (Keller 1955, 27). Keller's guidebook recommended taking an extra wagon loaded with grain, "forty or fifty bushels of corn, oats or barley" to feed teams in an early month of travel before grass sprouted on the plains.

Fuel for cooking and heat was the last of the three major trail requirements. Except for travel in the mountains and along river bottoms, much of the trip west passed through treeless regions. Across prairies and plains, where wood wasn't available for fuel, grazing buffalo obligingly deposited huge quantities of dung, what the French voyageur called *bois de vache* (cow wood). For the American, it was "buffalo chips," and when dry, they made a good cooking fire.

Wagon companies stopping for a midday nooning or evening camp released young children to gather up the prize. Intense rivalries developed to see who could be first to collect the three bushels needed to cook a family's meal. Some women, new to the experience of cooking with dried manure, didn't share the younger generation's hands-on enthusiasm. But early, and awkward, attempts to handle chips with a pair of sticks usually gave way to a more cavalier attitude. Since normal spring travel on the plains meant plenty of storms, threatening rain clouds inspired a scramble to get buffalo chips undercover before they became a soggy mess. Across areas of the plains where buffalo weren't obliging, dried prairie grasses like tall-stalked Indian tobacco provided a backup fuel for cooking fires.

From Central Wyoming westward, scrubby, pale blue-green sagebrush covered the flatlands and low hillsides. An early 1850s emigrants' guide described sagebrush as fuel:

> *The stalks are found from one fourth of an inch, to three or four inches in diameter. It does not generally grow more than three or four feet high. After growing a few years, the stalks apparently break off at the surface of the earth, and seem entirely dead, while the tops are in full vigor. In this condition it makes very good fuel (Keller 1955, 9).*

Even coal was sometimes available for cooking and heat. T. H. Jefferson's 1849 *Map of the Emigrant Road from Independence, Missouri to San Francisco* gave the location of anthracite coal deposits in the Deer Creek area of present-day Wyoming, between Fort Laramie and Independence Rock. There, emigrants dug the black rock from exposed seams along weathered bluffs and wasted riverbanks.

Although emigrants could survive on cold rations for a time, the availability of water and forage had an immediate effect on wagon travel. Both were absolute necessities. If one or the other were not available at an evening campsite, drivers unhitched their teams, herding them and the rest of their livestock to the nearest source. At the peak of wagon travel in the early 1850s, emigrant journals reported driving livestock two or three miles off the trail to find ground that hadn't been grazed over by preceding wagon companies (Platt and Slater 1963, 9). That meant moving livestock to grass or water at the end of the day, adding another four to six miles travel for the animals and those who had to drive them. If the evening's halt had to be made at a dry or grassless camp, emigrants hitched up their teams early in the morning and traveled on until they found forage and water for their livestock. Then they could think about breakfast. Rumored availability of water or grass often determined which trails a wagon company traveled over or avoided. The later in the season a wagon company started, the more critical that decision was likely to be.

Besides potential shortages of water, forage, and fuel, all wagon companies dealt with two great geographical obstacles to western travel, rivers and mountains. River crossings were a challenge from start to finish, along all western trails. In the 1852 edition of *Travelers Guide Across the Plains Upon the Overland Route to California*, its readers were informed that "unless they pass through Salt Lake Valley, they will not find more than a half dozen bridges between the States and California" (Platt and Slater 1963, 2). A few years before, they wouldn't have found any.

In the early years, without bridges or commercial ferries across a river, wagon companies had two options: fording, if it was shallow enough, or, in deeper water, a temporary ferry built by the emigrants themselves (figure 10). When rivers ran high or the current was too swift, a wagon company might "lay by" until river levels dropped, but eventually the river had to be crossed, one way or another. Fording was the first choice. Men on horseback scouted a river for likely crossing points. Where rivers were shallow enough to ford but the banks were high, men cut them out or built rock ramps to get the wagons down to the river. Before attempting to ford, there were several ways of elevating a wagonload of provisions. "Blocking up" raised the wagon box an extra foot above the running gear. Taking up the bottom planks of a wagon bed and fastening them on top of the sideboards raised the load about two feet (Stewart 1962, 155). But both of these options raised a wagon's already high center of gravity, a dangerous situation bumping over the invisible hazards on a river bottom. One wagon wheel lifted over a hidden rock or dropped into a pothole was enough to tip it, spilling passengers and cargo into a life-threatening tangle of canvas, floating equipment, harnesses, and panicked wagon teams. Chaining many wagons together in single file was a method of fording a wide or fast running river that could carry a lone wagon away (Hunsaker 2003, 83). Like mountaineers roped together, the theory was that if one slipped, the weight and momentum of the group would carry them all across safely. A single river or stream might be crossed many times, particularly in mountainous regions, where river channels meandered from side to side between narrow canyon walls. There, travelers had no choice but to make many fords to get to solid ground on the alternating meander banks. River bottoms were notorious for being brush choked and swampy. When necessary, emigrants built "brush bridges" from grass, sticks, brush, logs, and dirt thrown over these wet, muddy bottomlands. Traveling under such conditions was a trial for man and beast.

Most western emigrants couldn't afford to spend time on constructing regular bridges they would use only once, unless they were simple and fast. One quick method was to split a log and lay the two halves, flat side up, across a small stream at the width of a set of wagon wheels. For larger rivers too deep to ford, constructing a ferry was the only other choice. In the early years this was a do-it-yourself project. A wagon box detached from its running gear and floated across a river made the easiest ferry. Emigrant guidebooks recommended having wagons built with watertight boxes, but if none were available, a leaky wagon box could be made watertight by caulking the cracks with cloth or paper soaked with pine tar or hot pitch (Hunsaker 2003, 81). Another method of waterproofing was the wagon traveler's version of the native bullboat, where the outside of the wagon box was covered with sewn rawhide.

With a rope tied to each end, a properly waterproofed wagon box ferried up to a ton of cargo across a river. A small company of about a dozen wagons—each carrying between fifteen hundred and two thousand pounds of supplies and equipment—required hauling a single ferry back and forth across the river between nine and twelve times. That didn't include the rest of the disassembled wagon boxes and running gear—or the company's complement of men, women, and children—all of which had to be ferried across. Then, too, draft animals and livestock had to be prodded across the river. Even with a small company, a river crossing was a tiresome, time-consuming, and sometimes dangerous task.

In May of 1853 Amelia Knight's wagon company arrived on the east bank of the Elkhorn River, the first major river crossing west of Council Bluffs on the Missouri. She was anxious to cross, but fresh in her memory was a scene she had witnessed a few days earlier. The leader of an earlier wagon company had drowned attempting to ford cattle across the Elkhorn. Amelia remembered watching that wagon company retreat slowly eastward, the widow lying desperately ill in her wagon bed surrounded by her fatherless children. Her thoughts were with "those who perhaps a few days earlier had been well and happy as ourselves..." Fortunately, Amelia, her family, and the rest of the train made it across the Elkhorn, and she left a record of the experience:

> *Sunday morning. Still waiting to cross, there are three hundred wagons in sight, and as far as the eye can reach, the bottom is covered, on each side of the river, with cattle and horses, there is no ferry here, and the men will have to make one out of the tightest wagon bed...everything must now be hauled out of the way head over heals...then the wagons must be all taken to pieces, and then*

> by means of a strong rope stretched across the river, with the tight wagon bed attached to the middle of it, the rope must be long enough to pull from one side to the other, with men on each side of the river to pull it, and in this way we have to cross everything a little at a time, women and children last, and then swim the cattle and horse...It is quite lively and merry this morning...(Knight 1986, 42–43).

Along heavily wooded river bottoms, wagon companies had the option of temporary river ferries made from cottonwood dugouts, sometimes as many as eight, pinned together with wooden pegs through a crossbeam at each end. Men rolled—or lifted if there was enough manpower available—wagons onto rail-like planks fixed across the ferry and wide enough to support the wagon wheels. Large ferries like these carried two loaded wagons across a river at a time using sweeps, oars, towropes, or any combination of these.

Although cutting down trees and hollowing out logs to make dugouts took time, using a ferry to move wagons and provisions across a river avoided some of the unloading and reloading, disassembly and reassembly of wagons.

By the 1850s commercial ferries—decked-over dugouts or flat-bottomed bateaus—became more prevalent along key river crossings. River crossings by commercial ferry reduced the risk of loss of livestock, cargo, and humans. Gustavus Pearson, heading for the gold fields of California in 1849, made a river crossing five miles above Saint Joseph, Missouri, at a place called Upper Ferry. Pearson's wagon was loaded on to the ferry with three others. He remembered a simple and ingenious method used by ferrymen to move their craft across the river:

> The motive power of the scow-shaped, flat-bottomed boat was the strong current of the river. A large hawser was fastened to a tree on the bank some distance up stream from the crossing, and was

attached by a smaller rope to both ends of the boat. By changing the angle at which the water strikes the upper side of the boat, it moves back and forth across the stream. This change is easily and quickly made by a block and tackle playing freely on the rope attached to both ends of the boat (Pearson 1961, 16).

With the west-facing end of the ferry angled upstream, the force of the river swung it on its long tether toward the west bank. Angling the east-facing end of the ferry upstream swung the ferry back to the east bank, again using the deflection of the river off the angled side of the ferry to force it across. Pearson paid five dollars per wagon to cross the river but, like many other emigrants, swam his oxen across to save money. In addition to an expense, commercial ferries became bottlenecks at key river crossings during the peak years of emigrant travel. It was a problem that started at the jumping-off points along the Missouri River and eventually spread to all the important river crossings of the West. Thaddeus Dean, waiting to cross the Missouri at Council Bluffs in the spring of 1852, wrote home, "I shall probably have to stay here a week or more as the chances for crossing the river are all taken for a long time. There are some ten or twelve ferry boats running, but they cannot begin to work fast enough, something over 10,000 teams have arrived & they continue to arrive" (Dean 1979, 8).

For travelers to the Pacific West, mountains crossings posed an even more formidable geographical challenge than rivers. After crossing the Rockies, the journey of emigrants to the valley of the Great Salt Lake was done, but for those continuing on to California and Oregon the worst came last. California-bound trains followed the Humboldt River westward to face the wall of granite that makes up the eastern flank of the Sierra Nevada. Oregon trains traveled northwest along the Snake and west down the Columbia River to the equally formidable volcanic peaks of the Cascades. Nearing the end of the journey, low on supplies and with worn-out teams and

PART 5 — THE AMERICANS—OVERLAND BY WAGON

wagons, trail-weary emigrants faced their most daunting challenges. In the early years emigrants followed mountain trails only wide enough for foot travel—narrow forest trails winding around obstacles and up steep slopes, where even pack animals could barely travel. With enough maneuvering room, double- or triple-teamed wagons could be hauled up a considerable incline. But under trail conditions of the early years, maneuvering room was as much of a challenge as a steep slope, even for a single team. Moving down a steep slope required extra precautions to avoid the danger of a runaway wagon. Wagons fitted with special locking chains, attached to the wagon bed and looped through a wheel spoke, kept them from turning. Called a rough lock, the chained wheels created drag when traveling down a mountainside; the steeper the descent, the more wheels were locked. On very steep slopes, logs or poles chained in front of a set of wagon wheels slowed the downhill slide as well.

To avoid steep ascents and descents, mountain trails moved obliquely across a slope whenever possible. That mitigated one problem and created another. Rachel Taylor, traveling through Idaho's Cascade Mountains on a hot August day in 1853, wrote, "In the afternoon the roads were very bad. One place particularly was so sideling that they tied ropes to the sides of the wagons and held with all their power to keep the wagons from rolling over" (Taylor 1986, 175).

The word *sideling*, mentioned in Rachael's diary, referred to a trail sloped sideways. Early trails, those used for foot travel or pack animals, were only single, narrow tracks. Wagons moving across a mountain slope, on a sidling trail, had one set of wheels on the track, while the wheels on opposite side were either higher or lower, tilting the wagon downslope. Again, with a wagon's already high center of gravity, a sideling trail multiplied the danger of tipping and losing a wagon and team down a steep mountainside. To keep a wagon from tipping on a trail that was both sidling and steeply descending, men stood precariously on the rough-locked, uphill wagon wheels as the whole rig slid to the bottom of the slope.

The first true wagon road through the mountains—surveyed, cleared, and graded, with bridges, etc.—didn't appear until the late 1850s. Before that emigrants hacked and cut trails through narrow canyons strewn with rocks, boulders, and windfall timber barricades wide enough for a wagon to pass. They scraped trails along slopes with pick and shovel, cutting trees along the trail low enough for a wagons running gear to clear. Even so, there were places along early mountain trails where a wagon and team could not pass. Then, overland wagon companies faced a situation analogous to French voyagers, in canoes when they came to some impassable obstacle. The solution in both cases was the same—portage. On water or in the mountains, when faced with impassable obstructions, the means of transport—canoe or wagon—along with all its cargo, had to be packed around the obstacle. In extreme circumstances wagon companies had to unload every wagon, take each apart, load what they could on their draft animals, pack what was left on their backs then carry all their supplies, equipment, and wagons in pieces until they found a place to reassemble their wagons, reload cargo, harness their teams, and continue on to the next obstacle. And for Oregon- and California-bound emigrants, the majority of that came near the end of the trail when, after months of overland travel, teams were weakest, supplies lowest, and travelers exhausted.

River crossings and mountains slowed travel considerably, adding to a sense of anxiety that only increased as emigrants moved westward. Journal entries often referred to the need to be "getting on," "getting through," or "pushing ahead." One reason for concern was the shadow that hung over all westward emigration from 1846 onward. And that was the fate of the Donner Wagon Company, who spent a winter locked in the High Sierras by an early snowfall. With considerable loss of life, and facing starvation,

PART 5 — THE AMERICANS—OVERLAND BY WAGON

many resorted to cannibalism. Everyone knew the gruesome tale—how time lost, bad luck, bad decisions, and an attempt at an untried trail brought eighty-nine men, women, and children to such a desperate situation. A few years after that fateful experience, Joseph Ware's *Emigrants Guide to California* counseled,

> *We would earnestly advise you to oppose any experiments in your party, in leaving the regular route to travel to try roads said to be shorter. You will get to California in good season if you keep straight ahead. If not, you may lose a month or so of time, and experience the fate of the Donner's party...Lose no time foolishly on the road, that can be spent with profit to yourself and teams... (Ware 1932, 31)*

As wagon companies approached the Rocky Mountains, still less than halfway to California or Oregon, the first sight of snowy peaks hammered home the soundness of Ware's advice. Stick to known trails and don't dawdle. California-bound emigrants should cross the Sierras no later than the beginning of October.

The other pressure that could get travelers up early and on the trail was the sheer number of western emigrants beginning with the gold-rush years. At its peak, western immigration put seventy thousand people on the trail in a single year—all starting within about a two-month window of opportunity to make it to California or Oregon before snow closed mountain passes. In 1849 Elisha Perkins, camped at the forks of the Platte, observed,

> *Looking back from our camping place the plain looks like a camping ground of a great army. Trains of all kinds are stretched far as the eye can reach, some camped & others making preparations to do so, & the scene is quite animated & exciting. We are bound to keep ahead of them all & shall make an early start tomorrow (Perkins 1967, 41).*

Three years later, seventeen-year-old Abigail Scott, also crossing the plains, wrote in her diary, "Ahead of us, emigrant's wagons, cattle, and horses jammed the road as far as the eye could see. Behind us, it was the same. The Plain was a living, moving mass, struggling towards Oregon" (Hunsaker 2003, 134–135). In the peak years, emigrants and their livestock swept along the trail like a plague of locusts devouring every usable resource in a swath miles wide. Wagon companies in the main body could count on crowded campgrounds, jammed fords and river ferries, fouled or no water, dust not only from their wagon company but those in front and behind, and scarce forage for their teams and livestock. In 1853 two women, one on the California Trail and the other on the Oregon Trail, recorded their common frustration of traveling in that great wave of immigration.

Mary Burrell, crossing Nevada's desert, wrote, "We are troubled with to many slow trains ahead & behind & we are obliged to travel among them & be afflicted with their dust" (Burrell 1986, 249). In the Oregon Country, five hundred miles to the northwest, Amelia Knight, on a narrow mountain trail jammed with wagons, echoed that sentiment: "There was a slow poking train ahead of us, which kept stopping every five minuits [sic], and another behind us which kept swearing, and hurrying our folks on..." (Knight 1986, 73). Everyone wanted to be the first on the trail in the spring and to move fast enough to stay ahead of the pack. Unlike in the early years, when wagon companies waited for the grass to come up on the plains in May, emigrant guides of the 1850s advised getting an earlier start by carrying extra grain to feed wagon teams until forage was available. With enough grain a wagon company could start as early as the beginning of April and hopefully avoid the mob of travelers to come. Several guidebooks suggested the imprudence of too much haste, counseling "laying by on the Sabbath." Although many wagon companies began their journeys following this advice, for religious as well as practical reasons, most gave

PART 5 — THE AMERICANS—OVERLAND BY WAGON

way to the reality of time, resources, and the elements. If Saturday night found a company in an area without water or forage, they, by necessity, had to move on Sunday.

When the desire to "push ahead" reached a fever pitch, it overcame common sense. An entry in the diary of Oregon-bound Ezra Meeker recorded a scene familiar to any modern highway commuter:

> *Drivers often lost their heads and ruined their teams by running them to hard. There seemed on many days to be a stampede in the attempt to rule the road, to get ahead. It was against the rules to pass the team ahead of you. A wagon that had withdrawn from the line and stopped beside the trail could get in line again, but while we were moving, it could not cut ahead of the wagon in front of it. Now, though, whole trains would try to out run others in front of them, and their poor exhausted teams would simply give out (Hunsaker 2003, 160).*

More prudent heads, as they moved westward into the unknown, kept an anxious watch for signs of exhaustion in their draft animals. Even with the best of care, mules and oxen succumbed to the hardships of such a long and arduous journey. One man, in 1849, tried counting dead oxen he passed along trail. In a six-day period passing through western Wyoming, the total was 160 rotting oxen lying along the road (Perkins 1967, 71). In the less than two days it took to cross the Forty Mile Desert of western Nevada, he counted 130 to 140 more dead (Perkins 1967, 120). That only included oxen, not dead mules, cows, and horses. The stench of rotting animal carcasses was a common topic in emigrant journals as wagon companies moved across western deserts and into the mountains.

Loss of a single draft animal, for whatever reason, could seriously slow a wagon if no replacements were available. Mules came in teams of two and oxen in yokes of the same number. Losing one animal meant losing the whole team or yoke, reducing pulling power by one third in the average three-yoke or team wagon. Wagon companies that brought extra animals soon found that livestock herds trailing behind couldn't move as fast as a wagon train alone. The larger the herd, the slower it moved—as well as the wagon company to which it belonged. Without extra livestock it wasn't uncommon to see a milk cow pressed into service to fill one side of a yoke.

As time and the seasons passed, delays of any kind caused uneasiness and a sense of foreboding. Wagon breakdowns, from wear and tear, brought emigrant companies to a halt. Moving from the humid East into the dry West, wood shrank. Metal *tires* that rimmed wooden wheels separated unless they were wetted every day. Once sprung, metal rims had to be fired on the trail, reset on the wheel, and doused with water to shrink the tires to fit the wheel. Wagon undercarriages took considerable strain on rough trails and were most often in need of repair. One unlucky traveler along the Platte River road recorded the following calamity:

> *We went along finely till abt 10 oclock when our leading mule becoming frightened at something by the side of the road shied suddenly to the right & turned so short that we had no time to stop him till crack! crack! away went the tongue of our wagon! broken nearly off but fortunately in long splinters... We cut up raw hide into strips & first nailing a piece of hickory on the broken side, we wrapped it well with the raw hide which as it becomes dry will shrink & tighten & over this by means of a contrivance I learned at sea wound a new rope over the raw hide as tight as the hemp would bear straining & to all appearance the tongue is about as strong as ever (Perkins 1967, 36).*

PART 5 — THE AMERICANS—OVERLAND BY WAGON

That repair took about two hours. Traveling a few more miles, the wagon company entered a steep depression. On the descent, the same wagon had an axletree break loose, one end digging into the ground, while the other end "stove right through the bottom of our wagon body into a bag of flour" (Perkins 1967, 44). The second accident took about six hours to repair, including unloading the wagon, replacing the broken axletree, and reloading the wagon. In this case the repair was made under the best of trail conditions; a spare was available with plenty of help, including a skilled wagon maker and a blacksmith. That six-hour repair along with the two hours lost repairing the splintered wagon tongue must have made a very long day.

Carrying for the sick and injured added to travel delays. On the trail, with heavy wagons constantly on the move, injuries from falling under wheels were common, especially with children. Cholera—called camp fever—and typhoid fever were particular problems in the peak years of western emigration. Human waste from the large numbers of people crowding the trails carried the bacteria from these diseases into sources of drinking water. Poor sanitary practices were another factor. But wagon companies had to keep moving, to push on. The dead were buried and the sick and injured loaded onto wagons or, in some extreme cases, left behind. There was one "illness" delaying the wagon company of Hannah King in 1853 for which she had little sympathy: "Camped—I hope not for the night. One of the sisters is ill [pregnant] so we wait for her—how foolish of women to be in that way on Such a Journey as this! but some people consider nothing but their own appetites Bah!!" (King 1986, 218). It wouldn't stretch the imagination to envision the kind of trip Mr. King had.

Chapter 14

Conclusion

Those who knew Hannah Tapfield King would have been more likely sympathetic with her position. Forty-seven years old when her wagon company reached the Green River, she'd been "in that way" ten times. Six of her children died before reaching adulthood. A Mormon convert, Hannah, her husband, Thomas, and four surviving children left their home in Cambridge, England, in January of 1853. She and her family sailed across the Atlantic to New Orleans then up the Mississippi by riverboat to Keokuk in the extreme southeasterly tip of Iowa. From there the King family began the overland journey to Salt Lake City (King 1986, 184). Hannah had been encouraged to write from an early age by her father and would eventually publish works in poetry and prose, in addition to her overland diary. Besides the normal concerns of extended wagon travel, the record she kept of her trip west dealt with more homely subjects. With three daughters, ages nineteen to twenty-two, Hannah kept a wary eye out for amorous fancies, real and imagined. Of even greater concern was her youngest child,

PART 5 — THE AMERICANS—OVERLAND BY WAGON

thirteen-year-old Thomas King Jr. He was a sickly boy, and Hannah constantly referred to the state of Thomas's health in her journal. But the entire family made it to the valley of the Great Salt Lake, and Thomas grew into a healthy young man, who, before he left his teens, witnessed and eventually participated in some remarkable changes in the West.

The journey west became less daunting as time passed, at least for those with money. Most river crossings added toll bridges or ferries. Settlers took up land along established trails, turning to farming and ranching to supply the emigrant trade with flour, beans, bacon, fresh fruit, and vegetables along with additional livestock, grain, and forage for their teams. More trading posts sprouted along the major routes west. Improvements were made on the trails. When Thomas King was sixteen, businessmen in Stockton, California, raised five thousand dollars to open a new route across the Sierra Nevada, called the Big Tree Route. Stockton boosters anted up, hoping to draw settlers to their town. Their new road boasted eight bridges, one of which was seventy feet long and fourteen feet wide (Stewart 1962, 314).

Two years later, in 1858, when Thomas King turned eighteen, the first overland stage line left Saint Louis, Missouri, for its twenty-eight-hundred-mile trip through Texas, west across southern New Mexico, Arizona, and California then north to San Francisco. Officially known as the Overland Mail Company, it was more popularly referred to by the name of its owner, John Butterfield. His contract to carry the US mail stipulated that Butterfield's stages make the run in twenty-five days or less. Butterfield employees surveyed, graded, built bridges and ferries, dug wells, and built two hundred way stations along the route (Hollon 1957, 216). Stages carried passengers and mail twice a week across the West at an average speed of five miles an hour. And they traveled day and night. Except for meals, the schedule limited stops to no more than ten minutes every twenty miles to change teams (Greene 1994, 11).

CONCLUSION

In the summer of '58, while Butterfield's stages raised dust across the Southwest, far to the north, chief engineer Fredrick Lander was hard at work on another ambitious project. Hired by the newly formed Department of the Interior, Lander's job was to oversee the US government's first real effort to improve travel and transport along the California and Oregon Trails. Congress authorized a sum of $300,000 to make improvements along what it referred to as the Fort Kearny-South Pass-City of Rocks-Honey Lake Wagon Road. Lander named it the Pacific Wagon Road for short. His charge was to make a road out of many hundreds of miles of trail, beginning at Fort Kearny on Central Nebraska's Platte River. The new road followed the old trail almost to South Pass in what is now western Wyoming. From there, Lander surveyed a new, 250-mile northerly route to Fort Hall, bypassing one of harshest stretches of the old trail—the fifty-mile alkali desert between South Pass and the Green River. Eventually dubbed Lander's Road or Cut-off, this new section became the object of much attention throughout the 1858 work season. To add to the complement of surveyors, lumbermen, and bridge builders, Lander sent his agent, John Justus, south to Salt Lake City for additional help (Wight 1993, 45). Justus returned with forty-seven men, including Cornish miners, recently converted to the Mormon faith. With picks and shovels, plows, scarpers, dump carts and wagons, Lander's crew headed into the wilderness. To calculate distances, they brought along a light, eighty-pound contraption they called the measuring wagon, with an odometer attached to its wheel. By the end of the season, Lander's company had traveled 230 miles, excavated over sixty-two thousand cubic yards of earth, and cut through a mile of solid rock and twenty-three miles of dense mountain forests (Wight 1993, 48). And in that first year alone, western emigrants estimated at thirteen thousand were dogging the heels of the road builders. The following year, Lander turned an inconvenience into an advantage by offering tailgating (and hungry) emigrants flour

PART 5 — THE AMERICANS—OVERLAND BY WAGON

in exchange for their temporary labor on the road. When the winter of 1858–59 halted work in the West, Lander went east to compile a printed emigrant's guide for the new road—with accurate mileages from landmark to landmark, along with recommendations for finding water, grass, campgrounds, and fuel.

Heading west once again in the spring for the new construction season, Lander's party found itself saddled with a somewhat zealous young man, Albert Bierstadt (Wight 1993, 82). Arriving at Gilbert's Station, southern tip of the Wind River Range and eastern terminus of the Lander Road, Lander dropped off his supply of emigrant guides to be handed out to anyone interested—and, probably with some relief, young Bierstadt, who wandered south with a couple of comrades to do some picture painting. Working through the summer of 1859, Lander's crews completed the new cutoff to just east of Fort Hall in southeastern Idaho, where it met the old trail. From Fort Hall they moved west, improving the trail as they went along the Snake River then southwest, following the Raft River to City of Rocks near where the present-day borders of Idaho, Utah, and Nevada meet. The following year Lander's crews arrived in Honey Lake—near the present-day town of Susanville—in northeastern California. Fredrick Lander and his men had completed what would have been considered in that era the first true "road" west to the Pacific coast.

A year after Lander's start, Lieutenant John Mullan and party made their way east from Fort Walla Walla on the upper Columbia River to cut what Congress had authorized as a military road across the Bitterroots of northern Idaho and over the plains of western Montana to the road's terminus at Fort Benton on the Missouri River. Completed in 1862, the 624-mile-long, fifteen- to twenty-foot-wide Mullan Road included ferries and bridges—several over two hundred feet long, spanning the many rivers and streams along the route. As a way West from the jumping-off points along the Missouri, Mullan's wagon road was a small part of the total journey to the Pacific, the majority of which was by water.

Once an out-of-the-way trading post owned by the American Fur Company, Fort Benton became the head of navigation for steamboat travel on the Upper Missouri by the early 1860s. But to get to Fort Benton, a western traveler shoving off from Saint Louis was in for a two-month-long, twenty-four-hundred-mile meandering river trip, dodging snags, sawyers, sand, and gravel bars all the way. A little over eighteen hundred miles upriver from Saint Louis, on the flat plain where the Yellowstone flowed north to its confluence with the Missouri, sat the most important American Fur Company trading post on the northern plains. Fort Union had been in operation for more than thirty years before Mullan completed his road. It was last stop on the river before Fort Benton, and beyond that point—in addition to the other river hazards—low river flow added to the complement. Riverboat pilots called this final 370-mile stretch a "rainwater creek" (Bundy and Hall 1978, 122). Although four steamboats tied up at Fort Benton in 1862, none made it all the way in 1863 due to low water, their cargos transferred to ox trains for the rest of the trip.

Steamboats built for Mississippi River traffic drew too much water, and once on a sand bar, Mississippi side-wheelers stayed there. A new design class, called "mountain boats," with shallower drafts and stern-wheels, didn't run aground as often, and when they did, they were more likely to be backed off with the wheel mounted behind. When all else failed, mountain boats could literally drag themselves over impassably shallow stretches of water by what was called "grasshoppering." Mountain boats had two large poles suspended vertically over the bow for this maneuver. When lowered one end down to the riverbed, pulleys attached to the poles lifted the bow clear of the river then tilted forward to drag the craft a short distance ahead, and the process repeated until clear of

PART 5 — THE AMERICANS—OVERLAND BY WAGON

the obstacle. Tall tales recalled riverboat pilots grasshoppering through dark and stormy nights only to find, with the light of day, that they had traveled ten miles inland. With the end of the Civil War and the introduction of mountain boats, travel to the Oregon Country via the Missouri River-Mullan Road took off.

Change was coming to the West at an exponential rate. In the short span between the completion of the Lander and Mullan Roads, small, wiry, and tough mounted men were racing on horseback between Saint Joseph, Missouri, and Sacramento, California, along the Pony Express Trail. Hannah King's son, Thomas, whose precarious health had made his survival on the long trip west doubtful only a few years before, was one of them.

Beginning in the spring of 1860, "the Pony," as it was commonly called, carried wafer-thin messages from the Missouri River to the Pacific in ten days or less. Begun as an offshoot of the established freighting company of Russell, Majors, and Waddell, the Pony Express required its riders to be under twenty-one years old and 125 pounds. And they had to sign a pledge not to drink, use profane language, or fight. The company established roughly two hundred express stations along the route, on average ten miles apart. Starting at a home station, a rider stopped at swing stations just long enough to change horses. After forty or fifty miles' hard travel, the express rider had a short rest at his second home station. Then, picking up the return mail, he retraced his route before the workday (or night) ended. Each express rider carried mail within his defined route, part of a giant relay, a steady stream of messages flowing in opposite directions over the same bed.

The romance of the Pony Express captivated the American spirit as much then as it does now. Young Samuel Clemens, aboard a stagecoach crossing the Great Plains, recorded the excitement at the approach of an express rider:

CONCLUSION

Away across the endless dead level of the prairie a black speck appears against the sky, and it is plain that it moves…In a second or two it becomes a horse and rider, rising nearer—growing more and more defined—nearer and nearer, and the flutter of the hoofs comes faintly to the ear—another instant a whoop and a hurrah from our upper deck, a wave of the rider's hand, but no reply, and a man and horse burst past our excited faces, and go winging away like a belated fragment of a storm! (Twain 1987, 64)

In less than a decade, communications from east to west had gone from months by wagon to weeks by stage then days by Pony Express rider. And by the autumn of 1861, the express rider was history. Messages traveled from coast to coast in seconds via the first transcontinental telegraph line. Before the end of that decade, an even more momentous turning point in western travel and transport dramatically changed the West, quickly and forever.

It began in the middle of the Civil War, a new kind of western road but, starved for men and materials, moving at a snail's pace westward from Omaha on the Missouri River and east from Sacramento at the foot of the Sierra Nevada. With the end of the war, the road advanced rapidly, over 1,776 miles, crossing the Great Plains, the Rocky and Sierra Nevada Mountains, and the alkali deserts between. When it was finished it linked the railroads of the East with the shipping ports along the Pacific Ocean.

The road bed itself was an engineering marvel, even without considering what would pass over it. It was one that, more than any other before, defied the natural features of the western landscape. Rather than going around obstacles or following the natural undulations of the earth, it cut, filled over, or tunneled through them. Flat and wide and nearly level in length, it would never be allowed to rise or fall more than a hundred feet in a mile of travel, even when crossing the heights of the Rocky and Sierra Nevada

PART 5 — THE AMERICANS—OVERLAND BY WAGON

Mountains. Accomplishing such a feat took thousands of laborers, Chinese moving east and ex-soldiers and Irish emigrants moving west. Hundreds of miles ahead of the advancing roadbed, surveyors staked out the course. Behind them came crews of tunnel and bridge builders, crossing deep ravines with spindly trestles, cutting their way through mountains too steep to cross. Graders followed with picks, shovels, one-horse scrappers, and two-wheeled dump carts, blasting the high points low, hauling away the rubble to make the low points high. In the rear, and for every mile of graded roadbed completed, tracklayers put down twenty-five hundred crossties and four hundred steel rails weighing 560 pounds each, all fastened together with four thousand spikes. Behind them came the steam locomotives and gaudy posters announcing the "Great Event." In May of 1869 it was a "Rail Road from the Atlantic to the Pacific" that promised to take passengers from Omaha "Through to San Francisco In less than Four Days, avoiding the Dangers of the Sea."

Humans had traveled the West on foot for tens of thousands of years, mounted on horseback for a few hundred, and now, for the first time, under mechanical power at unimaginable speeds. Almost overnight the "rail road" broke the western barrier of space and time. Railroads transported federal troops quickly across the land to subjugate native populations, carried buffalo hunters west and hides east until there was nothing left to hunt, and then sold the now-vacant lands of the Great American Desert to emigrants who swarmed west to farm and ranch. It was there in the Great Plains, not the Pacific coast that the frontier ended.

This middle land, between the eastern prairies and the Rocky Mountains, became the last frontier for native peoples, never fully exploiting the plains until the coming of the horse, and then for only a few short generations before being shut up in reservations. These were the dry grasslands that turned back the last of the Spanish conquistadors, one traveling from the east and

CONCLUSION

the other from the west, both to misfortune. And from their beginnings in the Canadian high country, it was the end point for French trappers and traders, their territory sold out from under them by Napoleon Bonaparte to an infant American nation. It was the Great American Desert hurried across by early, farsighted American wagon companies, their vision limited to the Pacific West, blind to the prize under their feet. But within a few decades of the coming of the railroad, "The red grass had been ploughed under and under until it had almost disappeared from the prairie...all the fields were under fence, and the roads no longer ran about like wild things, but followed the survey section-lines..." (Willa Cather, *My Antonia*).

Bibliography

Adney, Edwin Tappan, and Howard I. Chappelle. *The Bark Canoes and Skin Boats of North America.* Washington, DC: Smithsonian Institution Press, 1983.

Aikens, C. Melvin. "The Far West." *Ancient North Americans.* Ed. Jesse D. Jennings. San Francisco: W. H. Freeman and Company, 1983. 149–201.

Alarcon, Hernando de. "Report of Alarcon's Expedition." *Narratives of the Coronado Expedition.* Ed. George P. Hammond. Albuquerque, NM: The University of New Mexico Press, 1940. 124–55.

Allen, J. L. "New World Encounters: Exploring the Great Plains of North America." *Great Plains Quarterly* [Lincoln, NE] 13.2 (Spr. 1993): 69–80.

Ambrose, Stephen E. *Nothing Like It in the World.* New York: Simon & Schuster, 2000.

Anonymous. "Relacion Del Suceso." *Narratives of the Coronado Expedition.* Report of the Events. Ed. George P. Hammond. Albuquerque, NM: The University of New Mexico Press, 1940. 284–94.

Bakeless, John. Ed. *The Journals of Lewis and Clark.* New York: Mentor, 1964.

Baldwin, Percy M. "Fray Marcos de Niza and His Discovery of the Seven Cities of Cibola." *Spanish Borderlands Sourcebooks, Vol. 9: The Native American and Spanish Colonial Experience in the Greater Southwest.* Ed. David H. Snow. New York: Garland Publishing, Inc., 1992. 35–66.

Bandelier, Adolph F. *The Discovery of New Mexico by the Franciscan Monk Friar Marcos de Niza in 1539.* Trans. M. T. Rodack. Tucson, AZ: University of Arizona, 1981.

Bandelier, Adolph F. *The Gilded Man.* NY: D. Appleton & Co., 1893.

Barnard, Edward S. Ed. "Rails Transform the Nation." *Story of the Great American West.* Pleasantville, NY: The Reader's Digest Association, Inc., 1977. 246–69.

Belknap, Keturah. "Commentaries." *Covered Wagon Women.* Ed. Kenneth L. Holmes. Vol. 2. Glendale, CA: The Arthur H. Clark Co., 1983. 189–229.

Bellin, Jacques Nicolas. *Charting Louisiana: Five Hundred Years of Maps.* Map of the Red River, 1764. Ed. Alfred E. Lemmon, John T. Magill and Jason R. Wiese. The Historical New Orleans Collection, 2003. 113.

Benson, Guy M., William R. Irwin, and Heather Moore. *Exploring the West from Monticello: A Perspective in Maps from Columbus to Lewis and Clark.* Charlottesville, VA: University of Virginia Library, 1995.

Biedma, Luys Hernandez de. "Relation of the Conquest of Florida." *Narratives of the Career of Hernando de Soto in the Conquest of Florida.* Ed. Edward Gaylord Bourne. The American Explorers Series II. New York: AMS Press Inc., 1973.

Black, Mary Louisa. "Seven Months on the Oregon Trail, 1864." *Covered Wagon Women.* Ed. Kenneth L. Holmes. Vol. IX. Spokane, WA: The Arthur H. Clark Company, 1990. 55–86.

Blakeslee, Donald J. *Along Ancient Trails: The Mallet Expedition of 1739.* Niwot, CO: University Press of Colorado, 1995.

Blakeslee, Donald J., and Robert Blasing. "Indian Trails in the Central Plains." *Plains Anthropologist* 33.119 (1988): 17–25.

Blankenship, J. W. "Native Economic Plants of Montana (1905)." *An Ethnobiology Source Book: The Uses of Plants and Animals by American Indians.* Ed. Richard I. Ford. NY: Garland Publishing, Inc., 1986. 1–30.

Bloom, Arthur L. *Geomorphology: A Systematic Analysis of Late Cenozoic Landforms.* Englewood Cliffs, NJ: Prentice-Hall, Inc., 1978.

Branch, E. Douglas. *Westward: The Romance of the American Frontier.* NY: D. Appleton & Co., 1930.

Broughton, Jack M., and Floyd Buckskin. "Racing Simloki's Shadow: The Ajumawi Interconnection of Power, Shadow, Equinox, and Solstice." *Earth & Sky: Visions of the Cosmos in Native American Folklore.* Ed. Ray R. Williamson and Claire R. Farrer. Albuquerque, NM: University of New Mexico Press, 1992. 184–92.

Brown, Robert. "On the Vegetable Products, Used by the North-West American Indians as Food and Medicine, in the Arts, and in Superstitious Rites (1868)." *An Ethnobiology Source Book: The Uses of Plants and Animals by American Indians.* Ed. Richard I. Ford. NY: Garland Publishing, Inc., 1986. 378–96.

Bryant, Edwin. *What I Saw in California.* Minneapolis, MN: Ross & Harris, Inc., 1967.

Bundy, Rex, and Edith Thompson Hall. "The Missouri and the Yellowstone." *Water Trails West.* Ed. The Western Writers of America. Garden City, NY: Doubleday & Company, Inc., 1978. 113–28.

Burchardt, Bill. "The Arkansas River and the Red." *Water Trails West.* Ed. The Western Writers of America. Garden City, NY: Doubleday & Company, Inc., 1978. 29–42.

Bureau of Land Management, Wyoming State Office. *Guide to the Lander Cut-Off, Oregon Trail, 1857 [Cartographic Material].* Cheyenne, WY: Bureau of Land Management, 1998.

Burland, C.A. *North American Indian Mythology.* New York: Peter Bedrick Books, 1985.

Burrell, Mary. "Council Bluffs to California." *Covered Wagon Women.* Ed. Kenneth L. Holmes. Vol. VI. Glendale, CA: The Arthur H. Clark Co., 1986. 225–61.

Cahokia Mounds State Historical Site. Collinsville, IL: Illinois Historic Preservation Agency, 2005.

Carr, Lucien. "The Food of Certain American Indians and Their Methods of Preparing It." *An Ethnobiology Source Book: The Uses of Plants and Animals by American Indians.* Ed. Richard I. Ford. NY: Garland Publishing, Inc., 1986. 155–90.

Carter, Kate B. *Utah and the Pony Express.* Salt Lake City, UT: Utah Printing Co., 1960.

Castaneda, Pedro de. "Castaneda's History of the Expedition." *Narratives of the Coronado Expedition 1540–1542.* Ed. George P. Hammond. Albuquerque, NM: The University of New Mexico Press, 1940. 191–283.

Castetter, Edward F. "The Domain of Ethnobiology." *An Ethnobiology Source Book: The Uses of Plants and Animals by American Indians.* Ed. Richard I. Ford. NY: Garland Publishing, Inc., 1986. 158–70.

Cather, Willa. *My Ántonia.* Boston: Houghton Mifflin Co., 1995.

Chaffin, Tom. *Pathfinder: John Charles Frémont and the Course of American Empire.* NY: Hill and Wang, 2004.

Chamberlain, Von Del. "The Chief and His Council: Unity and Authority from the Stars." *Earth & Sky: Visions of the Cosmos in Native American Folklore.* Ed. Ray R. Williamson and Claire R. Farrer. Albuquerque, NM: University of New Mexico Press, 1992. 221–35.

Chappell, Philip E. *A History of the Missouri River: Discovery of the River by the Jesuit Explorers; Indian Tribes Along the River; Early Navigation and Craft Used; the Rise and Fall of Steamboating.* Kansas City? 1905.

Chardon, R. "The Elusive Spanish League: A Problem of Measurement in Sixteenth-Century New Spain." Notes and Comments. *Hispanic American Historical Review* [Durham, NC] 60.2 (May 1980).

Charlevoix, P. F. X. "History and General Description of New France." *Charlevoix's History of New France.* Ed. John G. Shea. New York: Francis C. Parker, 1962.

Charting Louisiana: Five Hundred Years of Maps. Ed. Alfred E. Lemmon, John T. Magill and Jason R. Wiese. The Historical New Orleans Collection, 2003.

Chartkoff, Joseph L. "A Rock Feature Complex in Northwestern California." *American Antiquity* 48.4 (1983): 745–60.

Coe, Michael, Dean Snow, and Elizabeth Benson. *Atlas of Ancient America.* New York: Facts on File Publications, 1986.

Cohen, Paul E. *Mapping the West: America's Westward Movement 1524–1890.* NY: Rizzoli International Publications, Inc., 2002.

Coleman, Louis C., and Leo Rieman. *Captain John Mullan: His Life.* Ed. B. C. Payette. Montreal, Canada: Payette Radio Limited, 1968.

Colton, Harold Sellers. "Prehistoric Trade in the Southwest." *Scientific Monthly* 52 (1941): 308–19.

Colville, Frederick V. "Notes on the Plants Used by the Klamath Indians of Oregon (1897)." *An Ethnobiology Source Book: The Uses of Plants and Animals by American Indians.* Ed. Richard I. Ford. NY: Garland Publishing, Inc., 1986. 87–108.

Cordell, Linda S. *Prehistory of the Southwest.* London: Academic Press, Inc., 1984.

Coronado, Francisco Vasquez de. "Letter of Coronado to the King." Letter. *Narratives of the Coronado Expedition 1540–1542.* Ed. George P. Hammond. Albuquerque, NM: The University of New Mexico Press, 1940. 185–90.

---. "Letter of Coronado to Viceroy Mendoza, August 3, 1540." *Narratives of the Coronado Expedition, 1540–1542.* Ed. George

P. Hammond. Albuquerque, NM: University of New Mexico Press, 1940. 162–78.

---. "Letter of Coronado to Viceroy Mendoza, March, 8, 1539." *Narratives of the Coronado Expedition, 1540–1542*. Ed. George P. Hammond. Albuquerque, NM: University of New Mexico Press, 1940. 42–44.

Coulter, Tony. *La Salle and the Explorers of the Mississippi*. NY: Chelsea House Publishers, 1971.

Crazier, Lola. *Surveys and Surveyors of the Public Domain 1785–1975*. Washington, DC: US Government Printing Office.

Cutter, Donald, and Iris Engstrand. *Quest for Empire: Spanish Settlement in the Southwest*. Golden, CO: Fulcrum Publishing, 1996.

Dale, Harrison Clifford. *The Ashley-Smith Explorations and the Discovery of a Central Route to the Pacific, 1822–1829*. Glendale, CA: The Arthur H. Clark Co., 1941.

Dean, Thaddeus. "Letters." *A Journey to California: The Letters of Thaddeus Dean*. Ed. Katherine Dean Wheeler. Tampa, FL: American Studies Press, 1979.

Decker, Elly. "Of Spheres and Shadows." *The Story of Time*. Ed. Kristen Lippincott, et al. London: Merrell Holberton, 1999. 96–131.

Denhardt, Robert M. *The Horse of the Americas*. Norman, OK: University of Oklahoma, 1975.

DeVoto, Bernard. *The Course of the Empire*. Cambridge, MA: The Riverside Press Cambridge, 1952.

Dobyns, Henry F. "Part I: The First Americans." *The Settling of North America*. Ed. Helen Hornbeck Tanner. NY: McMillan, 1995. 10–31.

Dodge, Richard I. *Our Wild Indians*. New York: Archer House, Inc., 1959.

Earle, Timothy. "Paths and Roads in Evolutionary Perspective." *Ancient Road Networks and Settlement Hierarchies in the New World*.

Ed. Charles D. Trombold. Cambridge: Cambridge University Press, 1991. 10–16.

Earle, Timothy. "Positioning Exchange in the Evolution of Human Society." *Prehistoric Exchange Systems in North America.* Ed. Timothy G. Baugh and Jonathan E. Ericson. New York: Plenum Press, 1994. 419–37.

Ehrenberg, Ralph E., John A. Wolter, and Charles A. Burroughs. "Surveying and Charting the Pacific Basin." *Magnificent Voyagers.* Ed. Herman J. Viola and Carolyn Margolis. Washington, DC: Smithsonian Institution Press, 1985. 165–87.

Emerson, Ellen R. *Indian Myths.* Minneapolis: Ross & Haines, Inc., 1965.

Escalante, Silvestre Velez de. "The Dominguez-Escalante Journal: Their Expedition Through Colorado, Utah, Arizona, and New Mexico in 1776." Ed. Ted J. Warner. Salt Lake City, UT: University of Utah, 1995. 1–153.

Espinosa, J. Manuel. "The Recapture of Santa Fe, New Mexico, by the Spaniards, December, 29–30, 1693." *Spanish Borderlands Sourcebooks, Vol. 9: The Native American and Spanish Colonial Experience in the Greater Southwest.* Ed. David H. Snow. New York: Garland Publishing, Inc., 1992. 387–408.

Flint, Richard, and Shirley Cushing Flint. Ed. *Documents of the Coronado Expedition, 1539–1542.* Dallas, TX: Southern Methodist University Press, 2005.

Ford, Richard I. "Human Disturbance and Biodiversity: A Case Study from Northern New Mexico." *Biodiversity & Native America.* Ed. Paul E. Minnis and Wayne J. Elisens. Norman, OK: University of Oklahoma Press, 2000. 207–22.

Franklin, Benjamin. "Preface." *Poor Richard's Almanac* [Philadelphia] (1758).

Frazer, Robert W. *Forts of the West.* Norman, OK: University of Oklahoma, 1965.

Frink, Margaret A. "Adventures of a Party of Goldseekers." *Covered Wagon Women: Diaries and Letters from the Western Trails 1840–1890.* Ed. Kenneth L. Holmes. Vol. 2. Glendale, CA: The Arthur H. Clark Co., 1983. 55–169.

Galm, Jerry R. "Prehistoric Trade and Exchange in the Interior Plateau of Northwestern North America." *Prehistoric Exchange Systems in North America.* Ed. Timothy G. Baugh and Jonathan E. Ericson. New York: Plenum Press, 1994. 275–305.

Gatty, Harold. *Nature is Your Guide.* New York: E. P. Dutton & Co., Inc., 1958.

Gentleman of Elvas. "The Narrative of the Expedition of Hernando de Soto." *Spanish Explorers in the Southern United States.* Ed. Theodore H. Lewis. New York: Charles Scribner's Sons, 1907.

Gibson, Robert. *The Theory and Practice of Surveying.* New York: Evert Duyckinck, 1814.

Gilbert, Martin. *American History Atlas.* N.Y.: The Macmillan Co., 1969.

Gill, S.D., and I. F. Sullivan. *Dictionary of Native American Mythology.* Santa Barbara, CA: ABC-CLIO, Inc., 1992.

Golay, Michael, and John S. Bowman. *North American Exploration.* Hoboken, NJ: John Wiley & Sons, Inc., 2003.

Graham, R. B. Cunninghame. *The Horse of the Conquest.* Norman, OK: University of Oklahoma, 1949.

Greene, A. C. *900 Miles on the Butterfield Trail.* Denton, TX: University of North Texas Press, 1994.

Hafen, LeRoy R., and Ann W. Hafen. *Handcarts to Zion: The Story of a Unique Western Migration 1856–1860.* Glendale, CA: The Arthur H. Clark Company, 1960.

Haggard, J. Villasana. *Handbook for Translators of Spanish Historical Documents.* University of Texas, 1941.

Hajda, Yvonne. "Southwestern Coast Salish." *Handbook of North American Indians: Vol. 7.* Ed. Wayne Suttles. Washington, DC: Smithsonian Institution, 1990. 503–17.

Hall, Dorothy. "Castano de la Sosa's Expedition into New Mexico in 1590." *Spanish Borderlands Sourcebooks, Vol. 9: The Native American and Spanish Colonial Experience in the Greater Southwest.* Ed. David H. Snow. New York: Garland Publishing, Inc., 1992. 351–76.

Hammond, George P. "Introduction." *Narratives of the Coronado Expedition, 1540–1542.* Ed. George P. Hammond. Albuquerque, NM: University of New Mexico Press, 1940. 1–33.

Hammond, George P., and Agapito Rey. "Don Juan de Onate, Colonizer of New Mexico, 1595–1628." *Spanish Borderlands Sourcebooks, Vol. 9: The Native American and Spanish Colonial Experience in the Greater Southwest.* Ed. David H. Snow. New York: Garland Publishing, Inc., 1992. 239–349.

Hammond, George P. Ed. "Relacion Postrera de Cibola." *Narratives of the Coronado Expedition, 1540–1542.* Albuquerque, NM: University of New Mexico Press, 1940. 308–12.

Harshberger, J. W. "The Purposes of Ethno-Botany." *An Ethnobiology Source Book: The Uses of Plants and Animals by American Indians.* Ed. Richard I. Ford. NY: Garland Publishing, Inc., 1986. 73–81.

Harvard, V. "Drink Plants of North American Indians (1896)." *An Ethnobiology Source Book: The Uses of Plants and Animals by American Indians.* Ed. Richard I. Ford. NY: Garland Publishing, Inc., 1986. 33–46.

Hassig, Ross. "Leagues in Mexico Versus Leagues in Florida: How Good Were Estimates?" *The Hernando de Soto Expedition History, Historiography, and "Discovery" in the Southeast.* Ed. Patricia Galloway. Lincoln, NE: University of Nebraska Press, 1997.

---. "Roads, Routes, and Ties That Bind." *Ancient Road Networks and Settlement Hierarchies in the New World.* Ed. Charles D. Trombold. Cambridge: Cambridge University Press, 1991. 17–27.

Henderson, Norman. *Rediscovering the Great Plains: Journeys by Dog, Canoe, and Horse.* Baltimore, MD: The Johns Hopkins University Press, 2001.

Hill, William E. *The Mormon Trail: Yesterday and Today.* Logan, UT: Utah State Univ. Press, 1996.

Hines, Celinda. "Life and Death on the Oregon Trail." *Covered Wagon Women.* Ed. Kenneth L. Holmes. Vol. VI. Glendale, CA: The Arthur H. Clark Co., 1986. 77–134.

Hodge, F. W. Ed. "The Narrative of Alvar Nunez Cabeza de Vaca." *Spanish Explorers in the United States.* Ed. J. Franklin (Gen. Ed.) Jameson. New York: Charles Scribner's Sons, 1907.

Hodge, Frederick Webb. Ed. "Handbook of American Indians North of Mexico: Part 1." *Bureau of America Ethnology.* Washington: Smithsonian Institution, 1907.

Hodge, Frederick Webb. Ed. "Handbook of American Indians North of Mexico: Part 2." *Bureau of America Ethnology.* Washington: Smithsonian Institution, 1907.

Hollon, W. Eugene. "Great Days of the Overland Stage." *The American Heritage Book of Great Adventures of the Old West.* New York: American Heritage Press, 1957. 211–21.

Hough, Walter. "Environmental Interrelations in Arizona." *An Ethnobiology Source Book: The Uses of Plants and Animals by American Indians.* Ed. Richard I. Ford. NY: Garland Publishing, Inc., 1986. 133–55.

Hunsaker, Joyce Badgley. *Seeing the Elephant: Voices from the Oregon Trail.* Lubbock, TX: Texas Tech Univ. Press, 2003.

Iberville, Pierre LeMoyne de. "Journal of the Voyage Made by d'Iberville to the South Coast of Florida in 1699." *Iberville's*

Gulf Journals. Ed. Richebourg G. McWilliams. Tuscaloosa, AL: The University of Alabama Press, 1981.

Indiana Dept. of Transportation. *Construction Procedures Part I.* Distance Measurements - Pacing. 2012 <www.in.gov/indot/files/ED_ConstructionProceduresPart1CertifiedTechManual_2012>.

International Museum of the Horse. 2006 <www.imh.org/imh/bw/mule>.

Irving, Washington. "A Tour of the Prairies." *Washington Irving: Three Western Narratives.* Ed. James P. Ronda. NY: The Library of America, 2004. 3–162.

Jackson, A. T. *Picture Writing of Texas Indians.* Anthropological Papers II. Ed. J. E. Pearce. Austin, TX: The University of Texas, 1938.

Jackson, Kenneth T. *Atlas of American History.* N.Y.: Charles Scribner's Sons, 1984.

Jagger, Cedric. *The World's Greatest Clocks.* London: Hamlyn Publishing Group, 1977.

Jennings, Jesse D. "Origins." *Ancient North Americans.* Ed. Jesse D. Jennings. San Francisco: W. H. Freeman and Company, 1983. 25–67.

Jett, Stephen C. "Observations Regarding Chartkoff's California's 'Rock Feature Complex.'" *American Antiquity* 51.3 (1986): 615–16.

Keller, George. *A Trip Across the Plains and Life in California.* Oakland, CA: Biobooks, 1955.

King, Hannah. "My Journal." *Covered Wagon Women.* Ed. Kenneth L. Holmes. Vol. VI. Glendale, CA: The Arthur H. Clark Co., 1986. 183–222.

Knight, Amelia. "Iowa to the Columbia River." *Covered Wagon Women.* Ed. Kenneth L. Holmes. Vol. VI. Glendale, CA: The Arthur H. Clark Co., 1986. 33–75.

Kopper, Philip. *The Smithsonian Book of North American Indians: Before the Coming of the Europeans*. Washington, DC: Smithsonian Books, 1986.

Krober, A. L. *Cultural and Natural Areas of Native North America*. Berkeley, CA: University of California Press, 1963.

Lafferty, Robert H. III. "Prehistoric Exchange in the Lower Mississippi Valley." *Prehistoric Exchange Systems in North America*. Ed. Timothy G. Baugh and Jonathan E. Ericson. New York: Plenum Press, 1994. 177–213.

Laguna, Frederica de. "Tlingit." *Handbook of North American Indians: Northwest Coast*. Ed. Wayne Suttles. Washington, DC: Smithsonian Institution, 1990. 203–28.

Lamb, Ursula. *Cosmographers and Pilots of the Spanish Maritime Empire*. Aldershot, Hampshire, Great Britain: Variorum, 1995.

Large, Arlen J., Center for Great Plains Studies. "How Far West Am I: The Almanac as an Explorer's Yardstick." *Great Plains Quarterly* [Lincoln, NE] 13.2 (Spring 1993): 117–31.

Larsen, Clark Spenser, and George R. Milner. Eds. *In the Wake of Contact: Biological Responses to Conquest*. New York: John Wiley & Sons, Inc., 1994.

Larrabee, Aimee, and John Altman. *The Last Stand of the Tallgrass Prairie*. NY: Friedman/Fairfax Publishers, 2001.

Leigh, Edward. *Three Diatribes: First of Travel, or a Guide for Travelers Into Forein (sic) Parts, Secondly, of Money or Coyns, Thirdly, of Measuring Distance Betwixt Place and Place*. London, 1671.

Lemmon, Alfred E., John T. Magill and Jason R. Wiese. Eds. "The Entrance of the Missisipi at Fort Balise Taken in the Kings Ship "Nautilus" in the Year 1764." *Charting Louisiana: Five Hundred Years of Maps*. New Orleans: The Historical New Orleans Collection, 2003. 89.

Lewin, L. G., Huff. *How to Feed an Army: Recipes and Lore from the Front Lines*. New York: Harper Perennial, 2006.

Lewis, G. Malcolm. "Indian Maps: Their Place in the History of Plains Cartography." *The Great Plains Quarterly* 4.2 (Spring 1984): 91.

Linklater, Andro. *Measuring America: How an Untamed Wilderness Shaped the United States and Fulfilled the Promise of Democracy.* NY: Walker & Company, 2002.

Lipe, William D. "The Southwest." *Ancient North Americans.* Ed. Jesse D. Jennings. San Francisco: W. H. Freeman and Company, 1983. 420–93.

Malinowski, Sharon, Anna Sheets, and Linda Schmittroth. Eds. "The Great Basin/Southwest." *U.X.L Encyclopedia of Native American Tribes.* Vol. 2. Detroit: U.X.L, 1999.

Malinowski, Sharon, Anna Sheets, and Linda Schmittroth. Eds. "Arctic & Subarctic/Great Plains/Plateau." *U.X.L Encyclopedia of Native American Tribes.* Vol. 3. Detroit: U.X.L., 1999.

Malinowski, Sharon, Anna Sheets and Linda Schmittroth. Eds. "California/Pacific Northwest." *U.X.L Encyclopedia of Native American Tribes.* Vol. 4. Detroit: U.X.L, 1999.

Malouf, Carling. "Prehistoric Exchanges in the Northern Periphery of the South West." *American Antiquity* VI (1940–41): 115–22.

Malville, J. McKim. *Prehistoric Astronomy in the Southwest.* Boulder, CO: Johnson Printing Co., 1993.

Mason, Otis T. "The Human Beast of Burden." Annual Report of the Smithsonian Institution Part II. Washington, DC: The Government Printing Office, 1887. 237–95.

Mason, Otis Tufton. *Primitive Travel and Transportation.* Report of the National Museum for 1894. Washington, DC: Smithsonian Institute, 1894.

Mathien, Frances Joan. "Political, Economic, and Demographic Implications of the Chaco Road Network." *Ancient Road Networks and Settlement Hierarchies in the New World.* Ed. Charles

D. Trombold. Cambridge: Cambridge University Press, 1991. 99–110.

Maynard, Theodore. *De Soto and the Conquistadores*. NY: AMS Press, Inc., 1969.

McCaig, Robert. "The Great Canoe Trail." *Water Trails West*. Ed. Donald Duke. Garden City, NY: Doubleday & Company, Inc., 1978. 1–14.

McCleary, Timothy P. *The Stars We Know: Crow Indian Astronomy and Life Ways*. Prospect Heights, IL: Waveland Press Inc., 1997.

Meeker, Ezra. *Ox-Team Days on the Oregon Trail*. Younkers-on-Hudson, NY: World Book Co., 1925.

Mendoza, Antonio de. "Letter from Viceroy Mendoza to Fernández de Oviedo, October 6, 1541." *Documents of the Coronado Expedition, 1939–1942*. Ed. Richard Flint and Shirley Cushing Flint. Dallas, TX: Southern Methodist University Press, 2005. 309–16.

Mendoza, Viceroy Don Antonio de. "Instructions to Alarcon, 1541." *Narratives of the Coronado Expedition*. Ed. George P. Hammond. Albuquerque, NM: The University of New Mexico Press, 1940. 117–23.

---. "Instructions to Fray Marcos De Niza." *Narratives of the Coronado Expedition*. Ed. George P. Hammond. Albuquerque: The University of New Mexico Press, 1940. 58–62.

Milanich, Jerald T. *The Hernando de Soto Expedition*. NY: Garland Publishing, Inc., 1991. Vol. 11 of *Spanish Borderlands Sourcebooks*. Trans. Buckingham Smith. Ed. David Hurst Thomas.

Miller, Jay, and William R. Seaburg. "Athapaskans of Southwestern Oregon." *Handbook of North American Indians: Vol. 7*. Ed. Wayne Suttles. Washington, DC: Smithsonian Institution, 1990. 580–88.

Moorhead, Max L. *New Mexico's Royal Road: Trade and Travel on the Chihuahua Trail.* Norman, OK: University of Oklahoma Press, 1958.

Morisawa, Marie. *Streams: Their Dynamics and Morphology.* NY: McGraw-Hill Book Company, 1968.

Morison, Samuel E., and Henry S. Commager. *The Growth of the American Republic.* New York: Oxford University Press, 1962.

Morison, Samuel Eliot. *Admiral of the Ocean Sea: A Life of Christopher Columbus.* Boston: Little, Brown and Company, 1942.

Moulton, Gary E. Ed. *The Journal of the Lewis and Clark Expedition.* Lincoln, NE: University of Nebraska Press, 1983–2001.

Murie, James R. *Ceremonies of the Pawnee.* Washington, DC: Smithsonian Institution Press, 1989.

Nabokov, Peter. *Indian Running: Native American History & Tradition.* Santa Fe, NM: Ancient City Press, 1981.

Nasatir, A. P. *Before Lewis and Clark: Documents Illustrating the History of the Missouri, 1785–1804.* Saint Louis, MO: Saint Louis Historical Documents Foundation, 1952.

National Park Service, Dept. of the Interior. *The Big Fill Trail: Golden Spike National Site.* Western National Parks Association.

---. *Golden Spike National Historical Site Utah.* Government Printing Office, 2007.

Champagne, Duane. Ed. *Native America: Portrait of the People.* Detroit, MI: Visible Ink Press, 1994.

Nebenzahl, Kenneth. *Atlas of Columbus and the Great Discoveries.* N.Y.: Rand McNally, 1990.

Newberry, J. S. "Food and Fiber Plants of the North American Indians (1887)." *An Ethnobiology Source Book: The Uses of Plants and Animals by American Indians.* Ed. Richard I. Ford. NY: Garland Publishing, Inc., 1986. 31–46.

Newcomen. "Land Measurement in the Sixteenth Century." *Newcomen Society Transactions* 31 (1955–59).

Nilsson, Martin P. *Primitive Time Reckoning: A Study in the Origins and First Development of the Art of Counting Time Among the Primitive and Early Culture Peoples.* Lund, Sweden: C. W. K. Gleerup, 1920.

Ninza, Fray Marcos de. "Report of Fray Marcos De Ninza." *Narratives of the Coronado Expedition, 1540–1542.* Ed. George P. Hammond. Albuquerque, NM: University of New Mexico Press, 1940. 63–82.

Niza, Fray Marcos de. "Report of Fray Marcos de Niza." *Narratives of the Coronado Expedition.* Ed. George P. Hammond. Albuquerque: The University of New Mexico Press, 1940. 63–82.

Norall, Frank. *Bourgmont, Explorer of the Missouri, 1698–1725.* Lincoln, NE: University of Nebraska Press, 1988.

Palmer, Edward. "Food Products of the North American Indians." *An Ethnobiology Source Book: The Uses of Plants and Animals by American Indians.* Ed. Richard I. Ford. NY: Garland Publishing, Inc., 1986. 404–28.

Pearson, G. C. *Overland in 1849: From Missouri to California by the Platte River and the Salt Lake Trail.* Ed. Jessie H. Goodman. Los Angeles, CA: Privately printed, 1961.

Perkins, Elisha Douglas. "Gold Rush Diary." Ed. Thomas D. Clark. Lexington, KY: Univ. of Kentucky, 1967.

Phares, Ross. *Cavalier of the Wilderness: Story of the Explorer and Trader Louis Juchereau de Saint Denis.* Baton Rouge: Louisiana University Press, 1952.

Philbrick, Nathaniel. *Sea of Glory: America's Voyage of Discovery, The US Exploring Expedition 1838–1842.* New York: Viking, 2003.

Platt, P.L., and N. Slater. *Travelers Guide Across the Plains Upon the Overland Route to California.* San Francisco: John Howell Books, 1963.

Powers, Stephen. "Aboriginal Botany (1873–1874)." *An Ethnobiology Source Book: The Uses of Plants and Animals by*

American Indians. Ed. Richard I. Ford. NY: Garland Publishing, Inc., 1986. 373–78.

Pratt, Orson. "Interesting Items Concerning the Journeying of the Latter-Day Saints from the City of Nauvoo, Until Their Location in the Valley of the Great Salt Lake." *Exodus of Modern Israel.* Ed. N. B. Lundwall. Independence, MO: Zion's Printing & Publishing Co., 1947? 17–82.

---. *The Orson Pratt Journals.* Ed. Elden Jay Watson. Salt Lake City, UT: Elden Jay Watson, 1975.

---. "Resume of the Journey to the Rocky Mountains." *Exodus of Modern Israel.* Ed. N.B. Lundwall. Independence, MO: Zion's Printing & Publishing Co., 1947? 82.

Prescott, William H. *History of the Conquest of Mexico.* NY: The Modern Library, 1998.

Pritzker, Barry M. *A Native American Encyclopedia: History, Culture, and Peoples.* Oxford, England: Oxford University Press, 2000.

Quinn, David B. "Maps of the Age of European Exploration." *From Sea Charts to Satellite Images: Interpreting North American History through Maps.* Ed. David Bruisseret. Chicago: The University of Chicago Press, 1990. 41–65.

Ranjel, Rodrigo. "A Narrative of De Soto's Expedition." *Narratives of the Career of Hernando de Soto in the Conquest of Florida.* Ed. Edward Gaylord Bourne. The American Explorers Series II. New York: AMS Press, Inc., 1973.

Reinfeld, Fred. *Pony Express.* Lincoln, NE: University of Nebraska Press, 1973.

Robertson, R. G. *Competitive Struggle: America's Western Fur Trading Posts, 1764–1865.* Boise, ID: Tamarack Books, Inc., 1999.

Romain, William F. *Mysteries of the Hopewell: Astronomers, Geometers, and Magicians of the Eastern Woodlands.* Akron, OH: Univ. of Akron Press, 2000.

Russell, Israel C. *Rivers of North America.* NY: G. P. Putnam's Sons, 1898.

Santoro, Nicholas J. *Atlas of the Indian Tribes of North America and the Clash of Cultures.* NY: IUniverse, Inc., 2009.

Schwartz, Seymour I. *The Mismapping of America.* Rochester, NY: The University of Rochester Press, 2003.

Sever, Thomas L., and David W. Wagner. "Analysis of Prehistoric Roadways in Chaco Canyon Using Remotely Sensed Digital Data." *Ancient Road Networks and Settlement Hierarchies in the New World.* Ed. Charles D. Trombold. Cambridge: Cambridge University Press, 1991. 42–52.

Severin, Timothy. *Explorers of the Mississippi.* NY: Alfred A. Knopf, 1968.

Shelby, Charmion Clair. "St. Denis's Declaration Concerning Texas in 1717." *The Southwestern Historical Quarterly* XXVI. No. 3 (January 1923): 165–83.

Smith, Elizabeth Dixon. "The Diary." *Covered Wagon Women.* Ed. Kenneth L. Holmes. Vol. 1. Glendale, CA: The Arthur H. Clark Co., 1983. 111–55.

Snead, James E. "Ancestral Pueblo Trails and the Cultural Landscape of the Pajarito Plateau, New Mexico." *Antiquity* 76.293 (2002): 756–65.

Starr, Eileen, "Celestial Navigation Basics." *We Proceeded On.* [Great Falls, MT] 27.4 (November 2001): 12–18.

Stewart, George R. *The California Trail.* New York: McGraw-Hill Book Co., Inc., 1962.

Strentzel, Louisiana. "A Letter Form California." *Covered Wagon Women.* Ed. Kenneth L. Holmes. Vol. 1. Glendale, CA: The Arthur H. Clark Co., 1983. 247–70.

Sturtevant, William C., and Alfonso Ortiz. Eds. *Handbook of North American Indians: Southwest.* Handbook of North American Indians 9. Washington, DC: Smithsonian Institution Press, 1979.Suttles, Wayne, and Barbara Lane. "Southern Coast Salish." *Handbook of North American Indians: Vol. 7.* Ed. Wayne Suttles. Washington, DC: Smithsonian Institution, 1990. 485–502.

Swanton, John R. *The Indian Tribes of North America.* Washington, DC: Smithsonian Institution Press, 1968.

Swanton, John R. Ed. *Final Report of the United States De Soto Expedition Commission.* Reprint. Washington, DC: Smithsonian Institution Press, 1985.

Tarleton State University. "Shortgrass Prairie." Pictures and Descriptions of Vegetation Common to a Variety of High Plains Grasslands (NM, CO, WY, TX, & NE). Feb. 3, 2005 <www.tarleton.edu/~range/Grasslands/shortgrass%20Prairie/shortgrassprairie>.

Taylor, E. G. R. *The Haven Finding Art.* NY: American Elsevior Publishing Co., Inc., 1971.

Taylor, Rachel. "Overland Trip Across the Plains." *Covered Wagon Women.* Ed. Kenneth L. Holmes. Vol. VI. Glendale, CA: The Arthur H. Clark Co., 1986. 149–82.

Terrell, John Upton. *Traders of the Western Morning: Aboriginal Commerce in Precolumbian North America.* Los Angeles, CA: South West Museum, 1967.

Thrower, Norman J. W. *Maps & Man: An Examination of Cartography in Relation to Culture and Civilization.* Englewood Cliffs, NJ: Prentice-Hall, Inc., 1972.

Thrower, Norman J. W., and Malcolm G. Lewis. "Frontier Encounters in the Field: 1511–1925." *Cartographic Encounters: Perspectives on Native American Mapmaking and Map Use.* Ed. Malcolm G. Lewis. Chicago: The University of Chicago Press, 1998. 9–32.

Thwaites, Rueben Gold. Ed. The Jesuits. *Lower Canada, Abenakis, Louisiana, 1716–1727.* The Jesuit Relations and Allied Documents 67. Cleveland: The Burrows Brothers Company, 1900.

---. *Lower Canada, Crees, Louisiana, 1720–1736.* The Jesuit Relations and Allied Documents 68. Cleveland: The Burrows Brothers Company, 1900.

Trombold, Charles D. "An Introduction to the Study of Ancient New World Road Networks." *Ancient Road Networks and Settlement Hierarchies in the New World.* Ed. Charles D. Trombold. Cambridge: Cambridge University Press, 1991. 1–9.

Turner, Gerard L'E. *Elizabethan Instrument Makers.* Oxford, England: Oxford University Press, 2000.

---. *Nineteenth-Century Scientific Instruments.* Berkeley, CA: University of California Press, 1983.

---. *Scientific Instruments 1500–1900: An Introduction.* London: Philip Wilson Publishers, 1998.

Vega, Garcilasco de la. *The Florida of the Inca.* Ed. J. G. Varner and J. J. Varner. Austin, TX: University of Texas Press, 1951.

Vehik, Susan C., and Timothy G. Baugh. "Prehistoric Plains Trade." *Prehistoric Exchange Systems in North America.* Ed. Timothy G. Baugh and Jonathan E. Ericson. New York: Plenum Press, 1994. 249–74.

Vestal, Stanley. *The Missouri.* Lincoln: The University of Nebraska Press, 1996.

Ware, Joseph E. *The Emigrant's Guide to California. Narratives of the Trans-Mississippi Frontier.* Ed. John Caughey. Princeton, NJ: Princeton University Press, 1932.

Warhus, Mark. *Another America: Native American Maps and the History of Our Land.* New York: St. Martins Press, 1997.

Weddle, Robert S. "Soto's Problems of Orientation: Maps, Navigation, and Instruments in the Florida Expedition." *The Hernando de Soto Expedition.* Ed. Patricia Galloway. Lincoln, NE: University of Nebraska, 1997.

Wedel, Mildred Mott. *La Harpe's 1719 Post on the Red River and Nearby Caddo Settlements.* Austin: The Texas Memorial Museum, 1978. Bulletin 30.

Wedel, Waldo R. "The Prehistoric Plains." *Ancient North Americans.* Ed. Jesse D. Jennings. San Francisco: W. H. Freeman and Company, 1983. 202–41.

Wentworth, Edward Norris. *America's Sheep Trails.* Ames, Iowa: The Iowa State Press, 1948.

White, Leslie A. "Notes on the Ethnozoology of the Kersean Pueblo Indians." *An Ethnobiology Source Book: The Uses of Plants and Animals by American Indians.* Ed. Richard I. Ford. NY: Garland Publishing, Inc., 1986. 223–43.

Wight, Jermy Benton. *Frederick W. Lander and the Lander Trail.* Bedford, WY: Star Valley Llama, 1993.

Williamson, Ray A. "American Indian Astronomy: An Overview." *Stars Above: Sky Below.* Ed. Marsha C. Bol. Niwot, CO: Roberts Rhinehart Publishers, 1998, 65–94.

---. *Living the Sky: The Cosmos of the American Indian.* Boston: Houghton Mifflin Co., 1984.

Williamson, Ray A., and Claire R. Farrer. "Introduction: The Animating Breath." *Earth & Sky: Visions of the Cosmos in Native American Folklore.* Ed. Ray R. Williamson and Claire R. Farrer. Albuquerque, NM: University of New Mexico Press, 1992. 1–24.

Windes, Thomas C. "The Prehistoric Road Network at Pueblo Alto, Chaco Canyon, New Mexico." *Ancient Road Networks and Settlement Hierarchies in the New World.* Ed. Charles D. Trombold. Cambridge: Cambridge University Press, 1991. 111–31.

Winship, George Parker. "The Coronado Expedition, 1540–1542." *US Bureau of American Ethnology, 14th Annual Report, Pt. 1.* Ed. J. W. Powell. Washington, DC: Government Printing Office 1896, 1892–93, 329–598.

Wynter, Harriet, and Anthony Turner. *Scientific Instruments.* London: Studio Vista, 1975.

Zenk, Henry B. "Siuslawans and Coosans." *Handbook of North American Indians: Vol. 7.* Ed. Wayne Suttles. Washington, DC: Smithsonian Institution, 1990, 572–79.

Index

Alarcón, Hernando de, **88-89**
Añasco, Juan de, **127-129**
Anville, Jean Baptiste Bourguignon de, **138, 176**
Bellin, Jacques Nicolas, **151**
Bienville, Jean-Baptiste LeMoyne de, **161**
Bonaparte, Napoleon, **186, 255**
Bourgmont, Etienne Veniard, **156-157, 171-172, 177-178**
Bruyere, Andre Fabry de la, **163-164, 171-172, 177**
Bryant, William, **194, 195, 222-223**
buffalo, **5, 6, 19, 20, 21, 22-23, 25, 36, 38, 42, 45, 52, 60, 61, 63, 65, 72, 73, 76, 113, 114, 151, 199, 222, 223, 233-234, 254**
cache, **46-48**

Cartier, Jacques, **143**
Clayton, William, **194, 195, 196-197, 198**
communication
 fire, **170**
 interpreters, **109-111**
 runners, native, **76-78, 86-87, 90**
 Pony Express, **252-253**
 posting, **87-89, 198-201**
Coronado, Francisco Vasquez de, **83-84, 98, 101, 111-112, 130**
Courier de Bois, **xiii, 181**
Cross-Timbers, **155, 162**
Delisle, Guillaume, **176, 177**
deserts
 Chihuahua, **3, 24**
 Great Basin, **7, 8, 9, 13, 27, 28-29, 47, 54, 75, 198**
 Mohave, **7, 8, 9, 10, 54, 56**

INDEX

Sonora, **3, 7, 8, 9, 10, 15, 24, 105, 190**
Diaz, Melchior, **89-90, 105**
distance, measurement
   leagues, **47, 65, 89, 97, 103, 116-117, 119, 120, 152, 159, 175, 177**
   odometer, wagon, **196-198**
   pacing, **119-120**
   speed & time, **116-117, 119**
Domínguez, Fray Francisco Atanasio, **126**
elevation, measurement
   barometer, **204, 210-211**
   thermometer, **204, 210-211**
Fer, Nicholas de, **138, 176**
Fitzpatrick, Thomas "Broken Hand", **193-194**
Frémont, John C., **192, 194, 195, 202, 203**
Frink, Ledyard, **189-190**
Friscus, Gemma, **180**
forests, eastern hardwood, **3-4, 21, 75, 164, 172**
fuel
   buffalo chips, **61, 233, 234**
   coal, **234**
   grass, **234**
   sagebrush, **234**
   wood, **201, 230, 231, 233**
geographical fantasy
   Quivira, **24, 83, 111, 112, 125**
   Seven Cities of Gold, **82, 83, 88, 98, 116**
   Symmetrical Geography, **147**
   Western Sea, **147, 156**
geographical margins, xii, **10-11, 14, 20, 28-29, 75**
grasslands, **5, 22**
   Central Valley, California, **12, 14, 29**
   High Plains, **4, 6, 21, 24, 44, 149, 254**
   Llano Estacado, **152**
   prairies, **xii, xiii, 3, 5-6, 57, 60, 147, 153, 155, 164, 173, 178, 186, 187, 199, 216, 224, 232, 233, 253, 255**
   Willamette Valley, **12, 32, 54, 187**
Halley, Edmund, **174**
India rubber
   mattress, **222**
   water containers, **232**
Jefferson, T. H., **203, 234**
Joliet, Louis, **144, 145, 156, 172, 175**
La Renaudière, Philippe de, **171**
La Salle, Rene Robert Cavalier, Sieur de, **145-146, 151, 175**
Mallet, Paul & Pierre, **157, 163-164, 169**
maps & mapmaking
   Anville, Jean Baptiste Bourguignon de, **138, 176**

barometer, **204**, **210-211**
Bellin, Jacques Nicolas, **151**
cartography, French, **176-178**
  Delisle, Guillaume, **176**, **177**
  Fer, Nicholas de, **138**, **176**
  institutions for, **176**
  latitude & longitude, **xii**, **118**, **121-123**, **174**, **175**, **179**, **204-211**
  logarithms, **xiii**, **180-181**
  native, **34**, **63-65**
  plane table, **180**
  Preuss, Charles, **202**, **203**
  thermometer, **204**, **210-211**
  triangulation, **xiii**, **178-181**, **202-203**
  US Exploring Expedition, **202-203**
Marquette, Jacques, **148**, **150**
mountains
  Cascades, **3**, **7**, **13**, **14**, **31**, **49**, **149**, **224**, **239**
  Coastal, **11**, **12**, **29**, **30**, **32**
  crossing, **10-11**, **59**, **102-103**, **109**, **215**, **239-241**, **242**
  Rocky, **xiii**, **3**, **4**, **5**, **7**, **9**, **13**, **20**, **21**, **27**, **49**, **54**, **55**, **56**, **57**, **75**, **76**, **147**, **154**, **156**, **185**, **186**, **190**, **191**, **223**, **232**, **242**, **253**
  Sierra Nevada, **4**, **7**, **10**, **11**, **12**, **13**, **14**, **27**, **29**, **31**, **54**, **56**, **149**, **190**, **192**, **194**, **203**, **213**, **217**, **224**, **239**, **241**, **242**, **248**, **253**
mountain men, **xiv**, **186**, **190**, **193**, **223**, **224**
Narváez, Pánfilo de, **81**
native demography
  disease, **18-19**
  migratory tribes, **19**, **21**, **24**, **26**, **27**, **43**, **62**, **66**, **68**, **74**, **106**
  settled tribes, **xii**, **19**, **22**, **24-26**, **27**, **29**, **30**, **31**, **33**, **36**, **38**, **66**, **67**, **69**, **74**, **75**, **106**
native tribes
  Apache, **21**, **26**, **31**, **171**
  Arapaho, **21**
  Arikara, **21**
  Aztec, **xii**, **18**, **24**, **25**, **26**, **55**, **76**, **77**, **78**, **82**, **92**
  Blackfeet, **22**
  Cheyenne, **21**
  Chilua, **31**
  Chinook, **31-32**
  Chumash, **30**
  Coastal Salish, **31**
  Comanche, **21**, **64-65**
  Costanoan, **30**
  Crow, **21**
  Hidatsa, **21**
  Hopi, **25**, **54**, **82**

INDEX

Hupa, **31**
Kiowa, **21**
Mandan, **21, 133**
Navajo, **26, 31**
Osage, **21, 171**
Paiute, **27**
Papago, **25**
Pawnee, **21**
Pomo, **30**
Pueblos, Rio Grande, **24-25, 55, 58, 66, 72, 74, 75, 78, 82, 83, 84, 104, 111, 112, 185**
Shoshoni, **21, 27**
Sioux, **21, 145**
Tillamook, **31**
Ute, **27**
Wichita, **21**
Yahi, **29**
Yana, **29**
Zuni, **25, 54, 55, 102-103, 116, 125**
navigation
  almanacs, **121, 123, 174, 204, 205, 208, 209, 210**
  birds, **39**
  cairns, **61, 62, 173**
  celestial, **xiv, 121, 122, 123, 193, 206-210**
  dead reckoning, **114, 116, 120-121, 122, 174**
  divine intervention, **126-127**
  Home Centered Reference, **113-114**
  landmarks, man-made, **61, 62-63, 85, 88**
  landmarks, natural, **x, 34, 60-61, 62, 64, 65, 66, 67, 85, 87, 154, 178, 179, 181, 193, 194, 198, 201, 250**
  latitude & longitude, **xii, 118, 121-123, 174, 175, 179, 204-211**
  magnetic variation, **115, 174**
  plants, **40**
  prime meridian, **208**
  seaman's rutters, **194**
navigation, instruments
  artificial horizon, **204, 207-208**
  astrolabe, **xii, 123-124, 125, 128, 129, 136, 174, 179, 206, 207**
  chronometer, **205-206, 209, 210**
  compass, **x, xii, 39, 40, 60, 71, 109, 114, 115, 117-118, 120, 174, 178, 179, 193**
  crossstaff, **123, 128**
  octant, **206, 207**
  quadrant, **123, 124, 125, 204, 206, 207**
  reflecting circle, **206-207**
  sextant, **139, 193, 204, 206, 207**
navigation, training
  Jesuit Colleges, **xiii, 174-175**

Oñate, Don Juan de, **104**
plateaus
   Colorado, **4, 6-7, 9-10, 27, 54, 75**
   Columbia, **4, 6, 7, 9, 13, 31, 49, 54**
Poisson, Paul de, **166-167, 168**
portage
   canoe, **144, 145, 147, 157, 160, 162, 169**
   wagon, **241**
Pratt, Orson, **197-198, 199, 204, 205, 206-207, 209-210**
Preuss, Charles, **202, 203**
provisions
   foraged, **6, 8, 11, 12, 19-20, 21, 22, 26, 27, 28, 29, 30, 32, 39-41, 45, 56, 105**
   livestock, **94-95, 100-102, 232-233, 243**
   plundered, **83, 93, 105, 106-108**
   transported, **xi, 26, 39-42, 76, 100, 102, 104, 105, 167, 212, 221-223**
rivers
   Arkansas, **xiii, 6, 55, 83, 144, 146, 153, 154, 155, 156, 162, 163, 166, 173, 177, 181, 190**
   Canadian, **163**
   Colorado, **10, 24, 26, 47, 49, 52, 54, 55, 88, 89, 105, 125**
   Columbia, **7, 12, 14, 30, 31, 48, 49, 50, 51, 54, 75, 188, 191, 202, 203, 224, 239, 250**
   eastern vs. western, **5, 48, 146, 147, 148, 149, 150, 160**
   Humboldt, **54, 191, 194, 203, 214, 224, 239**
   Mississippi, **xii, xiii, 3, 4, 21, 48, 54, 55, 57, 73, 83, 96, 102, 104, 108, 110, 128, 129, 144-149, 151, 153, 154, 155, 156, 160, 161, 162, 165, 166, 167, 168, 175, 181, 185, 186, 247, 251**
   Missouri, **xii, 6, 21, 22, 48, 54, 55, 72, 75, 144, 145, 146, 148, 153, 156, 157, 161, 166, 168, 171, 173, 177, 178, 186, 188, 189, 190, 195, 198, 201-204, 216-219, 221, 223, 224, 227, 228, 229, 233, 237, 238, 239, 248, 250-251, 252, 253**
   Platte, **6, 21, 54, 140, 173, 177, 182, 189, 190, 191, 197, 198, 200, 210, 223, 224, 225, 242, 245, 249**
   Red, **xiii, 6, 112, 151, 153, 154, 155, 156, 161, 162, 166, 173, 175**

INDEX

Snake, **27, 54, 75, 191, 193, 202, 224, 230, 239, 250**
Sweetwater, **54, 191**
river, crossing
  baskets, **52, 58**
  bridge, **xiv, 58, 104, 226, 235, 236, 241, 248, 249, 250, 254**
  bridge, brush, **236**
  ferry, **51, 58, 103-104, 128, 226, 228, 235, 236-239**
  fords, **109, 173, 226, 235, 236, 237, 243**
  raft, **28, 58**
river, hazards
  floating logs, **148, 150-152, 160**
  sand bars, **160, 163, 251**
  sawyers, **150, 251**
  snags, **50, 150, 160, 251**
  water levels, **148-150, 153, 160, 165, 168**
roads & trails
  Big Tree Route, **248**
  California Trail, **191, 224, 227, 228, 242, 243**
  Lander Road, **249-250, 252**
  mountain, **102-103, 190**
  Mullen Road, **250, 252**
  native, **xii, 12, 13, 18, 26, 34, 38-39, 44, 53-56, 69, 75, 83, 98, 103, 173, 186, 190, 91, 193, 224**

Oregon Trail, **190**
  placement, **55-58**
Santa Fe Trail, **155, 169, 182, 190, 215, 219, 228**
sidling, **240-241**
Southern Route, **xiv, 190, 216**
stairways, **59**
Saint-Denis, Louis Juchereau de, **154, 175, 176**
shelter
  American, **215, 216**
  French, **160, 166-167, 174**
  native, **7, 17, 23, 28, 32, 41, 42-43, 56**
  Spanish, **90, 91, 109, 113**
Soto, Hernando de, **xii, 83, 90-92, 94, 96, 99, 100, 101-102, 104, 105, 108, 110, 112, 113, 121, 126, 127, 128, 129-130, 144, 172, 174**
South Pass, **54, 191**
Sublette, William, **191**
supply centers, American
  Fort Bridger, **200, 224, 225**
  Fort Hall, **194, 203, 213, 224, 225, 249, 250**
  Fort Kearny, **225, 249**
  Fort Laramie, **198, 210, 224, 225, 234**
supply centers, French
  Arkansas Post, **146, 154, 162, 163, 166**
  Biloxi, **146, 165**

INDEX

Cahokia, **146**
Fort New Orleans, **157**
Fort Saint Jean Baptiste, **154**
supply centers, native
   Dalles, **7, 49, 75**
   Missouri River settlements, **21, 72, 75**
   pueblos, **24-25, 55, 72, 74, 75**
   rancherias, **24, 25**
supply centers, Spanish
   Caribbean, **94-95, 97**
   Mexico, **xii, 18, 95, 97**
   native, **19, 83, 93, 106**
   ships, **xi, xii, 84, 85-86, 88, 89, 90-92, 94, 95, 105**
time, measurement
   chronometer, **205-206, 209, 210**
   moon, **69-70**
   nocturnal, **118-119, 135**
   pocket dial, **117-118**
   stars, **66, 68-69, 70-71, 118**
   sticks & knots, **64-65, 76, 77**
   sun, **66-67, 68, 69, 70, 209**
Tonti, Henri de, **146, 151, 154**
transport, land
   bearers, human, **36-38, 93-94, 102**
   buggy, Dearborn, **191, 216**
   carrettas, **104**
   carriage, spring, **216**
   draft animals, **xiv, 97, 187, 194, 196, 211, 214, 215, 216-219, 222, 230, 232, 241, 244-245, 251**
   handcarts, **219-221**
   pack animals, dog, **xi, 37, 43-44, 45, 46, 97, 214**
   pack animals, horses & mules, **xii, 42-43, 85, 94, 97-99, 112, 155, 157, 162, 163, 169-170, 190, 194, 213-215**
   railroad, **188, 253-254, 255**
   sleds, **46**
   stage, Butterfield, **xiv, 248-249, 253**
   travois, dog, **37, 43, 44-45, 59, 214**
   wagons, **x, xiii-xiv, 13, 147, 187, 189, 190, 191, 193, 194, 196-197, 198, 202, 203, 204, 213-216, 218, 219, 221, 224-226, 228, 230, 231, 233-238, 240-241, 243-246, 253**
   wheelbarrow, **212-213**
transport, water
   bateau, **164-165, 238**
   bullboat, **51-52, 133, 237**
   canoe, bark, **xii, 157-160, 162-164**
   canoe, dugout, **11, 12, 32, 33, 49, 50-51, 104, 160-161, 162-163, 165, 188, 238**
   canoe, plank, **11, 30**

INDEX

canoe, tule, **28**
Canots, maître, **158-159**
Canots, du nord, **158**
piraguas, **104**
ships, sailing, **x-xi, 60, 81, 84-85, 86, 88, 89, 90-92, 94-95, 105, 146, 179, 188-189, 202-203, 205, 253**
steamboats, **157, 227, 251-252**
travel guides
  letters, **xiv, 194, 199-201**
  guide boards, **193, 198**
  guide books, **194-196, 198, 233**
  maps, **see: maps & mapmaking**
  mountain men, **xiv, 193, 201, 223-224**
  native, **xii, xiv, 34, 47, 48, 61, 62-63, 93, 94, 109, 111-112, 113, 173-174**

US Exploring Expedition, **202-203**
Vaca, Cabaza de, **81-82**
Vivier, Father Louis, **168**
voyageurs, **xiii, 148, 157, 158, 162, 164, 165, 166-167, 168-170, 173, 181, 233**
Ware, Joseph, **189, 195-196, 242**
water
  alkali, **323**
  caching, **47-48**
  drinking straws, **168**
  locating, **39, 53, 61, 64, 173, 231-232**
  river sediment, **40, 168, 231**
  transporting, **38, 232**
  water holes & springs, **53, 56, 61, 64, 173, 195, 231**
  well, **231, 232, 248**

About the Author

Thomas A. Permar has a master's degree and PhD in forestry and forest biology as well as an English degree in creative writing. He lives in Morgan, Utah.